# Scientific Yogi

A scientific look at Yoga
A spiritual perspective on Science

## Tulsi Arora

Published by: NotionPress
#7, Red Cross Rd, Egmore,
Chennai, Tamil Nadu 600008
https://notionpress.com

# Scientific Yogi

Tulsi Arora

First Print: 2023 by Subbu Publications
Second Print: 2024 by NotionPress

All rights reserved

No part of this publication may be reproduced or transmitted in any form or by any means, electronic or mechanical, including photocopying, recording, or any other information storage or retrieval system, without permission in writing from the author.

The views and opinions expressed in this book are the author's own, and the publishers are in no way liable for the same.

Printed and Published in INDIA

*Spirituality is the Science of Reality.*
- Shri Ram Chandra

# Contents

# Introduction

The Sanskrit word for self-study is *swadhyaya,* a study related to the nature of the Self. *Swa* points to Self, and *adhyaya* means to study. This book is *swadhyaya,* a practical study of ancient Indian yogic culture and philosophy in the modern scientific context. Hence, this writing can be considered study notes and self-reflection. This study is also an aid to my spiritual practice or *sadhana.* Both *swadhyaya* and *sadhana,* like scientific research, are continuous, explorative and organic processes.

Yoga and other Indian knowledge systems are gaining popularity around the world. Seeing people from around the world quote insights from this heritage is fascinating. For my grandparents and parents, the authority of the traditional texts was unquestioned, and they held them in high esteem and approached them reverentially. The current generation, however, has developed a greater understanding and appreciation of the practicality of this knowledge for living a balanced life in the modern world.

Growing up, I paid little attention to the traditional customs or rituals, although I did wonder about the contents of the ancient texts. I found Swami Vivekananda's call to the youth motivating. He had walked all over this sacred land, inspiring millions of Indians to greater self-pride and self-reliance. His life and teachings are a glimpse into India's struggle to get over the hardships caused by invasions, colonisation and cultural decline. His instructions are relevant today as we rediscover our roots, decolonise our collective psyche, and find our evolutionary path.

Later in my life, when I started meditation, different concepts became easier to grasp, and clarity emerged.

Interestingly, meditation created an internal environment more conducive to exploring and learning. I am a science student and have continuously updated myself on the latest developments. Aided by meditation, I found a remarkable synthesis of ideas and concepts emerging from modern science and Yoga. To make sense of it and make this understanding coherent, I started this journey of *swadhyaya*. *Swadhyaya* is not a set of theories or philosophies but a practical approach where practice and knowledge go hand in hand.

Although this book provides an overview of ancient Indian spiritual teachings and discoveries in modern science, the emphasis is on self-discovery through practice, contemplation, and rationality. Sustained practice brings more clarity and helps one assimilate new ideas, a process that continues throughout one's lifetime.

Yoga means union. Yoga deals with realising our true nature as a direct inner experience of *Being,* an inner union with the *Highest.* What is the role of objectivity and rational thought in this journey? The science of Yoga shows that although each individual's path is solitary and uniquely travelled, the goal is the same. The objectivity of its philosophy and the commonality of purpose make Yoga highly logical and rational. Like a controlled experiment in science, the yogic experience of achieving the goal is reproducible and verifiable by anyone interested in this pursuit.

The book's first part deals with yogic philosophy, while the second deals with new concepts in science. The third part synthesises the two. The book draws many interesting parallels between the yogic and scientific approaches.

This book does not claim the originality of ideas but expresses a growing understanding of diverse concepts. Prominent authors, thought leaders, researchers and various yogic texts have been referenced, with due credit to the sources. I am only a student engaging in self-expression.

Realising the magnificence of our cultural heritage also brought with it the history of its decline and its associated pain. Working through tears and writing this book has been a cathartic process. It enabled me to see history in a larger context, analyse how consciousness works and see events more clearly and objectively.

Now, I see that with a peaceful heart and a clear mind, we can march towards the noble goal of *Vasudeva Kutumbakam*. As pain resolves, we can embrace ourselves and others without prejudice and judgements, thus freeing ourselves from the past. Only then can we be truly free.

Dedicated to Bharat, our cherished ancient motherland.

ॐ भूर्भुवः स्व तत्सवितुर्वरेण्यं
भर्गो देवस्य धीमहि
धियो यो नः प्रचोदयात॥

We meditate on the Pure Consciousness, which illuminates our entire being.  May it shine more brightly through our intellect so we may come to know the Self, our true nature.
- Gayatri Mantra from the Rig Veda

# Part 1

# Art and Science of Yoga
(Direct Perception and Experience)

# Chapter 1
# An Indian Perspective

## Indian Culture and Philosophy

India is an ancient land with historical continuity, changing geography, multiple *darshanas* and languages. It is the land of *avatars*, many gods, spiritual giants, royals, scholars, yogis, artists, warriors and a diverse population who have kept this unique culture alive across its unbroken chain for countless millennia.

Over these thousands of years, the people of Bharat (the ancient name for India) engaged in trade, cultural and knowledge exchange with the rest of the world. This exchange helped its cultural identity spread to vast regions, stretching from central to southeast Asia. In recent centuries, as recorded history shows, this land saw an influx of numerous groups of people: invaders, colonisers, persecuted minorities, tourists, pilgrims, traders, students and truth seekers. Many people assimilated with this land, and some went back, yet the inherent culture of this land and its indigenous people not only survived but has also thrived.

In 1947, India gained independence and forged ahead on the path of self-reliance and welfare for all its citizens. This resurgence is a testimony to the bravery, tenacity and deep-rooted spirituality of the people of this land. The best part is that despite facing a long period of external aggression, this land continues to give its message of peace, harmony and unity to the world. Scholars, archaeologists, astronomers, geologists, historians, and people from all walks of life are inquiring about the origins of Indian culture in the light of new science. Is it the unbroken

Harappan culture? Does it predate the Sindhu-Saraswati civilisation? What were the other population centres in the subcontinent of India during that time? How can we place the records of Mahabharata and Ramayana in our historical timeline?

In her book, *Ramayana Retold With Scientific Evidences*, Dr Saroj Bala presents her findings to date the Ramayana and recreates forgotten Indian history. In his book, *When Did The Mahabharata War Happen*, author Nilesh Oak looks at astrological references in the Vedas to date the Mahabharata war. The current estimates place the Vedas around 11000 years, Ramayana 7000 years ago and Mahabharata 5000 years ago.

Author Sanjeev Sanyal has written several books on reimagining Indian maritime history. The books *The Incredible History of the Indian Ocean* and *The Ocean of Churn* paint vibrant pictures of the thriving and bustling shipping routes in the Indian Ocean from Africa to Australia.

Another book by the author, *The Land of the Seven Rivers,* delves into the Sindhu-Saraswati region and how changing geography and climate affected the civilisation. These books prove beyond doubt the long history of commerce, culture and knowledge exchange that took place along the trading routes for millennia, even before the available written records.

In *In Search of the Cradle of Civilization,* authors Georg Feuerstein, David Frawley, and Subhash Kak trace the ancestry of the Vedic civilisation of India. They provide conclusive evidence that this ancient culture is thriving to date, preserving the old way of life.

The recent decoding of the Indus Valley script by author and mathematician Yajna Devam is the final brick in the wall of the Indian historical narrative, which is a continuing civilisation from antiquity with Sanskrit as its language. Our current history books will get churned in the light of these discoveries. This book, however, does not try to delve into the origins of the Indian Vedic civilisation; instead, it looks into the **essence** of its ancient teachings through the modern scientific lens. The Indian knowledge systems are now slowly becoming mainstream, and their efficacy and scientific foundations are coming to light.

The *Vedas, Upanishads, Puranas,* and *Itihasa* are the foundational texts of Indian culture. The *Rig Veda,* the oldest text known to humankind, is a UNESCO World Heritage site. These texts are so ancient that there is no consensus on dating them, although several authors have presented evidence to support their claims. Before being written down, teachers transmitted this knowledge orally from one generation to the next. How can we date this oral dissemination of knowledge?

Vyasa, the great scribe of Vedic literature, compiled and structured this knowledge about 5000 years ago; however, it existed long before his time. Inspired by these texts, ancient India developed an enormous library with works of diverse genres: poetry, history, yoga, psychology, mathematics, performing and visual arts, metallurgy, astrology, medicine, surgery, and philosophy.

With time, more books were added to this library as learned yogis and philosophers propounded their treatises, commentaries, expositions and explanations, which gave birth to different schools of thought called *darshanas.* These yogis were spiritual scientists who looked for direct evidence and saw each subject as a portal into the underlying reality. They saw Reality as a synthesis of all viewpoints, not as exclusive to anyone.

*Darshana* refers to 'direct seeing or perceiving', not just mentation or reading books. It requires one to gain knowledge by doing, experiencing, and becoming.

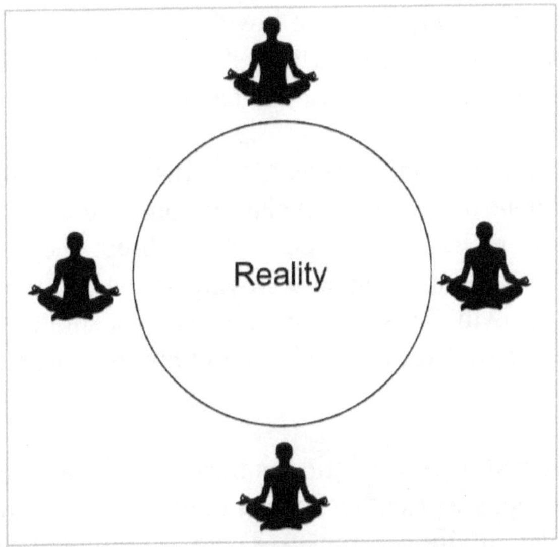


Darshana: multiple points of view of Reality

*Darshana* also requires one to develop an increasingly clear perception or pure cognition, thus refining the quality of the acquired knowledge itself. It is akin to cleaning the lens before making sense of what you see. In humans, the instrument of cognition is the mind; hence, mental clarity and purity of intent are essential prerequisites to gaining knowledge through direct perception. The yogis believed that knowledge of the Self was the highest knowledge, knowing which all became known. Hence, the inner pursuit of self-realisation was Yogi's goal, and knowledge was a byproduct of this direct realisation.

It is a matter of inner craving to discover this treasure trove of knowledge and practices in one's current place and time. A lifetime is not enough to uncover all the wisdom; however, self-study, meditation, and book study can speed up this process. Why meditation? Regular meditation can do wonders for a person's mind and heart. The mind becomes regularised, the heart attains a state of calmness, and an attitude of poise develops in facing all the diverse experiences of life. Understanding and wisdom become increasingly possible in this balanced state.

Further, meditation reveals the true nature of the object we meditate on. Such a revelation comes not as a thought but as a feeling and later as a direct perception. This understanding or inner knowing keeps evolving, mirroring our growth. This practice can more accurately be called a science of life, as applicable today as it was in the olden times.

All *darshanas* are valid, as they are just another viewpoint that looks at Reality from a unique perspective; therefore, Indian culture accepts all. There are essential similarities in all metaphysical and religious approaches worldwide. Ancient Indigenous cultures show many commonalities and even the later developed formal religions of the world speak the same truth, albeit set in a particular time and culture. This book deals with ancient Indian texts contextual to the author's time and place.

Having a viewpoint does not exclude, negate or demean other views. In an inclusive culture, one more viewpoint only adds to its beautiful diversity. In the book *Being Different*, author Rajiv Malhotra explains the Indian worldview as an unbroken continuity from aeons based on the foundational principles of Vedas. The Indian perspective is all-inclusive; it respects all, encompasses all and upholds the rights of all beings in the world. However, some researchers and indologists have misinterpreted and misunderstood it. It is in our interest to look for accurate ancient Indian perspectives, find the hidden wisdom therein and realise the truth through genuine inquiry, study and immersion.

In India, the most popular book loved by people from all walks of life is *Shrimad Bhagwat Gita*. It is part of one of the greatest epics of the culture, called *Mahabharata*. *Bhagwat Gita* means Lord's Song or Eternal Song. People often quote from the *Bhagwat Gita* to solve life's practical problems. This book generates wonder, inspiration and reverence in the readers. It answers profound questions such as: Who are we? Why are we here? What is the purpose of our lives? How do you make the right decision?

The fundamental question behind all *darshanas* is to find ways and means to solve the problem of life itself, to transcend suffering, pain, disease and death. Vedic texts describe this goal in three distinct terms: *moksha* (salvation), *mukti* (liberation) and *layaavastha* (mergence). Such a goal is not a religious idea but a practical quest because, in this culture, each individual looks at oneself as a Soul on an eternal journey of evolution, each life being just one experience of the embodied existence. The fundamental **quest** is to rise above the sorrows of the life and death cycle. In simple terms, *moksha* is a temporary relief from the life and death cycle, and *mukti* is freedom from it, as the soul continues on other planes of existence. *Laya Avastha* is the ultimate goal of union with the *Highest*.

The original text of ancient Indian literature is in the Sanskrit language. Sanskrit means 'well-formed or structured', and it is believed to be of divine origins as it was perfect from the very beginning, unlike other languages of the world, which have a history of gradual evolution and are still continuously changing. Due to this structured nature of Sanskrit, many of the works, whether orally transmitted or written down, have remained mainly unaltered. However, Sanskrit of Vedic times differed from later ages, and its originality got lost as other local dialects emerged in different parts of India. It is a matter of wonder if Sanskrit was perfect from the beginning or if it was standardised later by the great scholar Sage Panini, who wrote down the grammatical rules of the language. Some people believe that Sage Panini standardised it to retain its relevance and prevent further loss; however, it was perfect originally.

In the book *The True History and the Religion of India*, author Swami Prakashananda Saraswati also argues that Sanskrit is a divine language that was perfect from the beginning. He traces the origins and evolution of various European and Middle Eastern languages of the world and, by comparison, clearly shows evidence of the perfection of Sanskrit from the ancient past. Interestingly, Sanskrit has root sounds, and the words thus formed have root meanings. The relationship of object-sound-word-meaning is an integrated whole.

Do we need to learn Sanskrit before we can decode, make sense of it, and then apply the Vedic teachings? It will surely help to keep the language alive if we learn it, yet one is allowed the profound teachings of the Vedas despite a lack of knowledge of Sanskrit. Numerous scholars and linguists have produced translations of these texts in multiple languages. Knowledge of Devanagari or Hindi helps one understand some Sanskrit words that need help finding accurate translations in English. Interestingly, many such books have been available in digital versions and audio recordings in multiple languages in the past few years. It has become easy for anyone to access this content. The only prerequisites are interest and time. As stated earlier, along with book study, *sadhana* (spiritual practice) is needed to make the teachings alive and meaningful through direct experience. Also, nature does not insist on any language to reveal its secrets to a genuine seeker. Nature's language is not dependent on words; it is pure sound, form and vibration. More on this later.

Although most ancient Indian spiritual texts are written in poetic meter, they contain stories, conversations, or dialogues. These stories, like many found in all cultures worldwide, are allegorical. The stories reveal a wealth of knowledge using the words, context, and culture of the prevailing times. The events, characters, and settings are detailed, and the dialogue brings the concept alive. One example is Arjuna's dejection at the start of the *Mahabharata* War, as described in the *Bhagwat Gita*.

The text describes Arjuna's state of mind, his doubts, feelings, and inner conflict so the reader can genuinely empathise with his condition. It is a prelude to how Arjuna became the receptacle of the spiritual knowledge imparted by Shri Krishna before the commencement of the *Mahabharata* war. Interestingly, Arjuna poses many questions to Lord Krishna, who answers all his questions and then asks Arjuna to choose the right course of action. This is an excellent display of genuine inquiry, knowledge sharing, free will, and the teacher-disciple relationship.

Another example of elevating dialogue is the book *Ashtavakra Gita*, a sublime conversation between sage Ashtavakra and King Janaka that describes the condition of a seeker of higher spiritual attainment and realisation. It demonstrates the understanding, spiritual practice, and humility of an ageing King who took an unsightly teenage sage, Ashtavakra, as his teacher, which is heartwarming.

The word *Ashtavakra* translates as '8 deformities'. Ashtavakra, a young sage deformed from birth, had a body permanently bent in 8 different places. Reading these texts can elevate the mind of a prepared seeker, and practising and living these teachings can help reach the ultimate goal of self-realisation itself.

The *Kathopanishad* text is a lively dialogue between a young boy, Nachiketa, and Yama, the god of death. Nachiketa wants to know the secret of life and death, but Yama dissuades him by tempting him with material gains. The boy stands his ground and finally receives this secret knowledge from Yama. The reluctant Yama eventually becomes the Teacher of the young seeker. These stories brim with knowledge, philosophy, and guidance, yet they are heart-warming and humorous!

# Ancient Indian Literature

India has a vast library of extensive spiritual and philosophical literature. Many luminaries have since added to this ever-growing collection, bringing a new perspective. However, it is amazing that there is no claim of authorship of the ancient foundational texts. People attribute them to the great seers, sages and yogis of the yore. The sages themselves would say that they just 'heard' the knowledge in deep meditation. Hence, these original texts came to be known as *Shruti*, meaning 'that which is heard'. They would say these texts are divine in origin, not a product of the human mind.

This 'hearing' is not by the human ears; it is beyond the sense-perception. Then why call it 'hearing'? The actual deeper meaning of the word *Shruti* is to catch the higher vibrations as direct perception. These vibrations exist even today for anyone to 'hear' them. It would be hard to believe it could happen unless one has meditated and felt this opening up of knowledge and intuition. Yoga and meditation help us reach a higher level of consciousness where our perceptions are authentic, and we naturally become more attuned to higher vibrations.

Hence, *Shruti* was perceived by the great sages as vibrations in their mind and then later given a shape and form via the perfected language of Sanskrit. This knowledge was passed down over generations orally, and only much later was it written down. The superior mental abilities and the superfine consciousness of people of the ancient past to receive this knowledge and transmit it across generations orally is no small feat. One must have inner discipline and commitment for a lifetime to partake in this endeavour.

Sage Veda Vyas (a title for the person who reproduces the Vedas in written form, in different epochs of time) restructured, indexed and re-wrote all Vedas about 5000 years ago. Since then, many texts have survived, while some got lost. *Shruti* texts are, therefore, foundational texts of Indian knowledge systems. In the later period, several authors gave their commentaries, explanations and extensions on these foundational texts, which came to be known as *Smriti*, which means 'that which is remembered or from memory'.

Many teachers throughout the long history of the Indian civilisation have authored *Smriti* texts based on the evolving cultural and philosophical landscape of India. They reinterpreted the *Shruti* to suit the prevailing context of time and place. Many teachers, even today, guide us by putting this ancient knowledge in the current context of the 21st century, thus helping us understand the meaning of self and the world. In conclusion, *Shruti* is unchanging, while *Smriti* is its re-interpretation in the context of the prevailing time and space. Hence, *Smriti* should be understood within a suitable context.

## A Vast Library
A Brief Introduction to Ancient Indian Literature

Indian spiritual literature is vast and detailed, covering many subjects and points of view. These texts provide the framework for understanding India's culture, philosophy, history, and practices. For a list of some of the literature available today, see Appendix 1.

The quest for knowledge and realisation is ongoing; this research is a work in progress. One lifetime might not be enough to read and understand all of it; hence, people specialise in one branch of study rather than try to master it all. Interestingly, whichever branch of study you take up, the endpoint is the same: self-realisation, as if each branch is a *darshana* or point of view of the same eternal Reality.

The content is vast, and the capacity to grasp it is continuously evolving. Hence, discovering hidden gems in this extensive library is a lifelong project. One person might devote his entire life to perfecting a particular dance form and another to mastering a musical instrument. One might take up practical applications of yoga, while another might perfect his knowledge of herbal medicines. These endeavours are commitments of a lifetime that promote agency and creativity according to the individual's aptitude.

For example, it would take a lifetime of practice and dedication to become Shri Pandit Jasraj, a great artist who has been awarded multiple times for his contribution to Indian classical music. He could touch higher levels of consciousness through his music and give the listeners a glimpse. The listeners need to be open, allowing vibrations of the music to guide them. The listeners should also grasp the meaning of the words and have a reverential attitude to appreciate his music. Knowledge of melody or *raga* would be an added advantage.

It is generally believed that the complete list of all ancient texts is unavailable, as many of the works have been lost over millennia. However, there is consensus on the primary texts that still exist. Many of these are now available in multiple languages and digital versions. Even today, many organisations are devoted to keeping this knowledge tradition alive.

The literature classified as *Shruti* and *Smriti* comprises the following works:

| Shruti Texts | Smriti Texts |
| --- | --- |
| • 4 Vedas<br>• 5 Upa-Vedas<br>• 6 Vedangas | • 18 Maha-Puranas<br>• 18 Upa-Puranas<br>• 108 Upanishads<br>• 2 Itihasas |

In addition, there are numerous works of writing from many past teachers. Many great sages and saints lived in India in different epochs, working anonymously for the betterment of the world. We may not know them, but we feel gratitude toward them nonetheless. They are the unknown torchbearers of this precious heritage.

## Vedas

The most prominent texts in the *Shruti* are *Vedas*. The root word *vid* means knowing or knowledge. Then there are *Upa-Vedas,* which are supplementary texts to Vedas. *Vedangas* are multiple limbs of Vedas which help in understanding the primary texts. For example, *Vedangas* explain the Sanskrit language and its grammar. With knowledge of Sanskrit, one can read and understand the Vedas. But is just reading enough? Someone who does not know Sanskrit can still arrive at the same Vedic truths through direct perception and *sadhana*. Hence, practice and experience trump external knowledge; combined, they are a source of great joy. The *Upa-Vedas* are different branches or extensions of knowledge systems that help uphold the Vedic society, such as archery, music, architecture, medicine, and economics.

The Vedas are considered India's most ancient sacred texts but belong to the world as their spiritual heritage. They contain mantras or hymns in Sanskrit. Many Sanskrit scholars have translated these texts honestly. One crucial point is that various so-called Indologists have translated these texts in the past century. However, due to their lack of understanding of Indian culture and practices or the fact that their intention was not to learn but to colonise the Indian people, their translations may not be accurate or even respectful of the Indian ethos. So, a thorough and critical approach is needed to research and select books by authors who demonstrate a greater understanding of Indian culture rather than those who wear a coloured lens and critique the texts superficially. Someone who knows Sanskrit and the Indian ethos, who is a practitioner of its values and abides by its principles, can do justice to the translations.

A good tip is to refer to one's heart and see how the writing makes you feel to verify the authenticity of these translations. If it elevates you, shows you a clear path or points to the commonality of human experience and endeavour, then that is the right book to pick. If, on the other hand, it leaves you with feelings of comparison, lack of reverence or one-upmanship, then it is advisable to shun such literature.

How many ancient texts are read or used practically in the 21st century? Yoga and Ayurveda have now been recognised worldwide as holistic wellness practices. Mantras are memorised and recited by worshippers on special occasions or ceremonies even today. Personal development and corporate management workshops quote *shlokas* from *Bhagwat Gita*. The famous *Gayatri mantra* recited by many people comes from the *Rig Veda*. It is a prayer to the Sun to illuminate our minds just as it illuminates the material world. Fine-tuning the instrument of perception (mind) to realise pure knowledge is the basis of self-development. The mantras are recited in a prescribed poetic manner or meter. Knowing that the mantras praise the eternal divine, the recitation sounds soothing and comforting, although we may not understand the meaning completely.

New research on the science of vibrations of the mantras would be a wonderful inquiry. However, we can approach the Vedas to find meaning; we can look for pearls of wisdom and wealth of knowledge that corroborate our current scientific worldview and spiritual practice, like a modern *Smriti* or personal interpretation in the current times. Vedas are not trying to be understood. It is our desire to learn that propels us.

There is a general spiritual awakening taking place around the world, and it doesn't matter what one looks like, where one resides, or what external manifestations of their spiritual practice are there, as long as it elevates the individual, creates common ground, brings unity and peace, it is the right step. A common misunderstanding by onlookers is that those engaged in ritualistic worship or dress in a certain way are somehow different. Then there are some people searching for meaning and truth, living like a simple householder, who show no external signs of such an endeavour. Who can see what's inside another's heart? The tell-tale sign of people engaged in spiritual practice is an inquiring mind, honest living, compassionate heart and the idea of oneness with all beings in nature.

There are four Vedic texts: *Rig Veda, Atharva Veda, Sama Veda,* and *Yajur Veda*. Like many other spiritual texts worldwide, the Vedas are humanity's collective heritage. Notably, they have two parts: *Karma Kanda* and *Jnana Kanda*, which imply treatises for action and supreme knowledge, respectively.

| Treatise of Vedas | Part | Purpose |
| --- | --- | --- |
| *Karma Kanda* (Rituals) | *Samhita* | Mantras for various rituals |
| | *Brahmana* | Manual for using the mantras |
| *Jnana Kanda* (Knowledge) | *Aranyakas* | Philosophy of Vedas |
| | *Upanishads* | Essence of the Vedas |

Each additional part of the Vedas facilitates better practice and understanding of the mantras. The rituals are supported by a clear methodology, process, and materials. The philosophy behind the practice is then explained. Finally, the essence of the practice and knowledge is condensed and disseminated for easy comprehension.

This kind of progressive addition of supporting knowledge might have taken place gradually as per the need of the prevailing times, and when inquiring minds might have asked, 'Why do I need to do that?'. This inquiry is precisely how we must explain the logic behind every action in modern times to the curious student.

In the current context, we might think these rituals and practices are not mainstream, but if one observes this culture, one will find myriad practices and customs that stem from the Vedic *Karma Kanda Samhita*. In addition to these practices, the knowledge or philosophical essence of the Vedas referred to as *Vedanta*, has been the backbone of Indian philosophy from time immemorial. Teachers give contemporary analogies and explanations in each age, making the concepts relevant to the people.

Thanks to the many scholars and teachers who have translated these texts, Vedic knowledge has become more accessible to vast populations. The critical point is that we can realise this knowledge when we adopt Yogic practices to regulate our minds and live by these principles. Just an intellectual understanding will not suffice. So, are there any simple yogic practices suited to modern life or well-established in the current time and place? How can we adopt them in our daily lives to help us realise the eternal truths? These questions are dealt with later in this book.

**Upanishads**
*The Upanishad,* which translates to mean 'to sit nearby in reverence,' contains the essential ultimate knowledge of the Vedas. Ancient teachers imparted this knowledge to the prepared students, much like a lesson plan based on the Vedic syllabus. A typical lesson plan, like the ones in modern education, would have a concept, a story, a follow-up activity, and a reflection.

The teacher's role in preparing the students to assimilate this knowledge was equally important. In addition to imparting knowledge, the teacher was responsible for fine-tuning the students' instruments of cognition and perception through yogic practices.

*The Upanishads* contain the essence of the spiritual knowledge enshrined in the Vedas, which is revealed through some *mahavakyas*, great sayings or eternal truths. The following four *mahavakyas* epitomise the essence of the Vedas, which seekers must realise as a direct personal experience, not just as mental constructs. Contemplating these *mahavakyas* helps us distil ageless wisdom and expand our consciousness.

| Upanishad | Mahavakya |
| --- | --- |
| Aitareya (Rig Veda) | प्रज्ञानम् ब्रह्म (prajnanam brahma) Prajnana, the ultimate supreme spiritual knowledge or wisdom is Brahma |
| Mandukya (Atharva Veda) | अयम् आत्मा ब्रह्म (ayam atma brahma) This Self is Brahma |
| Chandogya (Sama Veda) | तत् त्वम् असि (tat tvam asi) You are Brahma |
| Brihadaranyaka (Yajur Veda) | अहम् ब्रह्म अस्मि (aham brahmasmi) I am Brahma |

What is referred to as Brahma in these statements? Brahma is the unity consciousness, our true essence.

## Puranas

The *Puranas* are considered *Smriti* texts. *Puran* is *pura + an,* where *'pura'* refers to ancient, and *'an'* means to tell. *Puranas* are records of antiquity. The *Puranas* relate to the events of ancient history and genealogical records of various gods, sages and royal families. Many of these accounts are relegated to mythology by historians due to a lack of archaeological or scientific evidence. The *Puranas* contain allegorical explanations of creation, different worlds or *lokas* and beings inhabiting these worlds. These events and interactions unfold the understanding of the underlying divine order that regulates the world.

The *Puranas* contain stories in which the protagonists are divine beings, sages, royal families, and some trouble-making entities. When we read the *Puranas*, it is difficult to recognise all the names and map the genealogy of the many ancient people. That is a topic for detailed research by itself. A text had to fulfil five conditions to qualify as a *Purana*. The five characteristics are:

1. *Sarga*- the creation of the universe.
2. *Pratisarga*- dissolution and recreation of the world.
3. *Manvantaras*- period of each *Manu*.
4. *Vamsha*- genealogies of gods, sages and royals.
5. *Vamshanucharita*- accounts of ruling dynasties.

It is postulated that around 5000 years ago, *Vyasa* (the scribe) compiled various folktales prevalent across India and gave them a coherent structure of *Puranas* in the form of 5 lakh shlokas. *Vyasa* also formatted the *Puranas* and made 18 divisions for better understanding. The stories and characters in these texts are symbolic and have a great depth of meaning. A critic can dismiss them, while a curious seeker can find the symbolism valuable. It depends on the attitude and the intent of the individual. To understand this anthropomorphic symbolism, one must learn the philosophy of the *Vedas* and *Upanishads*. The purpose of *Puranic* symbolism was to bring glorious spiritual truths into the cultural life of the population through tales and relatable imagery.

If the *Puranic* stories are not understood in the context of spiritual knowledge, one can get caught up in the complex names and events described and even question some of the actions. In these stories, characters' names, plot and setting point towards a duel within ourselves, between progressive and regressive forces within our nature.

One example of this anthropomorphic representation of spiritual truths through story-telling and imagery is Goddess Durga's story in the book *Durga Saptashati*, which contains 700 mantras. In this story, Goddess Durga defeats

the *asuras* or demons, who can be equated to the lower
tendencies in human nature. These lower tendencies are
misguided ego, attachment to senses, and false
identification. Our higher energies of intellect, devotion,
and detachment from the senses come to our rescue. These
symbolic truths are hidden in the names, characters, and
imagery.

These stories have a cultural role as an introduction to the
idea of divine reality beyond the limited perception of
human awareness. They also create an opportunity to
express devotion to the divine. The stories build a coherent,
united community of seekers, as we see in the grandiose
celebrations during Durga Puja by devotees wherever they
may be. The stories can also act as catalysts to propel us
towards actively seeking the goal of self-realisation. We
can also expand the scope of this worship and revelry by
applying the hidden, symbolic meaning in our lives. We can
do this through Yoga.

**Itihasa**
The word *Itihasa* means 'as it happened'. It is a factual
account of history, particularly related to two incarnations
of *Vishnu*, namely Rama and Krishna. Many archaeological
and geological findings have recently mapped the location
of kingdoms, cities, highways and landscapes mentioned in
these texts. The texts also contain astrological references,
which can date the events described when analysed using
modern satellite-based software systems. Many scholars are
looking at various pieces of evidence to recreate a narrative
of the true history of India; for example, the underwater
archaeological digs in the Arabian Ocean for the lost city of
Dwarka and the Astro-archaeological mapping of the
dried-up riverbed of river Saraswati. Interestingly,
advancements in modern science are taking us back to the
roots of ancient India.

*Itihasa* primarily contains two epics: *Ramayana* and *Mahabharata*. As the name suggests, *Ramayana* is the story of the life of Rama, the Prince of Ayodhya, and his journey across India to present-day Sri Lanka. *Mahabharata* is the story of Krishna and the epic battle of two royal clans of north India. These grand epics reveal the cosmic laws, the duties of a human being, the right way of living and the importance of yogic practices. The texts give a glimpse of the cosmic order and laws that are rigorous and irrefutable. Ancient society inherently respected and upheld this natural order and lived a life governed by these higher principles. What is this cosmic order?

# The Cosmic Order

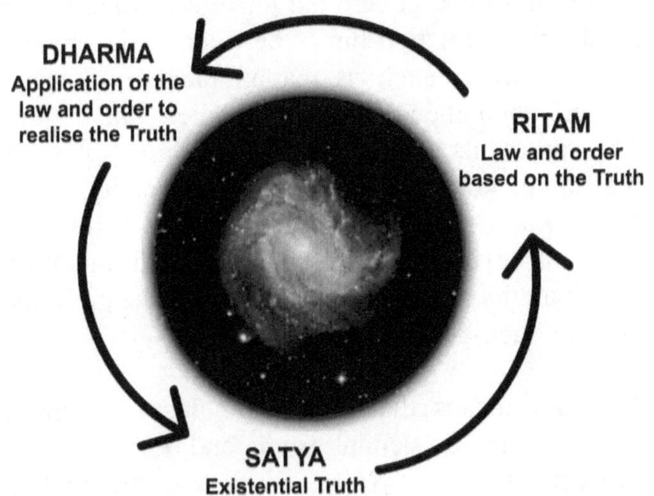



The universe has an underlying unchanging order. Its essential nature is *Satyam Shivam Sundaram*, which means Truth, Goodness, and Beauty. The universe is fundamentally one Truth; it is inherently Good and creates Beauty in all its constituent parts. The principle by which this cosmic order works is explained by the terms *Satya, Rta, and Dharma.* Let us try to understand these concepts.

**Satya** is the foundation of Reality, implying existential truth or *Being*. The entire Vedic approach searches for this existential truth, 'the first cause'. In common parlance, the word *satya* means to tell the truth, which, from a subjective point of view, can have many interpretations. *Satya*, mentioned here, however, is one integral concept; it is the very foundation of existence itself. In the final stage, nothing exists but *Satya*, the existential Reality, the One.

**Ritam** or *Rta* is the cosmic principle or order that operates within the realm of *Satya*. In other words, *Rta* is a set of natural laws that govern the universe. *Rta* also signifies the symbiotic relationship between different natural manifestations, such as matter, plants, animals, humans, natural phenomena, heavenly bodies, and higher beings. *Rta* represents the highest ethical principles and sound reasoning; goodness is its essential quality. At the subtle level, *Rta* defines how subtle matter forms, and at the physical level, *Rta* can be considered the blueprint by which atoms organise themselves to make gross matter. It is cosmic intelligence at work.

**Dharma** means that which upholds or supports. While *Satya* is the existential truth, and *Rta* is the governing principle based on *Satya, Dharma* is the application and understanding of *Rta* in the world. Humans apply it to function effectively, upholding truth, morality, ethics, equality and justice. *Dharma* is performing duty and doing what's right in a given context. It is a complex concept based on a person's location, time and stage in life. For personal gain, lying is *adharma* (opposite of *dharma*). Not telling the truth to save a life in another situation is *dharma*, as saving a life is ethical and aligned with *Rta*.

All actions and thoughts aligned with *Rta* and rooted in *Satya* comprise *Dharma*. In the modern context, the word *dharma* has come to mean religion, but in India, there is no fixed religion based on a set of beliefs and doctrines. *Dharma* is a practical application, a guiding principle to uphold the divine order. *Dharma* helps us align with *Rta* and finally leads us to the realisation of *Satya*, the existential Reality. Following the dharmic principles or not is one's choice, but then we become responsible for the effects of our choices, which further delves into the concepts of *Karma*, the law of action and its results.

# The Cosmic Order and the 33 Aspects of Creation

The Vedic people seemed to express their wonder and reverence for Nature by eulogising beautiful mantras, songs, and poetry in Her praise and performing *yajnas* (fire homage) to honour the gods who were considered a part of nature. As described in the *Puranas,* the creation stories use terms contextual to that time and era. The imagery is anthropomorphic and rooted in the culture of the time. We have modern scientific words for these concepts, and much of this vocabulary has become common knowledge today. But what would have been the case in antiquity? At that time, the language was Sanskrit, the terminology was symbolic, the explanation was visual, and the attitude was reverential.

The 33 *Koti* gods of Indian tradition are highly significant. They can be explained as powers of nature that sustain life. However, the word *Koti* is often misunderstood as one crore or 10 million, and 330 million gods would baffle anyone. The correct interpretation of *Koti* is supreme, type, or category. Although many explanations are available, the above flowchart depicts one logical interpretation.

The *Brihadaranyaka Upanishad* describes creation and its various aspects in great detail. The 33 supreme gods are different aspects of nature, considered reverential *devatas* or beings with unique divine qualities. They are regarded as protectors of *Rta* and maintain the cosmic order. These beings are considered sentient powers of nature in a symbiotic relationship with the human world. Vedic Indians identified, named, and communicated with these active principles of nature, which shows their higher cognitive and intuitive abilities. People pray to these gods and conduct *yajnas* to gain benefits and to improve their lives.

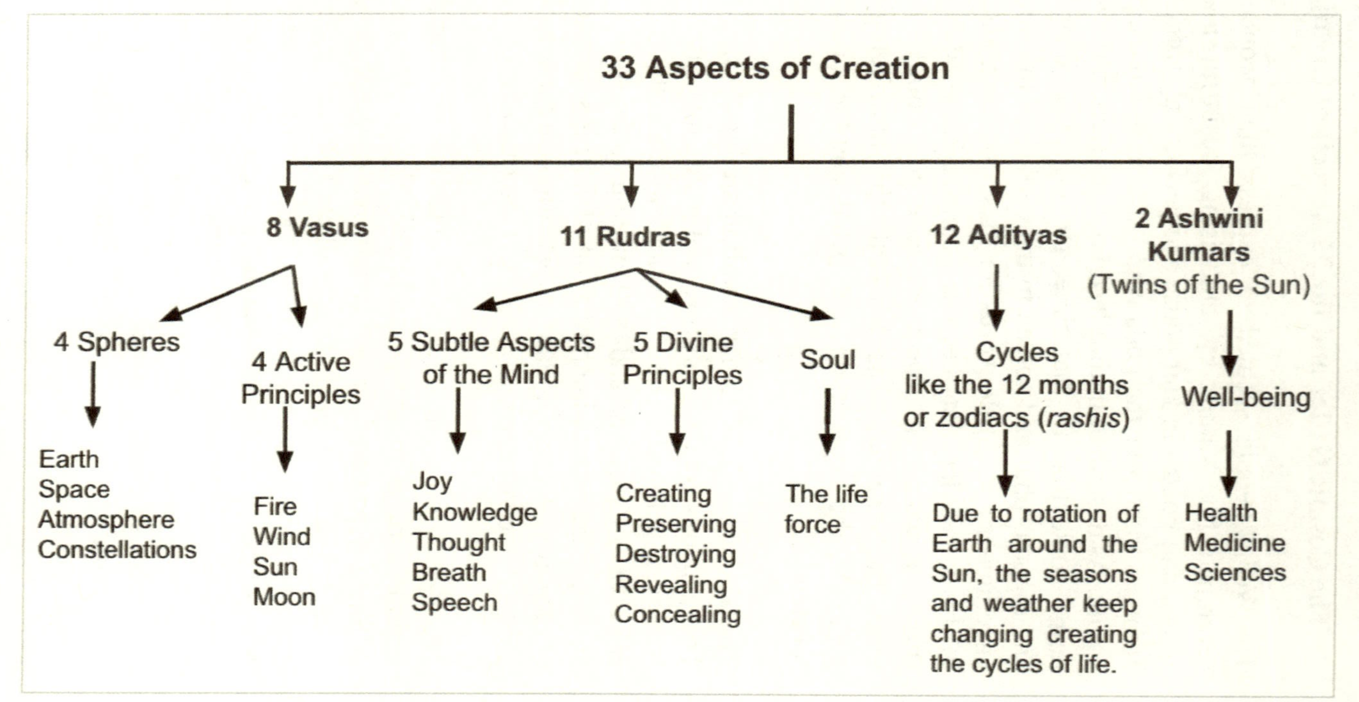

33 Aspects of Creation
8 Vasus
11 Rudras
12 Adityas
2 Ashwini Kumars
(Twins of the Sun)
4 Spheres
4 Active Principles
5 Subtle Aspects of the Mind
5 Divine Principles
Soul
Cycles like the 12 months or zodiacs (rashis)
Well-being
Earth
Space
Atmosphere
Constellations
Fire
Wind
Sun
Moon
Joy
Knowledge
Thought
Breath
Speech
Creating
Preserving
Destroying
Revealing
Concealing
The life force
Due to rotation of Earth around the Sun, the seasons and weather keep changing creating the cycles of life.
Health
Medicine
Sciences

However, these functionaries are of no help in pursuing Yoga and self-realisation, as the goal of Yoga is far beyond their level. These beings are also said to be striving for growth.

The first part of Vedas is *Karma Kanda,* which comprises rituals and practices praising the gods. For example, the Sun deity, in whose honour and worship *Surya Namaskara* is performed, is called by many names in the mantra: *Mitra, Ravi, Surya, Bhanu, Khaga, Pushan, Hiranyagarba, Maricha, Aditya, Savitra, Bhaskara* and *Arka.* Another way of worshipping the Sun is by offering water. Due to its heat, the sun evaporates from everywhere, collecting as clouds, and finally, the water is sent back to the human world as rainfall. This give-and-take (symbiotic relationship) is reflected in this worship.

Similarly, there are many such rituals and practices for different *devatas* of nature. These rituals, traditions, and customs are cultural and are not imposed on the population. Based on their understanding of the world and reality, people apply them. Starting from the level of performing rituals for the deity, chanting the mantras to feel their vibrations, looking for meaning in the mantras, and then developing an interest in the philosophy of Vedas, to finally reaching the summit of human spiritual potential in Vedanta, is the entire gamut of the Vedic worldview.

Each person's interest, aptitude and prior conditioning play a role in their application and understanding of the Vedas. Since people have different levels of experience and approach, there is unparalleled diversity in their approach to the Divine. We need not take this information about 33 gods at face value but use it to expand our idea of the inner and outer worlds. At the same time, we can marvel at the genius of the Vedic people who conceptualised it.

An explanation of the 33 principles is as follows:

1. *Vasus*- Physical aspects
   **-The 4 Spheres:** Earth, space, atmosphere, and constellations constitute the physical world observed with our eyes. The spheres comprise the arena of action for all life. What do you see around you?

   **-The 4 Active Principles:** Fire, wind, sun, and moon are the four active principles that support and influence life. They create constant change on Earth and in our lives.

2. *Rudras*- Subtle and Causal aspects
   **-The Subtle Elements of the Mind**: Speech, breath, thought, knowledge and joy are the subtle elements of the mind. They allow us to express ourselves, be self-aware, think, learn and be joyous. If unregulated, they can also cause suffering. The word *Rudra* implies both regulated and unregulated aspects.

   **-The 5 Divine Actions**: Divine intelligence creates, preserves, destroys, reveals, and conceals the world. The entire realm of knowledge is the search for the 'how and what' of these principles. People ask questions such as how the world is created, who created it, how it functions, how it is destroyed cyclically, and what the governing laws and causes are.

   **-The Soul**: The soul is our divine presence, the causal element.

3. *Adityas*- Cycles
   **-The 12 Months of the Solar Year**: *Aditya*, the name of the Sun, means 'bright'. Sun, the supreme deity of

our world, gives light and warmth and creates cycles needed to sustain life and order in the solar system.

4. *Ashwini Kumars*- Nurturance
   **-The Sun's Twins**: The *Ashwini Kumars* represent the Sun as the ultimate source of health, healing, and regeneration. The Sun gives life and also heals and maintains it.

Such an open-minded study of ancient texts can help us understand the perspective of the Vedic people. How curious, observant, inquiring and scientific these ancient people were to have come up with such a detailed exposition of the outer and inner worlds. Hence, it is necessary to approach this literature with reverence and scientific curiosity if one seeks the hidden pearls of wisdom. Of course, such a study is to be accompanied by *swadhyaya* (self-study) and *sadhana* (spiritual practice), so we can realise this knowledge through our direct experience with perseverance.

# Dharma and Religion

In addition to the 33 supreme deities, India has a pantheon of gods and goddesses that further confuse the uninitiated. Every region, town, village, and family has its deities, and even trees, anthills, caves, rocks, rivers, and plants are visualised as the essence of the same divine. We can say that Divinity lies in the eyes (or the heart) of the beholder.

While it is heartening to see such diversity, the question is- is it enough to be devoted to an image or an idea? The essence of Vedic teachings is to use an image to help the mind hold on to an abstract idea of the divine, but eventually, with yogic practices, one needs to go beyond the form and realise the formless essence within.

How many of us are seeking to go beyond the form? Are we just satisfied with a transactional relationship with the divine, where we seek fulfilment of our wishes in exchange for a ritual? Does the ritual give us the satisfaction of having done our religious duty? Or does it impact how we live, view ourselves and others, or the state of our consciousness? Before claiming to be the inheritors and caretakers of the Vedic heritage, we must dig deep enough to find its essence for ourselves.

As author Dr PY Deshpande described in his book *The Authentic Yoga*, humans have two natural propensities: biological urges and psychological tendencies, which naturally propel us. Survival and continuation of species are the biological urges as nature demands life to propagate. The human being, endowed with a mind, has psychological tendencies that comprise wonder and reverence. At the most basic level, wonder is a scientific inquiry into various tangible aspects of the creation, and reverence is awe at the creator of this magnificent universe.

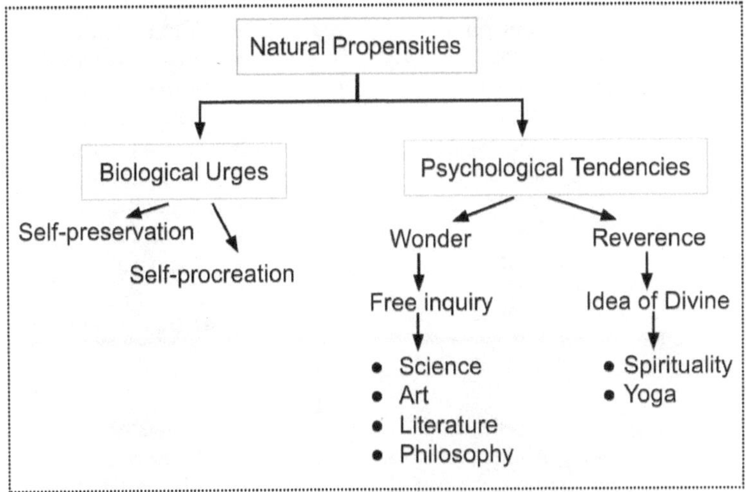


Of course, the basic physical need for survival trumps all. But when subsistence is not a problem, people explore their psychological propensities. They tend to wonder about this magnificent world and naturally develop reverence for its creator.

This basic psychological need for wonder and reverence has been manipulated into fear and guilt by exclusivist religious sects to keep people subdued and under control. It is a mental slavery where wonder transforms into dogmas, and reverence becomes blind faith and fixed belief patterns. In such a skewed approach, free inquiry, critical thinking, experimentation and experiential knowledge become the apparent casualties.

Let's use a quadrant chart to compare religion and science. Yoga is a scientific approach to the Divine. Religion without a practical approach is only a set of beliefs. On the other hand, science without reverence is also an unethical manipulation of natural laws.

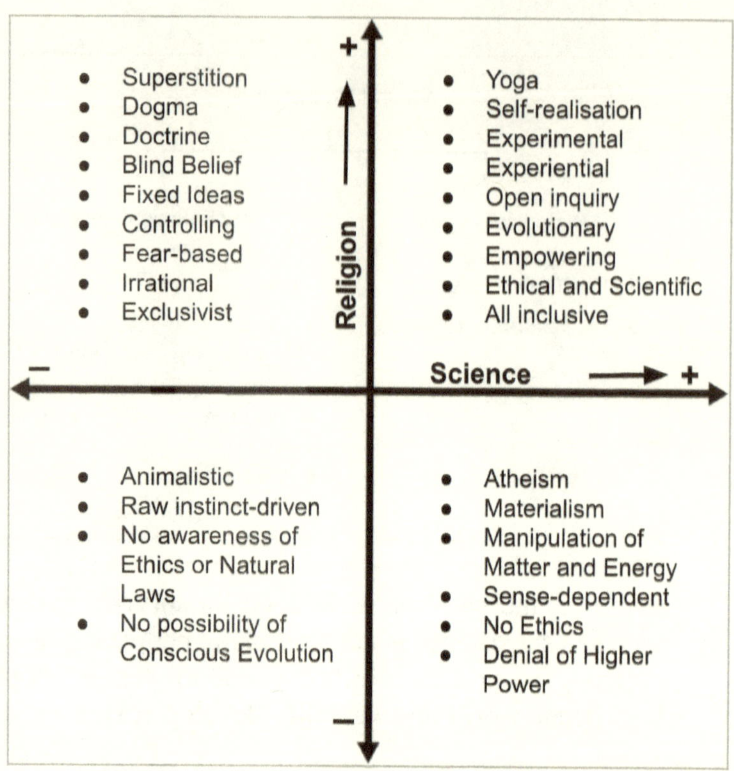


In this new era, the world is getting out of the clutches of fixed beliefs and moving towards rationality. But the chances are that people may choose to follow another religion or even 'secular science' due to dejection from one religion. We must question whether we are just transferring this tendency to hold fixed beliefs from one system to another. Or are we students and scientists extending explorative learning to all facets of life? We must remember that as science evolves, new perspectives develop. So, flexibility and synthesis are fundamental to science.

Ethical standards in scientific application are another critical aspect besides being open-minded. Science without ethical parameters can lead even the most rational person astray. Why don't we develop a scientific approach to the divine and incorporate ethical standards into modern science? Science can provide facts and logic, but only spirituality can show us higher human values. Both reason and ethics are fundamental aspects of being human, not rigid identification with fixed beliefs.

A lack of knowledge of Sanskrit does not hinder our connection to our ancient cultural roots. The core of this philosophy is that we are all One; it binds us and keeps our civilisation together. It is essentially pluralistic and universal in its embrace. Even today, stories from ancient texts are passed orally from grandparents to children. These stories also inspire popular picture books, songs, and movies.

One such fantastic book is *Tales from the Vedas and Upanishads* by Shri Kamlesh D Patel, also known as Daaji. This book is an excellent example of the reinterpretation of ancient knowledge in modern times, along with evolving spiritual concepts and practices. This evolutionary approach to *adhyatma,* or spirituality, is the hallmark of Vedic culture.

## Catharsis
Resolving the Pain of Recent History

Thus far in the book, we have looked at the fundamental ideas and texts of Indian culture and philosophy. While we may cherish the profundity of this vast civilisational heritage, we are tormented by this nation's history over the last millennium. It took some time to wash away the effects of this tumultuous history from my consciousness, with my eyes soaked in tears every day. In this section, I wish to express the feelings and ideas that might help the readers reach their catharsis and continue their journey without ill will or prejudice towards anyone. Any kind of prejudice is self-detrimental.

The traumatic history of our nation in the last 1000 years has seen barbaric invasions from West Asia and oppressive colonisation from Europe, followed by the partition of this secular land based on religion. Our parents and grandparents have stories about their experiences during the partition. People are still carrying this past and the associated pain in their conscious and subconscious minds. There are no simple answers to questions such as why it happened and what went wrong. We can try to make sense of the past, but we also need to **resolve** it by accepting it, learning from it and moving ahead, ensuring that we do not let it repeat. Never again! It requires both inner and outer strengths.

We must build on our strength, courage, self-confidence, and the societal strength of good governance, resources, and abundance. We must grow stronger in every possible way: physically, economically, educationally, militarily, technologically, and spiritually. We must leave no stone unturned in any facet of life and overcome any limitation, doubt, or lack. To overcome the external threat, we must unite.

The ancient texts talk about *dharma yuddha* or righteous war in antiquity. Under the mutually agreed rules of warfare, Kings and their armies fought to resolve disputes. The culture did not believe in inflicting undue harm on soldiers, even in wars. Hence, barbarism against civilians was totally out of the question. Several *Puranic* stories tell us how certain *asuric* (demonic) forces inflicting harm on the civilian population met with resistance and were defeated by *dharmic* (righteous) forces.

Invasion and colonisation of the entire world do not fall under righteous wars; they were a cruel and barbaric plunder of the civilian population. The tactics involved in invasion and colonisation included treachery, deceit, greed, plunder, brutality and a false sense of superiority. It started small, but it aimed to take total control of the resources and people of the oppressed land, eventually wiping out the local culture, economy and autonomy. The indigenous population of much of the world was disenfranchised, converted or killed during the colonial era.

During the invasion from West Asia, the Indian civilian population would undoubtedly have been alarmed by the extreme brutality of it. Not believing a specific god or book could get someone killed. How ironic this is in a land with diverse expressions of worship. Invasion was the rule of the sword, not *dharma*. The southern part of India escaped the severity of this onslaught, while northern India faced the maximum brunt of the invasions.

Following this mass persecution, lasting roughly 800 years, came 200 years of European colonisation in the later part of the 18th century, which exacerbated the poverty and misery of ordinary people. During this period, along with the cultural wealth and knowledge systems, natural resources were also sucked out of the country. The records of multiple famines in India during British colonial rule testify to the mass suffering. This prolonged suffering of 1000 years left India in dire straits.

Years ago, Bharat was known as a prosperous trading civilisation with the highest GDP and voluminous trade with the world. Then, it faced multiple attacks, was gradually invaded and colonised, and lost its wealth and freedom. What happened to the advanced weapons of warfare discussed in our epics? Did we lose the capacity to hold and harness the power of such weapons? How could swords and guns subjugate the Indian subcontinent?

People could argue that at some point in history, Indian society fell from its high traditional spiritual values into a state of lower consciousness. Had it been a strong, united and advancing civilisation, would such an invasion be possible? The jungle law dictates that the weak are subdued by the strong, so one could assume that the indigenous population was weaker than the invaders to have been subjugated by them.

At that time, the world's consciousness was not much different from the jungle law of the animal world, and the humane virtues of honesty, equality, rationality, and 'live and let live' vanished with time. Why did the consciousness of the human population fall to such a level that we saw invasion, dark ages, colonisation and world wars in the past 1000 years?

The peaceful indigenous populations were at the receiving end of this greed and cruelty sanctioned by greed and several fundamental ideologies. The invasion was a sustained and deliberate effort to pillage the resource-rich indigenous lands. Nationalistic historians, scholars and ordinary people, reeling under the pain of this torturous history, say that many great kings and freedom fighters fought against this foreign onslaught, sacrificing their lives. We are free today thanks to the brave efforts of our ancestors. As survivors and inheritors of this culture, we honour all those known and unknown souls. Standing up for freedom and equality in adversity is no small feat.

In the 19th century, when India was probably at its lowest point, the great sage Swami Vivekananda went around the nation trying to wake the oppressed masses. He spoke against corruption, greed, casteism, factionalism, inequality and superstition that had crept into Indian society, which was in survival mode, resigned to its dire fate. Swami Vivekananda wanted to instil self-confidence, courage, aspiration, patriotism and a sense of responsibility in the population. He wanted to see the revival of spiritual values in the nation through the age-old practices of Yoga. He wanted to see a free India, with each citizen realising their full potential. He recognised that the courage and ability to stand up and claim our freedom would come through realising our inner strengths.

Why did Swami Vivekananda try to impact people's minds? It is known that we can change anything from a higher level, not the same level. If we want to change our actions and habits, we should first change our thinking and behaviour. In short, a change in consciousness can create change at the physical level.

Unlike many other indigenous cultures worldwide, Indian culture has survived the onslaught of invasions and colonisation. Despite a fall in traditional values, partition, and ensuing poverty, the fundamental ideas of cultural unity and scientific spirituality from antiquity have brought this civilisation back on its feet and its people together. The sacrifices of the great freedom fighters and the ordinary people have brought us here today.

Now, India stands strong as one nation. The nation has a written constitution protecting human rights, and many laws have eliminated all regressive ideas from society which had seeped in during this dark period of 1000 years. Education and progressive ideas have replaced dogmatic and superstitious practices. There are equal opportunities for all people to become positive contributing members of society. All citizens enjoy the freedom of speech, can own property, vote, seek justice in the court of law, conduct business and live freely under the law of the land. The widespread infrastructure development and system reforms set into motion over the last decade promise a bright future for this country. We look forward to a uniform civil code, a practical education policy, and legal reforms. Greater vigilance is required to overcome factionalism, root out corruption and eradicate addiction. Is there a better way than Yoga to achieve a positive future for the nation and the world, the dream of the great Swami Vivekananda? Change your mind to change your life, he said.

Embracing the past, learning from it, working diligently in the present, and looking ahead with confidence and hope are the hallmarks of a Yogi. Can we be bogged down by identifications that are tied to the past? Who knows, as reincarnating souls, where we have been in the past in our many lifetimes? Where were we during the Vedic period, the great Itihasa period, the golden period of Indian maritime trade, the reign of many Hindu Empires, the invasions, the Dark Ages, the Industrial Revolution, colonisation, the world wars or the freedom struggle?

We are here now when India is surging ahead in the world, breaking off all shackles of the past. One human life seems very short for tethering ourselves to any one fixed identification. Unencumbered from the past, let each soul speak for itself by how it chooses to express its values in the current life, irrespective of culture, religion, country or race.

The Indian leaders and teachers who came along the way in each era kept the flame of spirituality burning, reinventing these age-old teachings to suit the societal context of that era. Some of the great teachers in the last 2000 years are Gautama Buddha, Guru Gobind Singh, Chaitanya

Mahaprabhu, Shri Ramakrishna Paramhansa, Swami Vivekananda, Shri Ram Chandra, Swami Sri Yukeshwar Giri, Paramahansa Yogananda, Shri Aurobindo and many a great sages and yogis. Some of the great leaders of the freedom movement were Rani Lakshmi Bai, Shivaji Maharaj, Subhash Chandra Bose, Vir Savarkar, Bal Gangadhar Tilak, Sardar Patel, Dr Ambedkar and many more.

Even today, great teachers and leaders are carrying the torch of this wisdom. The critical point is that despite all adversity, the essence of Vedic teaching has remained intact in India's cultural fabric. We now see a spiritual revival among the population, seeking the next level of evolution through yogic practices. Vedanta, the ultimate philosophy, has always been the bedrock of Indian thought. Understanding of Vedanta philosophy has grown in the 21st century, and Yoga has become popular again as its practical path.

It is fascinating to note that the teachings of Gautama Buddha became popular in the 5th century BCE, claiming a reformation of Indian society and doing away with its then-prevailing superstitious practices. This is just one example of the cultural regeneration of an ever-changing Indian society. Reformation and revival are part and parcel of any civilisation. In its life cycle, any system can rise and fall due to several factors because any system is as good as the people upholding it. If people and their level of consciousness fall, any system, whether religious, political, educational, administrative, legal, or social, is bound to fall too. Hence, people, not systems, are essential, and their understanding, approach and ethics are paramount. Today, as a civilisation based on dharmic principles, we need to connect to our roots and realise the profound teachings of our ancients to reclaim this lofty heritage.

Today's India is a melting pot of all spiritual systems. It is the sanctuary for the spiritual head of Tibetan Buddhism and a historic pilgrimage for Buddhists worldwide. Several Jewish, Persian (Parsi), Christian and Islamic communities have made India their home. Sikhs call it their motherland. Hindus and the entire NRI diaspora call it their natural homeland. As long as people see each other as equal partners on a journey, how does it matter what shape or form their worship takes?

The lives and original teachings of the great teachers, on whose names all world religions have been founded, contain wisdom. Their essence is also very similar to that of the Vedic texts. However, exclusivism, fundamentalism, and control cannot be part of any true spiritual system; they are distortions meant only for selfish political ends.

An essential point that needs to be re-stated is that there is no such thing as the formal religion of 'Hinduism', a name coined by observers. People of Hind are called Hindus, a name derived from the Sindhu River Valley civilisation. The civilisation spanning the vast geographical length and breadth of India (Bharat) is diverse and an admixture of many sub-cultures, languages and ethnicities. Religion, as per the typical connotations of the word, is not contextual to Indians. We use the word *dharma* to describe our spiritual worldview, which is as natural and eternal as life itself.

*Dharma* does not mean religion; it refers to doing what is right to uphold the divine order in a person's life at a given time and place. *Sanatana Dharma*, translated as Eternal Order or Natural Order, is the fundamental concept of Vedic culture in India. It is an organic, experiential, and all-inclusive concept that shows the path to the divine without rigid beliefs.

In his book, *India that is Bharat*, author J Sai Deepak clearly explains how Hindus are a group of people geographically located in the Indian subcontinent and have a civilisational continuity from ancient times. It is the living Vedic culture. Vedic culture is not a religion but a civilisational ethos deeply entrenched in our psyche. Like the other formal religions of the past couple of thousand years, *Hinduism* is not formally organised or defined by only one book or person. It is not headquartered anywhere, and no single authority exists. It does not proselytise.

Hindu people, however, are pluralistic and diverse and express their wonder and reverence in myriad ways. Vedas and the vast library of Indian spiritual texts are our heritage and world cultural heritage, too. All people worldwide, stripped of their long-held rigid beliefs, are inherently the same, belonging to an ancient culture, one humanity.

The Vedic culture is based on the philosophy of *Sankhya darshana,* and Yoga is its practical application.

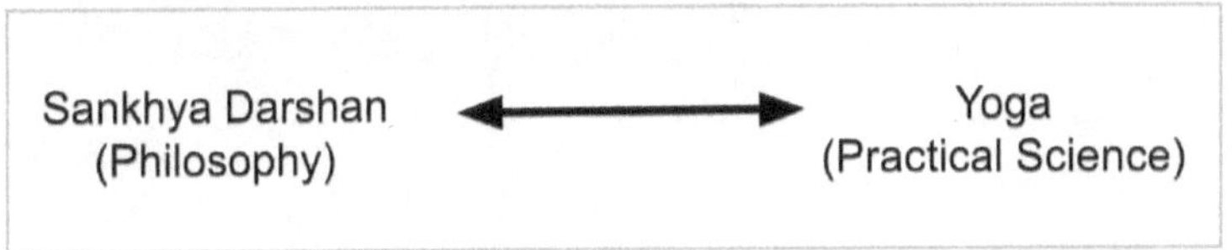


*Sankhya* is a Sanskrit word meaning 'number' or 'enumeration'. It describes the dualist philosophy that perceives the world as made up of matter (Prakriti) and pure consciousness (Purusha). We humans are embodied beings made of a synthesis of matter and pure consciousness. Yoga gives us a path to realising our essence as pure consciousness.

One need not be a Hindu to practice Yoga. Yoga transcends race, nationality, religion, gender, and age. It is a spiritual science and a universal heritage for the benefit of all humanity. Today, many Indians may not read the Vedic texts in their original form. However, this civilisation carries forward the Vedic spiritual teachings through its culture, values, and practices, which are universal in their application and embrace.

The spiritual renaissance worldwide is the next version of the same ancient spiritual tradition, carried forward with new yogic discoveries and methods, just like an evolving science. As yoga discovers new avenues, pathways, and processes, we must keep pace with it as the inheritors of this ancient tradition.

# The Dilemma of Ancient History

How old are the Vedas? The Vedic and Puranic records seem ancient, and the cosmological timescales appear vast. It is challenging to have a consensus on dating them, owing to oral transmission over several generations. Also, these texts are primarily about existential truth (*Satya*) and explain the ways and means to realise this timeless truth, rather than the chronological account of kingdoms, events and geographical locations, unlike much of the world's recent history. Scholars like Nilesh Oak and Dr Saroja Bala have used specific astronomical references from the texts of Itihasas to date them. However, there are a lot of unknowns about the timelines of the Vedas and Puranas.

One reason for this dilemma could be that we see history as a linear progression, with humanity evolving as time progresses. But is that view accurate? There are too many anomalies which create confusion and leave historians baffled. In the short run, we can see events linearly, but over extended time scales, we lose all context, and things become increasingly unclear and dumbfounding. It is similar to thinking that the Earth is flat from our tiny point of reference on its vast surface. Over a more considerable distance, we know that Earth has a curvature as we see a ship appearing on the horizon with the mast of the boat first coming into view. From a distant vantage point in outer space, we can see that the Earth is a sphere. So, when we look at history over 3000 or 5000 years, we see it linearly and try to assign meaning to what we find. For larger timescales, the evidence just goes haywire. If we zoom out to look at history as a cycle of rise and fall in human consciousness, we will arrive at a much better explanation.

Historians argue that early humans were hunter-gatherers, striving for the bare minimum resources for subsistence.

Over time, they developed agriculture and community living, and advancement in language, trade, craft, arts, and science ensued. One wonders, then, what happened to the knowledge that created the great pyramids of Egypt? How and why were they made? How is the largest pyramid's base perimeter proportional to the Earth's radius? How are the sides of the pyramid concave, and how is the curvature the same as the Earth? The theory of thousands of men lifting and transporting perfectly cut massive stone slabs using rudimentary tools seems less and less plausible. The evidence gathered through detailed studies has conclusively debunked the hypothesis that an entire army of men worked continuously and tirelessly for decades just to build a massive tomb. Far greater knowledge, technology, and awareness of purpose are at play in this project than we know.

How does the exquisite ancient Indian temple architecture show some fantastic stone work in precision cut pillars, geometry and sculpting? What can explain the perfection and alignment of such structures? Similarly, how and why were sites like Stonehenge, Nazca lines, Kailasha temple in Ellora caves and Aztec pyramids built?

If the ancient world was so cultured and advanced, then, based on linear progression, shouldn't we have developed further? Why is recent history full of wars, brutality, oppression and poor living conditions for most people? Historians point out that civilisations grow and decline, and the aggressors take over and assimilate the weaker ones. Even geological events can cause massive changes, and diseases can wipe out entire populations. These points are valid but don't explain changes in culture, knowledge and perception over vast periods. Shouldn't these grow overall despite the partial destruction? Shouldn't humans have evolved enough to understand that they can live harmoniously and nonviolently? Currently, the cache of modern weapons of mass destruction does not point towards evolution in clear thinking but rather in the ease of killing. Nor does the pollution and destruction of the natural environment show higher ethics in human society.

This paradox of evidence and narrative is solved by the theory of the cyclical nature of time as preserved in stories across multiple world cultures. The ancient Indians, Mayans, Aztecs, Greeks, Egyptians, Chinese and Persians all have kept accounts of the cyclical nature of time affecting human life in profound ways. In the Indian context, this time cycle is called Yuga. Each yuga has specific characteristics that impact human life. Yuga explains how human beings on Earth go through cycles of ascending and descending consciousness that create the rise and fall of civilisations, cultures and knowledge. Another explanation could be that at frequent intervals, the Earth sees such massive cataclysmic events that wipe out most of humanity, and the survivors have to rebuild from scratch every time, forgetting all previous advancements, hence the cyclical creation and destruction.

From one civilisation's subjective point of view, we can take a stand of being either a victim or an aggressor, inserting ourselves into the story. However, if we look, from a higher vantage point, at the rise and fall of humanity as a whole, we start to see patterns emerging which corroborate the Yuga cycle. The historical artefacts and archaeological evidence show that our ancestors had far more evolved intellect, ethics and spiritual powers. Along the descending cycle of the Yuga, humans devolved. By extrapolation, the human progeny will evolve in the ascending cycle of the Yuga. Maybe Earth has yet undiscovered records of multiple cycles of growth and decline of many ancient civilisations over many yugas.

# Yuga- Cycles of Time and Consciousness

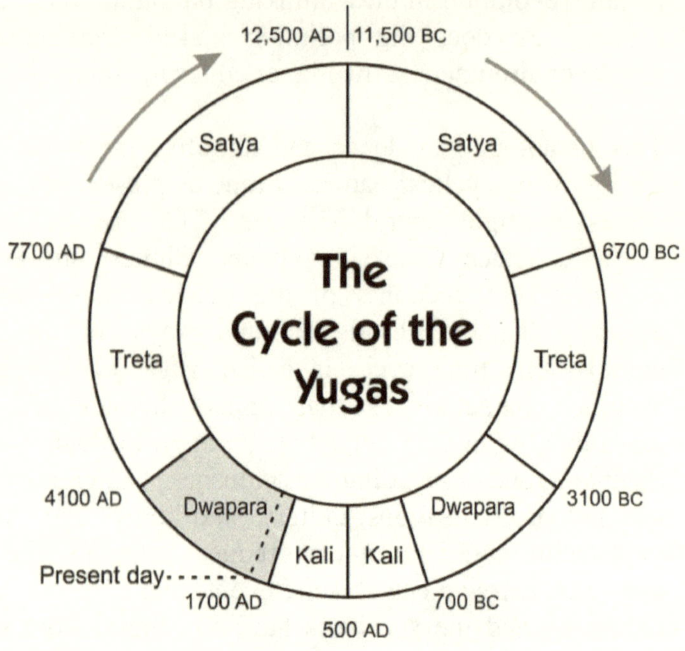



Image Source: The Yugas

In their book *The Yugas*: *Keys to Understanding Our Hidden Past, Emerging Present and Future Enlightenment*, authors Joseph Selbie and David Steinmetz give an insightful and intuitive exposition of the Yuga cycles. They present several facts and evidence to show how history in terms of human development is cyclical and not linear. Their work is inspired by the teachings of Swami Sri Yukteshwar Giri, who elaborated upon the yuga cycles in the early 18th century. He removed the discrepancy that had crept in calculating the yugas in traditional cosmology and explained how the one cycle of yuga spanned roughly 24000 years.

Swami Sri Yukteshwar Giri, the guru of Shri Paramhamsa Yogananda, also predicted the coming of the age of energy. He postulated that as human consciousness evolves, new science will introduce new electrical and magnetic energy concepts. He called this the coming age of divine magnetism, an idea explored later in this book.

In his other book, *The Holy Science*, Swami Sri Yukteshwar Giri also explains the similarities between various spiritual traditions. He points out that we fail to see their underlying unity as we do not understand these traditions and tend to view them in isolation. In his book, he finds common ground between the teachings of the Vedas and the Bible.

**Yuga**

What is a Yuga? A yuga cycle repeats four distinct periods; hence, one such complete cycle is called *chaturyuga* (*chatur* means 'of four'). Each half cycle is a period of ascent and the other half of descent, and a period of conjunction between them is called *sandhi*. The natural state of Satya yuga is self-realisation, a higher aspiration from the perspective of other lower yugas. In each yuga, humans aspire for greater fulfilment of their mental and spiritual potential, and it becomes increasingly difficult as we descend into Kaliyuga, the lowest yuga, also called the dark age.

When people in Satya yuga and Treta yuga lived a simple life, in tune with nature, in unity consciousness with higher capacities of intellect, intuition, telepathy and alchemy, they would not need massive infrastructure, technology, or machines. In the book, the authors argue that earlier yugas would have had a much smaller population than today, so it would not warrant mass manufacturing or agriculture. Physical evidence from Satya and Treta yugas is challenging to find as the people would have lived lightly on Earth, and the evidence might have been destroyed due to geological and climatic changes over long periods.

The associated qualities of the Yugas are as follows:

| Yuga Name | Years | Consciousness | Mental capacity | Dharma (Ethics) |
|---|---|---|---|---|
| Kali | 1000 | Passive | Dull | 25% |
| Dwapar | 2000 | Self-will, Self-interest | Awakened intellect | 50% |
| Treta | 3000 | Self-mastery | Intuitive intellect | 75% |
| Satya | 4000 | Self-realization | Direct perception | 100% |

A master archer will hit the target with an average bow and arrow, but an amateur will not achieve the result even with the best equipment. The analogy indicates that the secret of success lies in the archer's self-mastery, not just in the weapon's sophistication. So, a person in Satya yuga or Treta yuga could achieve any result through the sheer power of self-mastery, hence eliminating the need to exploit Earth's resources.

In Dwapara and Kali yugas, one expects to find physical evidence of civilisations, but it is difficult for modern historians to understand. In Kaliyuga, people can not fathom the construction of sites like Pyramids, Stonehenge, underwater city ruins near Gujarat or the Kailash temple in Ellora. These are a reminder of earlier glory days of human life on Earth when people lived with much greater inner potential expressed and realised. Kaliyuga is the age of ignorance. In the current ascending Dwapara yuga, we have seen tremendous population growth just in the last 200 years, aided by the mass production of food, eradication of diseases, harnessing energy from fossil fuels, and mass communication.

As per Swami Sri Yukteshwar Giri, the 1000 years from 700 CE to 1700 CE was the Kali-yuga, and we are now in Dwapara yuga, in the ascending phase of the cycle. Things can only get better from here. Post-1700 CE, human understanding evolved from matter to energy, corresponding to the change from mechanical work to an energy-powered world.

A couple of thousand years from now, the next stage will be that of higher mental powers like intuition and telepathy. And finally, after a few more thousand years, Satya yuga will come, where self-realisation will be an everyday experience of the entire human population. We do not have to wait to be reborn in Satya yuga to arrive at the lofty stage of full development of human potential; we can achieve our full potential here and now in this very lifetime. This is the ancient call of Yoga, as relevant today as at any other time on Earth.

**What explains the Yuga cycle?**
The entire creation, from macro to micro, is cyclical, one cycle inside another infinitely. From the perspective of time, we have seconds, minutes, and hours in our watch for practical timekeeping. The larger calendar calculates days, months, years, and yugas related to Earth's movements within our localised universe.

We have realised that the Earth, which seems stationary from our perspective, is moving at an enormous speed through space. All the heavenly bodies in the solar system and beyond are in a coordinated dance with each other.

Earth has three distinct movements:

1.  It spins on its axis every 24 hours, creating day-night cycles.

2.  It goes around the sun in a 365-day cycle, making a year. The tilt in its axis gives us the seasons.

3.  It wobbles on its axis like a top, producing a slow spin called the precession of the equinoxes. This creates a cycle of approximately 24000 years called 'the great year'.

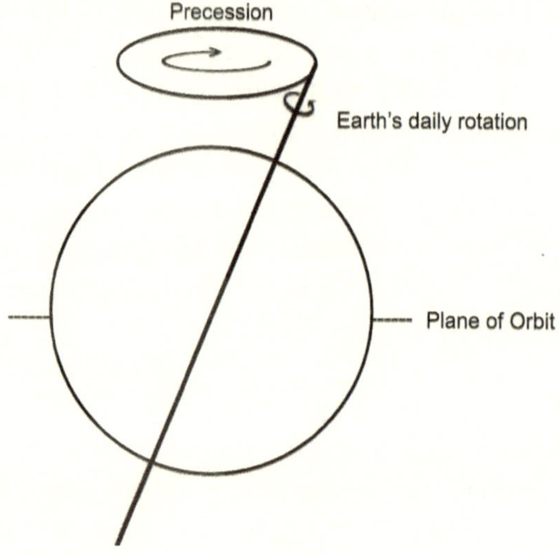


Although precession was known from antiquity, Sir Isaac Newton explained it scientifically in the 17th century. Earth's rotation creates an equatorial bulge, which causes the body to precess around the rotational axis like a spinning top. The Earth's axis of rotation traces a cone in space in approximately 24000 years. Due to this movement, the Earth's rotational axis points to a different north star every half cycle.

The precession is slow movement as it takes an average human lifetime to move each degree in the 360-degree cycle. Swami Sri Yukteshwar Giri explained Yugas by the Sun's movement around another massive heavenly body, let's call it the Central Sun. Sun traces an elliptical orbit around this Central Sun at one of the ellipse's foci. When our Sun is closer to the central Sun, we on Earth experience states of higher consciousness, and far from it, the consciousness levels dip. Even modern astronomers are pursuing the theory of our Sun being in a binary star system.

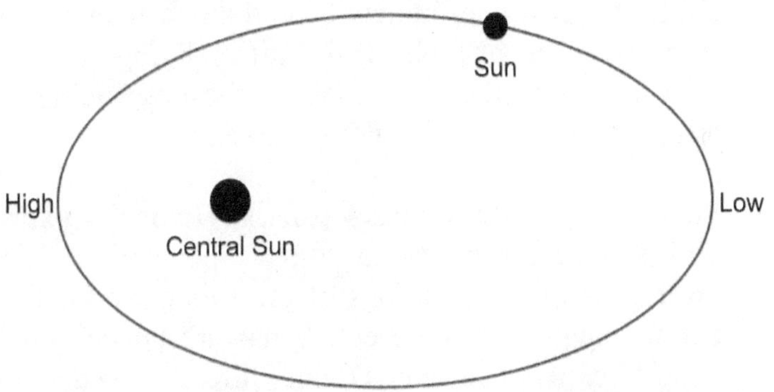


Whatever the cause of the Yuga cycle, the point is that the ancients could observe and measure these cycles of Earth. Although the precession was slow to observe, they calculated it, mapped it, and were aware of its effect on Earth. How did all this knowledge get lost to the extent that the medieval world held a geocentric viewpoint? Galileo, who saw through his telescope and proclaimed the heliocentric model, was persecuted. Even during Galileo's time, there might have been some yogis and curious scientists who would have known this fact. Then again, Yugas indicate the general collective condition of human consciousness, not that of a few individuals.

**Descending Yuga Cycle:**
In Satya yuga, humans were connected to their divine essence. They could understand their true potential and had excellent thought power. They could harness nature's energies and live peacefully. Then, in Treta yuga, they lost their connection with the divine essence but still possessed a mighty intellect and could, with little effort, experience the heightened awareness of Satya yuga.

Then came Dwapara yuga, when humans lost their higher intellectual capacity and had to contend with utilising natural energies. Finally, in Kaliyuga, humans lost the ability to grasp the subtlety behind the form and considered themselves as just physical entities living to satisfy the physical demands. Let's look at the descending cycle in terms of some stark changes observed:

**Satya Yuga**: 100% consciousness. Humanity experiences divine connection as a direct perception. There is awareness of the workings of the subtle world. Telepathic communication is prevalent. Vedas are unnecessary, as all people experience the Divine directly. Vedas exist in unmanifest form. The world's population is much smaller than today, and much of the northern world is under ice cover.

**Treta Yuga**: 75% consciousness. Humanity no longer experiences divine connection as a direct perception but can reach it with some effort. Intellect is intuitive, and awareness of subtle energy still exists. The Yogis intuitively receive the Vedas. They can use the mantras to tune into higher reality. Vedas are transmitted orally from one generation to the next. The population is still tiny compared to today, and the northern hemisphere is still under ice cover. Indigenous cultures develop their folktales and rituals for divine worship. In the Indian subcontinent, the grand epic of Ramayana plays out based on the concept of good defeating evil. This story teaches us that *dharma* and natural laws are above all.

**Dwapara Yuga**: 50% consciousness. Humanity no longer experiences divine connection but has a memory of it. Natural energies are harnessed, and higher consciousness is achievable only with great effort or *tapasya*. Only certain people can use Vedic mantras for gains. Communication is verbal and written. Vedas are written down so that there is a record for future generations. Cultures worldwide are connected, and there is trade and knowledge exchange. Large cities and towns with suitable infrastructure are created. In the Indian subcontinent, the grand epic of Mahabharata plays out. Through a story based on war and internal feuds between clans and families, we learn the philosophy of right living and how to forge a path for self-development through yoga.

**Kali Yuga**: 25% consciousness. Humanity no longer experiences divine connection but has a vague idea of the sacred as perpetrated by dogmatic religions. No one has the capacity to use Vedic tools. Knowledge of subtle energies is lost, and humanity harnesses only matter. Intellect is dull, and the masses are illiterate. Society is held hostage by superstition, fear and greed. Priestly class manipulates people for personal gain. Communication, whether verbal or written, is unreliable. Sanskrit is relegated as a legacy language, with few scholars. One group dominates another through invasion, imperialism and colonisation. Discrimination and inequality prevail between nations, within countries, communities, and families.

In the Satya yuga, when all humans were in touch with their divine essence and communicated telepathically, why would they need to write down Vedic texts that describe the spiritual truths and show how to connect to the divine? Vedic texts exist in each yuga cycle; their essence is vibrational, ever-existing. Vedas consist of mantras, which are tools to reach a focused state of mind where one becomes aware of higher realities, like an attunement device. Why would you need it in Satya yuga, where everyone is already in tune with the divine essence?

Mantras could be helpful in later yugas, particularly Treta, when human beings fell into a lower consciousness level and could no longer feel the connection to the divine. But by Dwapara, the mantras could be used only by a select group of people for specific worldly pursuits who could harness the potential of the mantras.

By Kaliyuga, no one had the potential to use the mantras correctly. Following the archer analogy, in Kaliyuga, no one had the self-mastery required to use the attunement tools of Vedic mantras. One must acquire some level of self-mastery to understand Vedic philosophy, use its tools, and apply them in life. From the Indian perspective, Kaliyuga is the lowest time in each evolutionary cycle. Indian society, being based on dharmic principles, has no history of oppressing other civilisations. Instead, it gradually declines from a high spiritually awakened state to a low state of ignorance, and invaders subjugate it. The long and hard-fought freedom struggle and the current decolonisation process prove the revival of truth.

**Ascending Yuga Cycle:**
We are now in the ascending yuga cycle. Science is pushing its boundaries to better understand the subtle realm. Yoga is returning to the modern world, giving people a much-needed method of connecting within. What will be in the future? No one can say, but we can extrapolate the ascending line and foresee positive growth. We can speed it

up with revolutionary yogic practices and co-create Satya yuga right here.

Moving from Kaliyuga to Dwapara yuga, we see apparent shifts in humanity's consciousness. From the dark ages, we move to the age of energy. From superstition and dogma, we move towards scientific temper and rationality. We see sovereign nation-states, education and literacy, and mass communication. We can harness energy from fossil fuels and renewable resources. We see a spiritual revival worldwide as people reconnect to their roots and natural wisdom. We see a large population living with relative peace, although there are still some parts of the world suffering from factionalism and terrorism.

Daaji, Heartfulness global guide, in an article titled *The planet was there before us and will be there after us*, published in the Heartfulness magazine in April 2022, writes that humans appeared on Earth at least 1,30,000 years ago. Daaji elaborates on human responsibility for the sustainability of life on Earth, pointing out that we don't need to save Earth; we need to save ourselves and our collective selves.

Apart from nature-friendly practices, he recommends reducing thought pollution to reverse negative environmental trends. What is inside is outside, too. Each person needs to work towards self-mastery, and when that is reflected externally, we naturally exhibit Earth-conscious behaviour. This is another example of creating change from a higher level. We could also surmise that 1,30,000 years of human life on Earth would equal at least five yuga cycles that humanity has seen, with consciousness levels descending and ascending 5 times. Overall, the duration that humans have been here on the Earth is minute compared to the large timescale of the planet's evolution.

# Visualising the Cosmos

In the previous section, we expanded our worldview by exploring the concept of Yuga cycles and examining humanity from a higher vantage point. In this section, we will stretch the limits of our imagination and visualise the vast cosmos from a scientific perspective. NASA has revealed amazing visuals of the cosmos that baffle us.

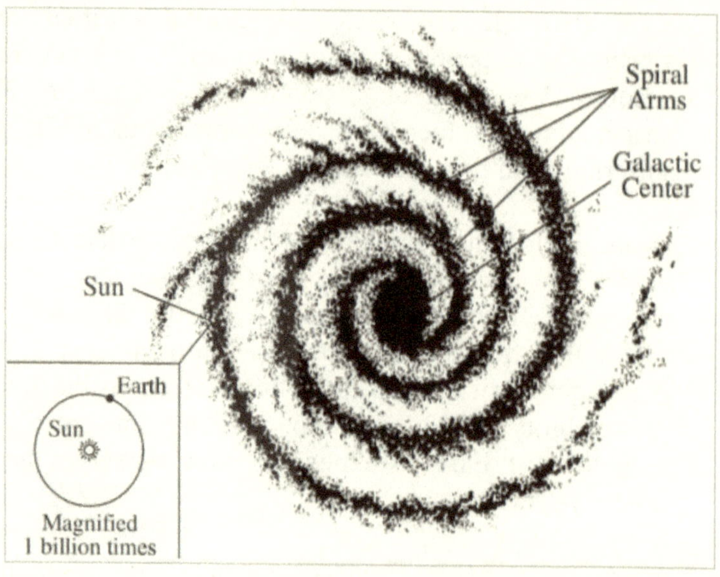


The cosmos is a perpetual motion of cycles inside cycles and overlapping cycles. All heavenly bodies are in relative motion to other bodies and subject to the collective effect of all the operating gravitational forces. The Moon revolves around the Earth, which revolves around the Sun. The Sun, moving at tremendous speeds along the galactic plane, tugs on its planets, which follow it in a helical orbit, like a vortex.

The Sun has the Sirius star system and the Pleiades cluster of stars in its interstellar neighbourhood. This entire collection is on the Orion spiral arm of the Milky Way galaxy, and the galaxy itself rotates around its galactic centre. The Milky Way and the Andromeda galaxy are part of the local galaxy cluster, which, in turn, is part of the larger Virgo supercluster of galaxies. The Virgo cluster is in the supermassive cluster of clusters of galaxies, newly named *Lineakea*, which means immeasurable heaven in Hawaii.

To wrap our brains around the enormity of the cosmos as revealed by modern satellites and deep space telescopes, let us look at some size and distance data:

**Earth**: The circumference of Earth at the equator is 40,075 km. Earth is 150 million km away from the Sun. Sunlight takes 8 min to reach Earth.

**Solar System**: The distance between the Sun and Pluto is 5.9 billion km. Light takes 5.5 hours to travel from the Sun to Pluto.

**Interstellar Neighbourhood**: The Sun has many stars in its neighbourhood. Sirius, twice the size of the Sun, is the brightest star in the night sky. Sirius is 8.6 light years from the Sun.

**Milky Way**: The Milky Way is 100,000 light-years across in its diameter. There are 100 billion stars in the Milky Way. The Sun is 25,000 light years from the galactic centre. The Sun takes 225 million years to orbit the galactic centre.

**Local Cluster of Galaxies**: The local cluster of galaxies contains 54 galaxies. The nearest galaxy, Andromeda, bigger than the Milky Way, is 220,000 light-years across.

Distance to Andromeda is 2.5 million light years from the Milky Way.

**Virgo Supercluster**: The Virgo cluster of galaxies spans 110 million light years. There are at least 100 galaxy clusters in the Virgo supercluster.

**Laniakea Super Massive Cluster**: Laniakea is 500 million light-years across with an estimated 100,000 galaxies.

**The Great Attractor**: The Great Attractor is the central gravitational point of the Laniakea supermassive cluster. The galaxies in Laniakea, perpetually in motion, appear to be pulled toward it.

Mapping has shown how all the clusters are finally moving towards The Great Attractor, and further inquiry on the why and how of these observations is ongoing. As published in an article in www.nature.com, a team led by Brent Tully, an astronomer at the University of Hawaii in Honolulu, charted the motions of galaxies to infer the gravitational landscape of the local Universe and redrew its map. The observable universe appears like a cosmic web where bright stars dot the entire firmament. The sheer vastness and complexity of this cosmology are enough to make one marvel with awe at the creation.

Ancient Indian cosmology gives interesting perspectives. In it, we find descriptions of the Earth as a globe rotating the Sun and the Sun moving in the plane of the Milky Way galaxy. There are indications in the texts that show a black hole as the centre of our galaxy. The term *Vishnu-nabhi* (navel of *Vishnu*) is used to define the galactic centre.

Notably, ancient Indian cosmology also describes 14 *lokas* or parallel worlds. Out of these 14 worlds or levels, seven are lower, and seven are higher worlds, which create a pair of octaves, with Earth in the middle where these two worlds intersect. Our telescopes cannot see these parallel worlds as they are at different vibrational levels. When we rise spiritually or vibrationally, we go to higher levels.

As above, so below. The seven *lokas*, seven musical notes, seven colours of the rainbow, and seven *chakras* in the body are all vibrational realities stratified by octaves. We are also aware of the vast timescales in the Mayan calendar. How did the ancient Indians and Mayans know about cosmic movements and create such massive time cycles as their cultural stories?

# The Dilemma of Modern Science

The dilemma of modern science is that the more we know, the more remains unknown. Specialisation in different branches of science and technology is progressing rapidly, which creates silos with little or no collaboration between various fields. More cooperation can unite diverse fields in a coherent picture of the observable world.

We want to map the farthest reaches of the universe, and we also want to find the most fundamental subatomic particles, and this is pushing the boundaries in both directions. Vedas say that the Ultimate is *Anoraniyan* and *Mahatomahiyan*, meaning smaller than the smallest and greater than the greatest. Will this search ever end as it stretches to infinity on both ends? Further, it throws up numerous questions that baffle us. We have progressively gone on to understand the physical Newtonian laws, thermodynamics, electromagnetism, atomic sciences and quantum theory, but we have yet to grasp the nature of matter and light completely.

Based on observed phenomena, we have developed technology to harness the potential of natural forces. Still, we need to explain the most basic questions, such as why light behaves like a particle when travelling, and when it interacts with other fields, why it acts like a wave. We cannot explain the observer's paradox: Why does the observer affect the measurements of subatomic particles?

Do the subatomic particles exist as probabilities, manifesting based on the stimulus? What is gravity? How are galaxies formed? Why do we label more than 80% of the universe as unknown dark matter and dark energy? What is matter, and how is it created?

Biology and modern medicine are still baffled by the human body and are treating the body symptomatically. Although there is a growing understanding of the human nervous system, it still does not explain the human mind's fundamental nature. Why do we call 98% of our DNA junk? What is consciousness? These questions push the scientific horizon from the level of manifest matter to the unseen energy and then further to unmanifest potentiality. A new field of energy medicine is emerging now, and traditional healing systems are also resurgent.

Scientists are now studying consciousness and are poised to break the barrier of reductionistic and materialistic approaches to science. It is now well known that all scientific discoveries happen when scientists have reached a state of mind which is 'in the flow' connecting to higher intuitive knowledge. The attunement inspires, and then the solution to the problem is worked out rationally. We need to raise our level of consciousness to grasp the subtle causes behind natural phenomena. In part 2 of the book, we will look at some discoveries in modern science and draw parallels with yogic teachings.

# Chapter 2
# Sankhya Philosophy

## A Culture of Inquiry

Humans always ask existential questions: Who are we? From where did we come? What explains the phenomenon we see around us and in us? What is the source of joy and sorrow? What is the point of living if death is inevitable? And many more.

Humans are inquirers by nature. Indian culture and philosophy are not a theoretical path with fixed ideas, dogmas, doctrines, or beliefs. They are a practical approach to understanding the science of life, setting a smart goal, adopting best practices, experimenting, asking questions, working on feedback loops, and then applying what is learned in life. In a word, this is called Yoga.

Yoga comes from the root word '*Yuj*', implying 'to join' or 'to unite'. Yoga is to be in union with your goal. All attempts to fix a higher goal and the steps followed to achieve it constitute Yoga. In a yogic system, the goal is the highest, which is to realise one's true nature. To understand the goal, we must first find out who we are.

In this culture of inquiry, we are encouraged to be yogis who experiment and find the result within ourselves. The yogi is a scientist who creates hypotheses, conducts experiments and gathers evidence. Finally, he corroborates findings by becoming the result he seeks. Since it is a subjective experience, how can it be an objective science? When more and more people find similar results with the practice, we can surmise that they followed a scientific process. Modern methods like the ECG, EEG, brain wave mapping, and sleep analysis show us the efficacy of these yogic practices. They show positive results by mapping the change in emotions and thoughts for all new and seasoned yoga practitioners. Like this, we can approach our traditional knowledge with a scientific temperament, an inquiring mind and a desire to experiment.

## The Science of Life

Modern science studies natural phenomena to determine the underlying laws so that we can harness nature's energy and resources. However, it has yet to explore the science of life, which deals with consciousness and goes beyond the observable universe into the subtle realm. The study of mind and behaviour is called psychology; however, the scientific study of consciousness is not yet mainstream. As an offshoot of ethics, consciousness has been relegated to the fold of religions. But that's changing now, in the 21st century.

Scientific attitude says we can approach any subject with an inquiring mind, asking questions, analysing, debating, experimenting and coming to conclusions based on our practical experience. We can have the same approach to the study of consciousness itself. Ancient Indian spiritual knowledge is scientific, and it deals with the evolution of consciousness. Labelling it as dogma, mythology, or a set of archaic rules is a common misunderstanding. It is time to strip away the superfluous and prejudiced ideas about consciousness, release it from the grip of religions and look at it scientifically. What is consciousness? We must first determine who we are to grasp the concept of consciousness.

# Who We Are

We are Jivas or living beings. We are a part of Nature (*Prakriti*) and created by it. Jiva has multiple layers or sheaths: gross, subtle and causal bodies. It is easy to understand these layers as having different densities.

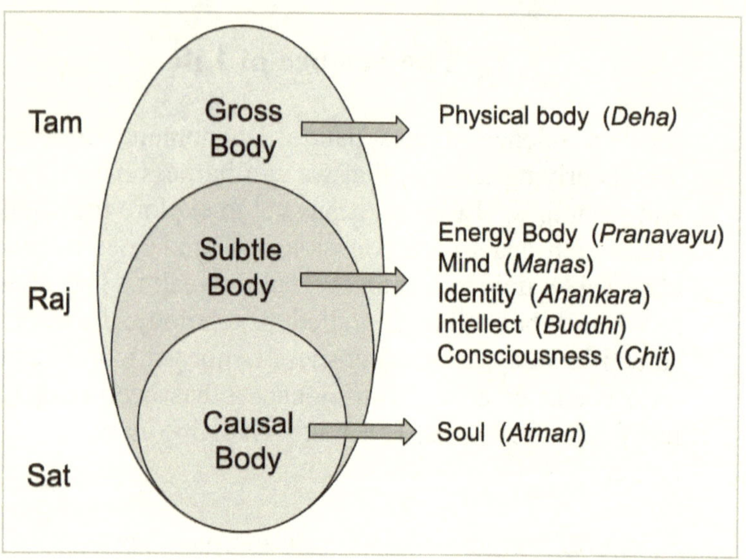


All living beings, animals, plants or minerals have these sheaths or bodies, although they are active to varying degrees. For example, humans have all three sheaths active, with a possibility of expansion of the subtle body. Animals have all three bodies active but to a lesser degree than humans and without the possibility of growth of the subtle body. Plants have their subtle bodies relatively dormant, while they do show some response to stimuli. Minerals, on the other hand, appear dense and inactive. All Jivas are bound by the three fundamental attributes of *Prakriti* (Original Nature) called *Trigunas*: *Sat*, *Raj* and *Tam*. *Trigunas* are described in detail later.

## Sheaths (*Koshas*) in a Human Being

**1. Gross Body** (*Sthula Sharir*)
It is also called the *Annamaya Kosha,* the physical sheath made of food. It is perceived through the five senses and comprises the five gross elements (*panchabhutas*): fire, air, water, space, and earth. It includes DNA, cells, nerves, tissues, skin, blood, bones, and organs.

**2. Subtle Body** (*Sukhma Sharir*)
The multiple layers of the subtle body are as follows:
(i) **Pranamaya Kosha***:* The vital force (*prana)* sheath is the flow of energy within us and a bubble of energy enveloping the physical body as its aura. *Pranamaya Kosha* comprises energy pathways (*nadis*) and vortices (*chakras*). It maintains movement and active functions of the body; it is the bio-energetic field. It powers both the body and mind.

(ii) **Manomaya Kosha***:* The mental-emotional sheath comprising the Identity (*ahamkara*) and Mind (*manas*) can not be perceived through the five senses. It is made up of subtle elements or *Tanmatras*: sound, touch, form, flavour and smell, which in turn co-relate to *Panchabhutas,* the five gross elements. *Manomaya Kosha* allows us to perceive, think, feel and have a sense of 'I-am-ness'.

(iii) **Vijnanamaya Kosha***:* The intellect (*buddhi*) sheath is the power of cognition in us. It also represents wisdom and intuition.

(iv) **Chit***:* Chit refers to consciousness, the agency or degree of awareness. Consciousness can move between all sheaths and locate our sense of awareness at any level. The entire yogic approach is to shift awareness from body-centric and mind-centric to soul-centric. This is the science of the evolution of consciousness.

3. **Causal Body** (*Karan Sharir, Atman*)

It is called *Anandamaya Kosha* and is made of bliss (*ananda*). It causes other sheaths, both gross and subtle. The senses or the mind cannot perceive it. Jiva realises itself as the *Atman,* or pure consciousness, when all impurities from the subtle and gross bodies are removed.

## More about *Pranamaya Kosha* (Energy Body)

*Pranamaya Kosha* is the energetic sheath in the subtle body. It comprises energetic pathways, which the yogis have perceived and described. These pathways, called *Nadis,* control all body functions. There are three main pathways: *Ida, Pingala,* and *Sushumna.*

*Pingala,* also called *Surya Nadi,* is associated with the sympathetic nervous system (left brain hemisphere) that directs action, logic, and reasoning. *Ida,* also called *Chandra Nadi,* is associated with the parasympathetic nervous system (right brain hemisphere), which controls rest and creativity. These two energies represent the duality in creation, defined by the masculine and feminine qualities or the yin-yang.

During the day, the left brain is active, supported by the right nostril breathing. The right brain is active at night, supported by the left nostril breathing. One nostril is dominant during the day and another one at night. Under stress, we can activate our right brain by consciously practising left nostril breathing. The right brain, associated with the parasympathetic nervous system, causes mental and physical relaxation. *Sushumna* is the central channel of energy that flows along the spinal cord and gets activated when *Ida* and *Pingala* are balanced.

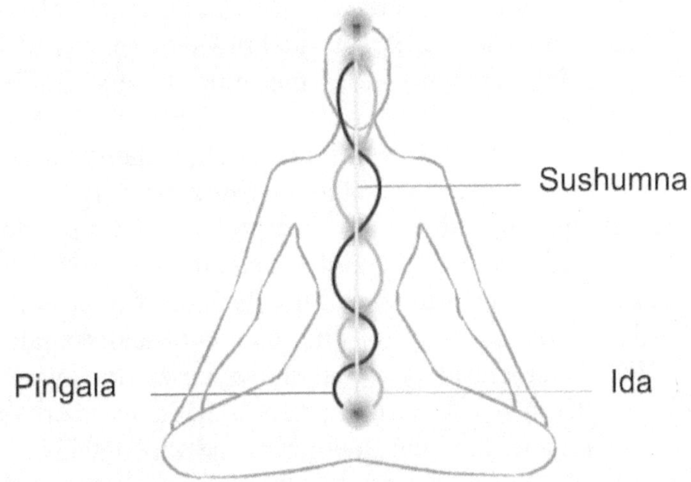


*Pranamayakosha* comprises five main energy flows called *prana vayus: apana, samana, prana, udana,* and *vyana.* Each *vayu* regulates specific processes in the body. *Pranamayakosha* is also associated with the five energetic processes of elimination, reproduction, movement, grasping with hands and speaking. Modern medicine looks at the physical body symptomatically, while disturbances in the energy body first cause most diseases. *Pranamayakosha,* or the energy body, can be balanced by following a simple and regulated life and with the help of a trained healer or practitioner.

## More about *Panchamahabhutas*, the 5 Elements
All matter in the universe is a combination of the five essential elements: Earth, Ether, Fire, Water and Air. Ayurveda describes this composition in detail. It is easy to see how our gross body or physiology comprises these five elements, but what about our mind? Is our psychology also in some way connected to these five elements? Our mind, being subtle, is influenced by the subtle forms of the same five elements.

In the book *Ayurveda and the Mind: Healing of Consciousness,* author David Frawley explains how these five subtle elements affect the mind in very simple terms. The mind is like space or ether; it is expansive, all-pervading, and can hold infinite shapes and forms. Mind's movement is akin to Wind or Air; its non-stop activities of perceiving, interpreting, judging, deciding, reacting emotionally and thinking are like the movement of air, in constant flux. The Fire element of light in the mind gives it the capacity for illumination or understanding. The Water element in the mind shows up as flowing emotions and feelings. The Earth element is the density or weight of accumulated thoughts, memories and attachments.

**Who Are We?**
The five senses allow us to see the gross body but not the subtle body. However, we know the subtle body exists because it enables us to think, feel, remember, and dream. Both the gross and subtle bodies cannot exist on their own. The prime mover, the Atman or the Soul, brings them into existence.

So, how will you answer the question, who are you? Will you say 'I am the body', describing the characteristics of the body in terms of name, age, gender, race, ethnicity, and appearance, or will you say 'I am the mind' and describe your academic and artistic achievements, thoughts and opinions? Both of these responses are true but incomplete unless you shift your identification to include the causal body and say, 'I am a Soul, essence of the divine, same as you!'

Identification with the Soul does not remove anything from your personality; it only adds another deeper perspective, in which you see yourself and others as souls while acknowledging that there may be differences in outer form and ideas. The inability to see ourselves and others as souls is the reason for strife and hatred in the world. But is just an intellectual understanding enough? Not really, but it is a good start. Yoga can give us a direct experience of it.

Indian yogic philosophy is about directly experiencing one's true nature (*Atman* or Soul). In this journey, with each meditation, we get closer and closer to identifying with our Soul, progressively deepening our experience. We then naturally move towards a harmonious world at peace with itself. Increasing proximity to the Soul creates inner harmony, peace, and happiness, thus naturally expressing harmony in the external world.

Trying to change the world by removing superficial differences of race, class, economic stature, ethnicity, politics, or opinions aims for an unreal utopian homogeneity, which results in perpetual conflict. Indian philosophy is practical. It avoids exaggerating superficial differences and focuses on the underlying unity. It actively promotes individual enterprise and diversity while being devoted to the well-being of the whole.

### *Atman* or Soul

*Atman* is pure consciousness, the essence of the One, *Param-Atman*.

*Ashtavakra Gita* uses an analogy of the Sun to describe attributes of pure consciousness. Just as the Sun gives light but does not interact with the objects it illuminates, pure consciousness animates everything but does not get mixed up with the objects. It is a witness. These beautiful words describe the Soul:

| Word | Meaning |
| --- | --- |
| *Sakshi* | Witness |
| *Vibhuh* | All pervasive |
| *Purnah* | Perfect |
| *Ekah* | Non-dual |
| *Muktah* | Ever free |
| *Akriyah* | Actionless |
| *Asangah* | Unattached |
| *Nisprhah* | Desire-less |
| *Santah* | Ever quiet |
| *Swa-prakashah* | Self-effulgent |
| *Niranjanah* | Taint-less |

The all-pervasive *Atman* witnesses. It is perfect as it is untainted by actions and their results. Since it is non-dual, it is self-contained and self-effulgent. It lacks nothing; hence, it is desireless and unattached.

# Creation: As Above, So Below

An oft-repeated adage in all mystical cultures is, "As above, so below." This saying points to the similarities between the macro and micro worlds, showing that we are in the creator's image despite the difference in scale or sheer magnitude.

The book *Truth Eternal* by Shri Ram Chandra of Fatehgarh describes the etymology of the words *Brahma* and *Atman*. Brahma is made from the root words *bruha* (expansion) and *manan* (contemplation), and Atman is made from the root words *ath* (movement) and *man* (thinking). Brahma is associated with contemplation and expansion, while Atman is associated with thinking and movement. If Atman represents the individuated essence of the Divine, then Brahma represents the Universal Principle or the Whole.

We are really in the image of the creator. Brahma has the same bodies or sheaths as the Jiva, only its collective, aggregated version. It is easier to visualise Brahma as the Principle of creation rather than a super-human being. Indian culture creates anthropomorphic symbols for all energies in Nature and calls them *devatas*. Brahma is depicted as a 4-headed human form sitting on a lotus, but to understand and realise what this form represents is a spiritual journey. The 4-heads represent the fact that being contemplative, Brahma has a 360° view. He is omniscient, with an all-pervasive unity consciousness.

The three bodies or sheaths of Brahma are named as follows:

1. *Virat*: The Gross Body. The visible universe, the cosmos, called *Virat,* is the gross body of Brahma.

2. ***Avyakrit:*** The Subtle Body. The universal mind or the one mind is the subtle body of the Brahma. It is called *Avyakrit* or *Antaryamin,* one who dwells within.

3. ***Hiranyagarbha:*** The Causal Body. Translated as 'golden egg', *Hiranyagarbha* is the causal body of the Brahma. It is the cause of the entire manifested and unmanifested creation.

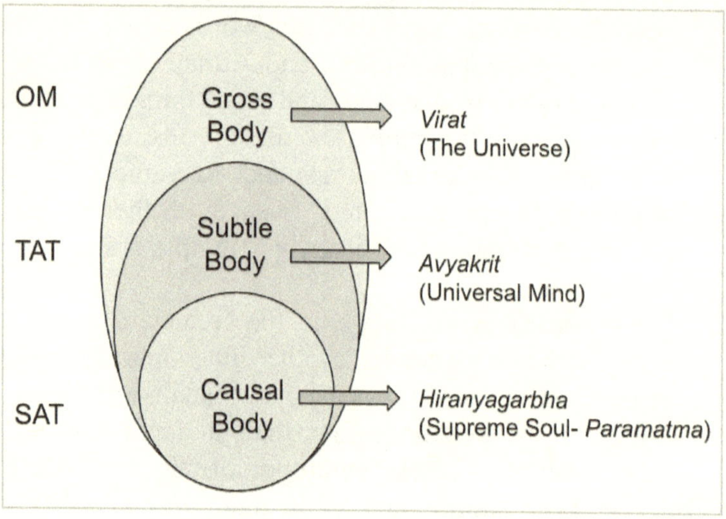


One could ask how Brahma came into being. Is there anything even beyond Brahma? The world created by Brahma is called the *Brahmanda Mandal.* What is beyond is called *Para-Brahmanda Mandal,* as the prefix *'para'* refers to before or beyond. So, there must be a prime cause that led to the creation of Brahma itself. Here, we come to the idea of the Absolute Source or Center, which is the primal cause of all creation, including Brahma.

The texts describe creation allegorically and visually: The eternal Absolute is Vishnu, who lies in the ocean of the *samsara.* Space already exists as a potential for the infinite manifestation of Vishnu. Vishnu creates Brahma from his *Vishunabhi* or navel. This is depicted as a lotus springing from Vishnu's navel. Brahma, in turn, makes the *Brahmanda Mandal* and everything in it. Brahma has a limited lifetime, however long it might be from the human perspective. Other indigenous cultures, such as the Mayans and Egyptians, also describe a central God that powers the world but remains still.

Sankhya Darshan explains Creation as follows:

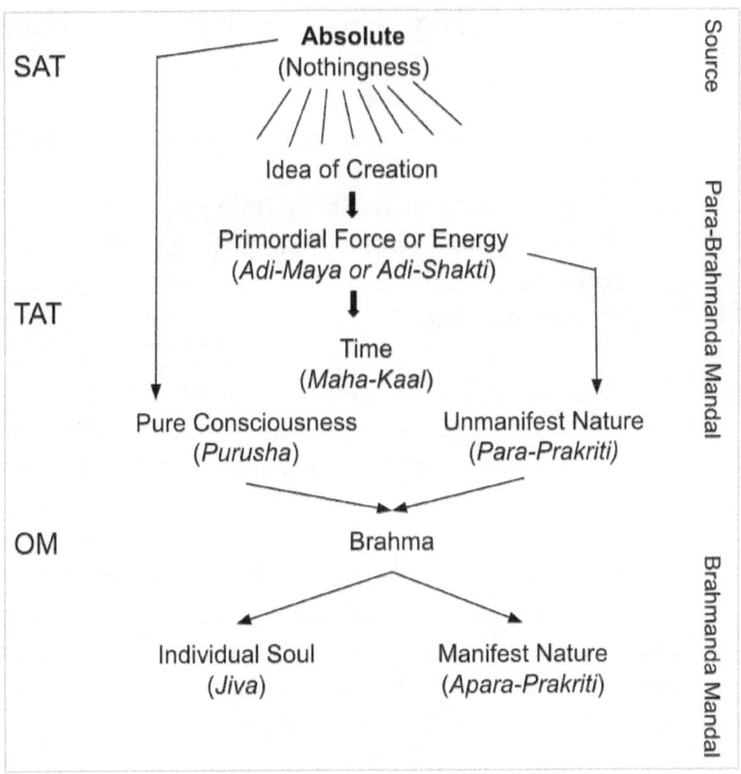


Absolute is Eternal and Unchanging. It is the Primal Cause of all Creation. It is the Source. When the idea of creation stirred in the Absolute, the Primordial Energy (*Adi-Shakti*) gushed out, creating Time (*Maha-Kaal*). The combination of Pure Consciousness (*Purusha*) and Unmanifest Nature (*Para-Prakriti*) led to the birth of Brahma in the unmanifest form. The unmanifest Brahma then became the cause of the entire manifest Universe. *Adi-Shakti* is the original energy of the primal Source that existed before creation and is the cause of creation at all levels. When this energy becomes the vital energy of life in a Jiva, it is called Prana.

As ancient Indian texts explain, creation is cyclical and has a vast cosmological timescale. Hence, the idea of creation, sustenance, and dissolution of the entire universe emerges.

**Visualising the Absolute**

There are two schools of thought to describe the Absolute:

1. *Nirguna* or *Nirakar* (Indeterminate Absolute):
   The *Nirguna* school describes the Absolute as a formless, quality-less, attribute-less, change-less and eternal principle.

2. *Saguna* or *Saakar* (Determinate Absolute):
   The *Saguna* school sees the Absolute manifested in its many forms with numerous attributes and qualities.

It is stated in *Srimad Bhagavad Gita* that while learned people can debate about the attributes (or lack thereof) of the Absolute, it is beneficial for an ordinary person to associate with a form and offer devotion (*bhakti*) to that personal form of the Absolute. It helps to conceptualise an otherwise abstract idea of divinity and focus one's attention on it. Hence, in India, we can look upon the Absolute in any form, shape, attribute or quality and yet be aware that all those forms, in essence, represent the form-less, attribute-less nature of the One. *Saguna bhakti* finally leads to *Nirguna bhakti.* Even in meditation, we can experience how the form dissolves into an inner experience of being.

It is also the essence behind '*namaste*', which says, 'I see, acknowledge and revere the divine in you'. *Saguna Bhakti* makes us see the divine in all beings in creation, thus laying the foundation for universal compassion, where all superficial differences dissolve, and we naturally connect to others at the heart level.

Whether one follows *saguna, nirguna* or even an agnostic school of thought, people in India exhibit unity in diversity, even in their expressions of divinity. This is pure universalism. It is the opposite of fundamentalism, where belief in one leads to the exclusion of others. When so many forms of the Absolute are visualised in a society, fundamentalism can divide and shatter it into pieces. Only the underlying unity of the formless essence of the divine can bind a culture together. This unity binds Hindu culture and allows space for diverse expressions of devotion and divinity.

The three prominent forms of the Absolute in Indian culture are Brahma, Vishnu, and Mahesh (Shiva). Each form is defined by its unique function: Creation, Sustenance, and Dissolution of the Universe. The Absolute and its many forms are, in essence, a combination of Principle (*Purusha*) and its associated Power (*Shakti*).

The Principle **IS** and Power **DOES**. Cultural symbolism shows the Principle as masculine and the Power as feminine. However, they are the same: Principle without Power will be ineffective, and Power without Principle can not exist. One cannot be without the other. Power can act and manifest in many ways, while the Principle stays as an inert potential without direct action (*Akarta*).

| Principle | Function | Power |
| --- | --- | --- |
| Absolute (Oneness) | Changeless Eternal Source | Adi-Maya or Adi-Shakti |
| Brahma | Creation- A | Saraswati |
| Vishnu | Sustenance- U | Lakshmi |
| Shiva | Dissolution- M | Parvati |

AUM (ॐ), also called *Shabda*, represents the primordial sound of Creation. Here, sound represents vibration. Per quantum physics, all matter is eventually energy, and all energy is vibration. Hence, everything has a specific vibration with an associated frequency and wavelength. It is as if each particle, planet or person has a certain *shabda*. We are also vibrating and producing our own 'unique sound signature'. Just as a vibrating tuning fork transmits its vibration to anything it comes in contact with, so do we. We can also tune in to each other's frequency. By the same logic, we can also raise our frequency to the level of the primordial sound *Shabda* or AUM (ॐ).

How do we do that? By living a regulated and honest life in tune with nature, we raise ourselves vibrationally. Simple, kind people radiate positive, loving vibes. But can we remain calm and kind even when faced with inner or outer conflict? Most of us need help through guidance, coaching, or practice to acquire and maintain a balanced state that helps us grow progressively.

One of the ancient yogic ways is to chant AUM (ॐ) to recreate the original sound vibration. Once we reach resonance with the original sound, our vibration rises to the frequency of the primordial *shabda*. Another way to raise our vibration is to be in tune with a Teacher who is already resonating with the primordial *Shabda*. To have the company of such a Teacher is a matter of grace and inner craving. Meditation on the heart under the guidance of a Teacher of such a high calibre can make this achievable within a short time. The Teacher comes down closer to our frequency level and then raises us by attunement with himself. The teacher descends to help raise the frequency of the seeker because it would be impossible for the seeker even to recognise the Teacher's highest frequency, let alone find attunement to it.

The book *Truth Eternal* describes creation as follows:

*"...The Real cast a shadow, and two spheres are formed. The current of the region of light flows to the region of darkness and back again. In this process, of the current flowing to and fro, another region is formed in the middle, which resembles the middle portion of a small drum, shaped like an hourglass."*

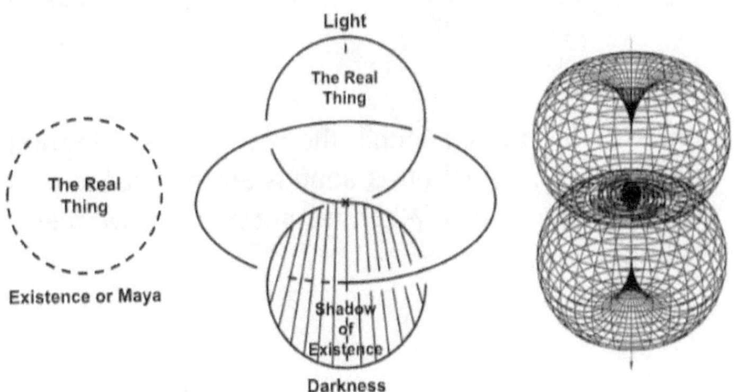


The images on the left are a 2D depiction of creation, while the one on the right is the current flow in 3D. The current flow in one part is clockwise, and in the other, it is counterclockwise. If we look at this scientifically, this 3-dimensional shape created by the current flow is called the torus.

In a torus, current flows out and in again, creating an hourglass-shaped void in the middle called the hyperboloid. The torus and hyperboloid are complementary geometries, like a negative image of each other. Together, they make a sphere. The current flows within the torus continuously between its inner and outer surfaces, as depicted below. Isn't it interesting that the current flow in the torus seems similar to the dynamic symbol for AUM ॐ, the primordial sound of creation? There is more discussion on the torus geometry later in the book.

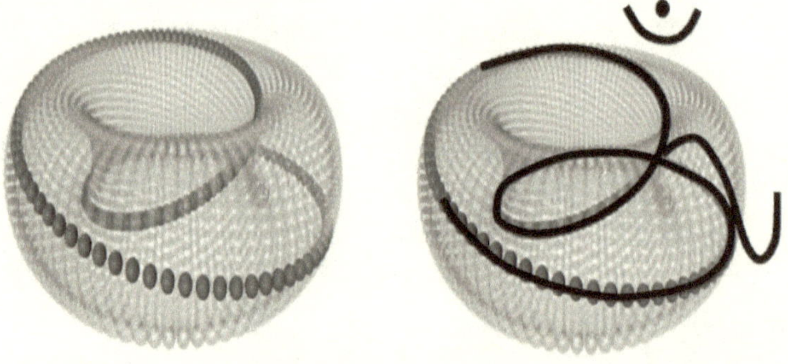

AUM is the sacred sound, the *shabda*, the vibration of the whole universe. All other sounds are embedded in it, but it is more than sound. When we attune to it, we feel centred, calm and poised.

# Creation of the Manifested World

*Brahmanda Mandal,* or the cosmic region, is the realm of illumination from where everything has emanated. *Brahmanda* has both manifest and unmanifest forms. The manifest form is the *Pinda-Pradesh* or the physical universe of matter. From the unmanifest, manifestation occurs. Just as the Soul is the causal body in the Jiva, which gives rise to the subtle and gross bodies, in Brahma, the causal body *Hiranyagarbha* gives rise to the *Avyakrit* and *Virat,* its corresponding subtle and gross bodies.

*Apara-Prakriti,* or the manifested world, is *Jada,* meaning it is inanimate, like a lump of clay. Brahma's light gives illumination and life to it, just like a potter who fashions a lump of clay into shape and purpose. Everything in nature comes into existence, is maintained for a while, and then destroyed. Like the potter analogy, the potter created the pot, then used it, and after some time, it disintegrated. The gradual disintegration is the process of entropy in any system. Everything in *Prakriti* renews in a cyclical process of creation, maintenance and destruction.

All matter goes through this cyclical process; hence, these three processes or states bind all matter. These three processes or states are called *Trigunas. Prakriti* is bound by *Trigunas- Sat, Raj,* and *Tam.* Since *Jivas* are part of *Prakriti,* all aspects of Jiva's physiology and psychology naturally come under the influence of these *Trigunas.* An atom manifests, stays for a while, and then disintegrates. The body is born, maintained for some time, and then dies or disintegrates.

These three qualities also bind the states of our consciousness: waking, dreaming and deep sleep states. We experience these three states of consciousness each day.

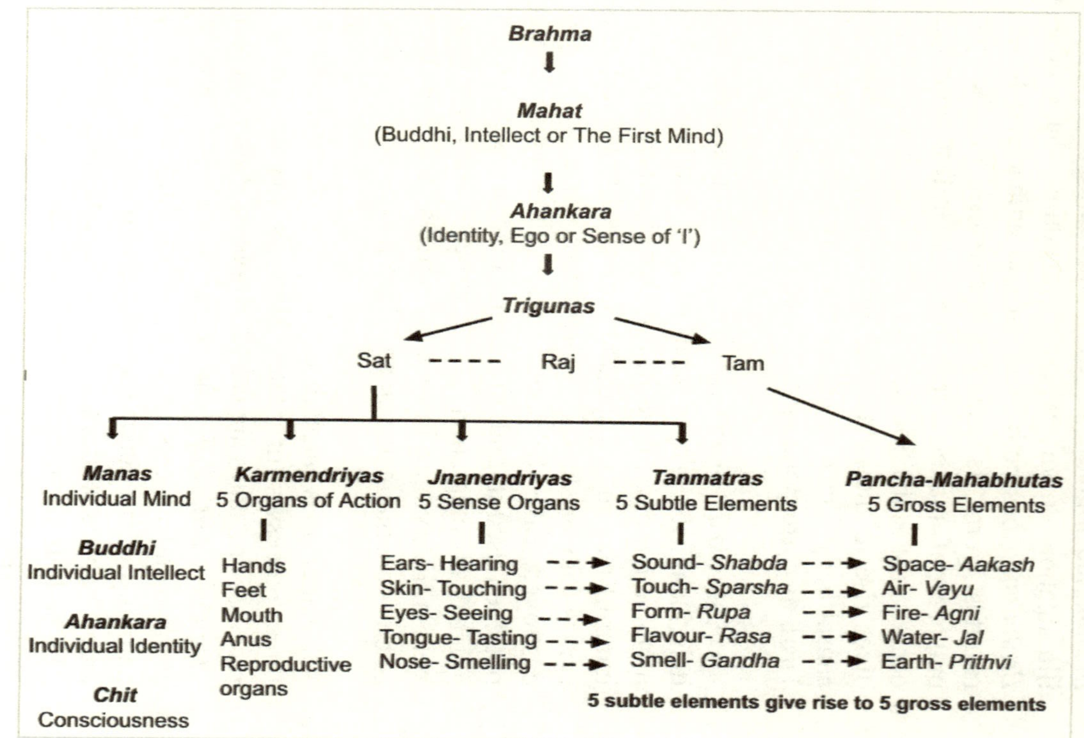

Brahma
Mahat
(Buddhi, Intellect or The First Mind)
Ahankara
(Identity, Ego or Sense of 'I')
Trigunas
Sat
Raj
Tam
Manas
Individual Mind
Buddhi
Individual Intellect
Ahankara
Individual Identity
Chit
Consciousness
Karmendriyas
5 Organs of Action
Hands
Feet
Mouth
Anus
Reproductive organs
Jnanendriyas
5 Sense Organs
Ears- Hearing
Skin- Touching
Eyes- Seeing
Tongue- Tasting
Nose- Smelling
Tanmatras
5 Subtle Elements
Sound- Shabda
Touch- Sparsha
Form- Rupa
Flavour- Rasa
Smell- Gandha
Pancha-Mahabhutas
5 Gross Elements
Space- Aakash
Air- Vayu
Fire- Agni
Water- Jal
Earth- Prithvi
5 subtle elements give rise to 5 gross elements

The Jiva has 24 components, which constitute its subtle and gross bodies. The 25th component is the soul itself, the causal body. The following flowchart depicts Jiva's constitution and the creation process from Brahma to Jiva.

Hence, in essence:
- Jiva is an embodied soul.
- Jiva has identity, mind, intellect and consciousness.
- Jiva has five subtle elements, *Tanmatras*.
- Jiva has five organs of action, *Karmendriyas*.
- Jiva has five sense organs, *Jnanendriyas*.
- Jiva has five gross elements, *Panchmahabhutas*, that comprise the physical body.

**Prakriti**

In Sankhya darshana, *Prakriti* is described by many terms:

| Word | Meaning |
| --- | --- |
| *Pradhana* | Main Cause |
| *Avyakta* | Unmanifest or dormant causes and effects |
| *Jada* | Material, gross or insentient |
| *Achetana* | Unconsciousness |
| *Maya* | Maya creates a boundary so that the effect is limited by the cause |
| *Shakti* | Power: It is in perpetual motion |

*Jada Prakriti*, or inanimate Nature, is infused with *Purusha* or Pure consciousness to give rise to the entire creation. By itself, *Prakriti* is inanimate. When *Purusha* merges with *Prakriti* and illuminates it, then creation occurs. Subtle elements are formed at subtle levels, and grosser elements are formed at gross levels. The English word used for *Prakriti* is Nature. We associate nature with flora and fauna or to define someone's inherent tendencies and behaviour. However, that is not what *Prakriti* denotes. *Prakriti* means the original condition at the time of creation, the original state. What manifests and continues later is the modification of the original condition, continuously changing. Hence, we see words such as *Pradhana* and *Avyakta* used as synonyms of Prakriti, which describe its original condition. *Prakriti* is in continuous motion from atomic to galactic levels; hence, it is called *Shakti*, the active power of creation.

The term *Maya,* commonly misunderstood as an illusion, also has a different meaning. *Maya* is the active energy that inherently limits the effects of each cause, thus maintaining order. Effects exist due to causes; however, we remain unaware of the causes and only experience the effects at the gross level, hence the illusion. Effects can manifest long after the cause, even in another lifetime, hence the unawareness. *Maya* ensures that the effect is precisely as per the cause, nothing more, nothing less.

Once illuminated, the entire purpose of *Prakriti* is to create opportunities for *Purusha* to free itself from *Prakriti*. This impulse in *Purusha* motivates the Jiva to strive for self-realisation. It also provides *Prakriti* with the impetus to create the right conditions for manifesting experiences that facilitate this realisation.

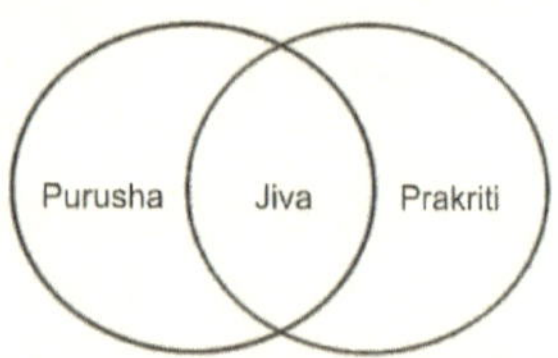

This is the reasoning behind trusting *Prakriti* to provide suitable situations in life. We say whatever happens, it happens for the best. That is why we need to accept situations in our lives and use them as stepping stones to achieving the goal of life, which is nothing but realising that each Jiva, in essence, is pure consciousness. It is the eternal witness, unchanging, unalloyed, and unmoved.

There are comparative attributes of *Purusha* and *Prakriti*:

| *Purusha* | *Prakriti* |
| --- | --- |
| Pure Consciousness or Soul | Nature |
| Sentient | Insentient |
| *Trigunatita* (beyond gunas) | *Trigunatmika* (with gunas) |
| Knower | Known |
| Inactive or Passive | Active or Dynamic |
| Seer | Seen |
| Free from all causes and effects | Primary cause |
| Unchangeable | Changeable |
| Without any consequence or result. | Full of all results. Cause of all manifestation. |
| Solitary | Multiplicity |

# The Three Attributes of Nature

*Prakriti* has three essential qualities - ***Sat, Raj, Tam***. These are called the *Trigunas*. Brahma is beyond the *trigunas*. Jiva, being part of *Prakriti*, is in the grip of *trigunas*. All Jivas have a predominance of one or the other *guna*, giving each a unique quality. Since we are a combination of these *gunas*, we exhibit different personalities based on the dominance of one *guna* or the other. Also, the *trigunas* are experienced in daily cycles; hence, balancing them is essential for a healthy life. *Trigunas* manifest in the following ways:

| Guna | Represents | State of conciousness |
|---|---|---|
| **Sat** Causal | **Soul** Bliss, consciousness, peace, stability, balance | **Deep sleep** *Sushupti* |
| **Raj** Subtle | **Mind** Knowledge, effort, activity, thought, contemplation | **Dream state** *Swapna* |
| **Tam** Gross | **Body** Existence, Inertness, physicality | **Waking state** *Jagrat Awastha* |

In human psychology, *trigunas* represent the states of consciousness during waking, dreaming and deep sleep. While awake, we are conscious and aware of ourselves and our thinking. In the dream state, there is some awareness as we tend to remember the dream afterwards, and at times, it feels real, too. During deep sleep, our awareness withdraws and rests in the Soul, beyond the conscious mind. We have no memory during deep sleep.

Yoga defines two higher states of consciousness beyond Sat, Raj and Tam. What happens when we meditate? In meditation, we feel rejuvenation similar to what we get from a deep sleep, but we are aware during meditation, while in a deep sleep, we have no awareness. This is the fourth state of consciousness, called *Turiya,* which we can acquire through sustained practice of meditation. In time, the *Turiya* condition becomes established in us at all times; then, we remain meditative even with our eyes open while going about our daily lives. Then, it becomes a higher state called *Turiyateet,* meaning beyond *Turiya.*

It is easy to understand the *Trigunas* as follows:
1.  **Sat** is Light, the presence of the Divine Principle.
2.  **Tam** is Dark, a shadow or reflection of the Divine Principle.
3.  **Raj** is Grey; mixed condition, arising out of Sat and Tam.

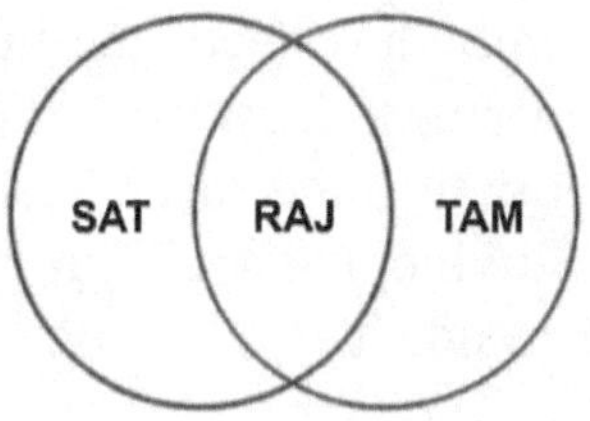


The entire world of action is Raj; it comes into existence through the interplay of Sat and Tam. Moving towards Sat means acquiring Sattvic qualities of awareness, balance, and harmony, while moving towards Tam means acquiring Tamasic qualities like inertia and dullness. Sat and Tam are the polarities in any system, and Raj is the state of flux between them.

As human beings, we have a physical body made up of *Prakriti* (Tam) and a causal body or *Atman,* which is the essence of the divine in us (Sat). The subtle body, or the mind (Raj), comes into existence through an interaction between Sat and Tam.

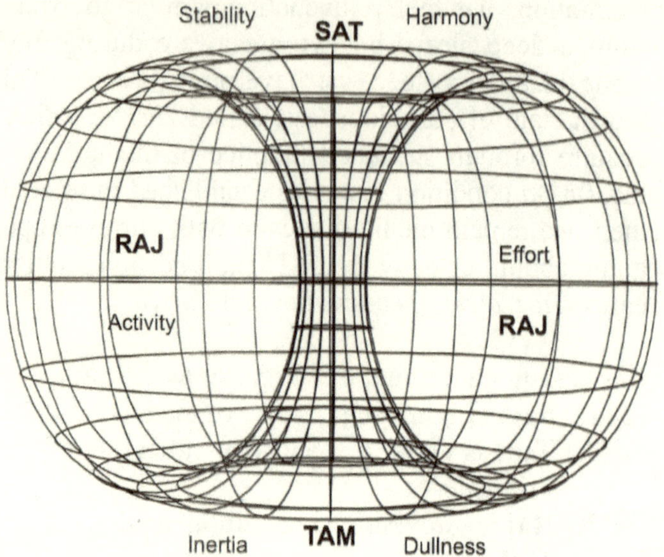


When a soul embodies itself, the mind comes into being. The mind enables us to know, think, choose, and act wisely. The most important thing to understand is that we are the essence of the divine, the soul, but ironically, this knowing is beyond the mind; it is a practical, direct experience, an inner perception of *being*.

*"Meditation evolves from thinking to feeling, feeling to being, being into becoming and finally going beyond."* -Daaji.

The physical body has specific survival needs and millions of years of evolutionary memory. To fulfil these needs, we must engage in action fueled by the direction and force of thought. Hence, Raj and Tam are natural and unavoidable for an embodied Jiva. So, what is the role of Sat? When Raj and Tam come under the influence of Sat, they demonstrate higher attainment. For example, we all need to eat food to live, but what matters is what we eat, how we eat, with what attitude we cook it, how we earn our livelihood, and how we offer food to our families and guests. Our intentions, attitudes, feelings and motivations can elevate a simple action to a lofty one. That is the role of Sat in our lives.

We are cognizant of the body and mind when we are awake. We continue to be aware of the mind as we dream while asleep, or when we wake up, we still have the memory of sleep and the dream. But what happens when we go into deep sleep? Our consciousness withdraws from the body and the mind to rest in the Soul. In this condition, we are naturally abiding in Sat. Due to deep sleep, our body and mind get rested and rejuvenated, we feel fresh, and our energy is restored. Since consciousness is withdrawn from the body and mind in the deep sleep state, we never know what happens to us while we are in deep sleep. Deep sleep brings us to Sat every night.

But the question is: how do we **consciously** bring about the attributes of Sat in our waking state? As we begin meditating on the heart, relaxing the body, regulating the mind and withdrawing the senses inward, we naturally bring forth qualities of Sat into our lives. This is Yoga. The condition in deep meditation is akin to the state of deep sleep, the difference being that we stay aware in meditation. That is why even a few minutes of meditation recharges us. Nature or *Prakriti* is an interplay of *trigunas*. Being born in the world, we are constantly under the influence of the *trigunas*. For any person, it is evident that when Rajasic and Tamasic qualities increase, it results in an imbalance in their life. What should we do? We can improve the Sattvic qualities to lead a fulfilling and balanced life by adopting yogic practices, a healthy diet, restful sleep, simple exercises, honest living and service to others.

# Karma: Levels of Action

There are different levels of action based on our attitudes, intentions, and *gunas*. We know that action performed with a lofty attitude will yield a lofty result, but is it possible to transcend the cause-and-effect cycle altogether? How is that possible? Let's explore the idea of action further.

In the waking state, when dull, inactive or materialistic, we exhibit Tamasic qualities. When the time for appropriate action is lost, inaction in the form of negligence, unfinished work, procrastination, delay and laziness can lead to dire consequences of guilt and shame, in addition to material loss. Hence, action (*karma*) is better than inaction (*akarmanyata*). Action promotes growth, while idleness is regressive, akin to death. The body's natural instinct is to act. But both action and inaction are riddled with associated consequences. How is that?

We get good or bad results when we engage in good or bad actions. Action, whether good or bad, if done with attachment, desire, and passion, is Rajasic, as it keeps us tied to the cycle of cause and effect. However, good actions (*punya karma*) are preferable over bad actions (*paapa karma*) as they eventually lead to good results.

One step better is engaging in good action while demonstrating balance, discrimination, and service. Then, we bring forth Sattvic qualities. However, it is still a golden cage of good results. We must undergo the effects of good results, however enjoyable they may be, as they also keep us tied to the cycle of existence. We are bound to physical existence until we exhaust all effects and no other causes remain. Is there a way out of the grip of cause and effect?

A higher state of steadfastness (*sthitaprajna*) is established in us when we can engage in desireless action, which *Shrimad Bhagavad Gita* describes as *nishkama karma*, an action that is free from cause and effect. Still higher than that is *vishisht karma* (or *vikarma* in short), where desireless action is done with love and devotion (*bhakti*). Even higher than that is *akarma,* where the idea of doer-ship is forfeited, and spontaneous, divinely inspired action gushes forth from us. Here is a recap of the terms that define types of action:

- *Akarmanyata*: Inaction due to lethargy, negligence or fear. It means the absence of action.

- *Punya and Paapa Karma*: A mix of good and bad actions done due to ignorance, desire, attachment, and prior impressions (*prarabdha*).

- *Punya Karma*: Good action done with good intention, discrimination, and contemplation.

- *Nishkama Karma*: Desireless good action done with non-attachment to the fruits of action.

- *Vikarma*: Desireless good action done with non-attachment to the fruits of action and done with love and devotion (*bhakti).*

- *Akarma*: Action done without the idea of doer-ship or even without the knowledge of the action and its fruit. This is the highest form of divinely inspired action where there is automatism and no self-identification with the action. Hence, it does not lead to the formation of any further causes.

To transcend the *trigunas* is a high attainment for a Jiva, and it is possible when the doer-ship is forfeited, and the Jiva engages in *akarma*, thus becoming an instrument of the divine possessing a divine will. In the book *Authentic Yoga*, author Shri PY Deshpande describes this state as **choiceless awareness** where one is free from the fruit of the action but not the action itself. The Sanskrit word for this state is *Sahaj Samadhi*. We become free from all the causes and their consequences.

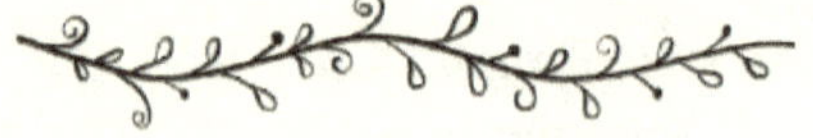

# Understanding Common Terms

Are there any principles or laws that govern the world? According to ancient Indian philosophy, the answer is yes; certain principles are active whether one is aware of them or not, whether one likes them or not. This world is not without purpose, fair rules, or accurate accounts.

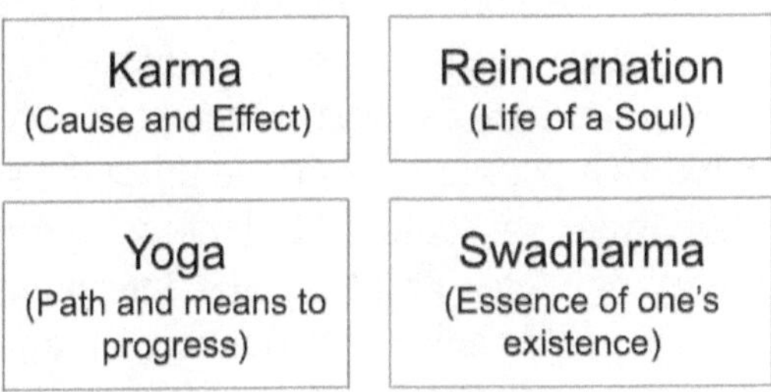


## Karma

Karma is a word recognised worldwide, and people interpret it according to their understanding. Generally, Karma is used in the context of action, good or bad luck, what we deserve, what goes around comes around, or cause and effect. While these interpretations might be valid, they are incomplete. As described previously, Karma refers to an evolutionary approach to action, where a human being can evolve from baser animalistic action through yoga to manifest the highest divine action.

The law of Karma is the foundation of free will. How can we have free will if we do not have the freedom to choose, think and act? But having free will, how can we be made responsible for our choices?

The theory of *samskaras* (impressions) explains the mechanism of the law of Karma in great detail. Each action, whether physical or mental, creates impressions or *samskaras* in our consciousness, thus 'disturbing or distorting' it. If you consider consciousness as a still lake, then each impression is a ripple on the surface of this lake. There are many ripples, and they can grow and spread out, creating interference patterns. The currents can even increase in power, giving rise to whorls and eddies, thus creating an ever greater distortion of consciousness.

Since consciousness is the agency of perception and awareness, these distortions prevent us from perceiving reality as it is, and we then create our interpretations of reality. No two people look at one thing the same way, as if they are wearing coloured lenses, giving rise to a multiplicity of ideas, opinions and interpretations. If these ideas have rigid self-identification, they can lead to disharmony, conflict and even fundamentalism. Hence, the root cause of all strife in personal life and the world at large is this distortion of consciousness and rigid identification with one's unique perception.

Repetitive actions and thoughts form habitual patterns, hardening impressions. These impressions become so ingrained that they lead to similar actions and thoughts, creating a vicious loop. The accumulated effect of these impressions is Karmic debt, which, like all debt, has to be paid off.

How can we pay off Karmic debt? There are multiple ways. First, we need to take responsibility for our condition in life, accept it, and live it with an open mind and heart. Second, we need to create a lifestyle that progressively minimises the formation of more impressions. Third, we can adopt Yogic practices that can help reduce this burden. Lastly, we can cry out in repentance and pray for divine guidance. A good cry does make one feel unburdened and light.

The need for change or growth is an inner cry for real freedom. Real freedom is when the karmic debt is paid off, and the auto-pilot of these impressions no longer leads us. This is the main reason we can only work on ourselves and change ourselves before offering advice to others. This is a solo game of purification of consciousness. With a purer consciousness, we can then be of help to others, too. When we change, the world changes to that extent, as the sum of all humanity's karmic debts is the world's collective karmic debt that guides its destiny.

**Reincarnation**

People have become disillusioned with doctrines that say, 'There is only one life, and at the end of that life, you will be judged and sent to either heaven or hell.' An increasing number of people worldwide are actively trying to understand the concept of reincarnation, as given in ancient yogic philosophy and ancient cultures. A greater need is felt to answer questions such as: Who am I? Why am I here? What is the purpose of my life? Why are people born a certain way? What is the guiding factor in steering my life? The law of reincarnation answers these questions.

I am a Jivatma, a Soul on a long journey through this cosmos to realise my true nature. My attempts will continue until I reach the goal. I am here because I chose to be born in a particular location, in a specific family, and with certain abilities best suited to paying off the karmic debt in this lifetime and realising my true nature.

Hence, irrespective of the conditions in my life, I must acknowledge that I am the cause of the debt that I carry, accept it wholeheartedly, and work diligently to pay it off. Paying off the karmic debt is a purification of consciousness so that the distortions created by choices (likes or dislikes) and thoughts (opinions and beliefs) are removed. If all the karmic debt is not paid off in one lifetime, the residual impressions become the cause of the next embodied life of the Soul.

It is becoming evident that in this 21st-century world with multiple distractions of media, consumerism, political instability, poor mental and emotional health and rigid ideologies, instead of working off the karmic debt, we end up adding to it, thus getting more and more mired in its self-tightening noose. So, the call of Yoga is here and now, and it is even more urgent in the current times. It makes complete sense to practice Yoga diligently. There is no other way out of this quagmire.

**Swadharma**

*Swa* means Self, and *dharma* refers to the righteous acts or duties that uphold the divine order. Ancient Indian philosophy says that however small or big, each entity has its inherent nature, its *raison d'etre* or the reason to be. That quality defines its *swadharma*. For example, the Sun shines, a warrior fights, a mother nurtures, a student learns, and DNA stores information. What would it do or be if not that? Similarly, each human being also has their *swadharma*, and it is worthwhile to define it for ourselves.

Since we have multiple sheaths or bodies that perform different functions, their reason for existence differs. What is the *raison d'etre* of the Soul? It exists to realise its true nature. It gives rise to the other sheaths for an embodied life form. Similarly, we can define the purpose of all sheaths, such as the body acts, the mind thinks, the intellect knows, identity gives us a sense of self, and consciousness, as the agency of awareness, makes us aware.

Hence, for each human, the first and foremost *swadharma* is to realise their true self, if possible, in this lifetime. To achieve this goal, it is in our interest to take care of ourselves holistically: keep the physical body in good health, educate ourselves, gain knowledge, regulate the mind, sharpen and refine our intellect, hone our unique skills, practice humility, and compassion and be of service. This is the evolution from animalistic tendencies to human-ness and divine qualities. Meditation on the heart is a simple way to this evolution.

With these unique and refined abilities, devoting oneself to the betterment of family, society, nation, and the world is also *swadharma*. Another word used interchangeably with *swadharma* is duty; duty to self and others performed with love and sincerity is *swadharma*. The ability to respond to the moment's call with utmost surrender is *swadharma*. Acting in all situations while upholding the highest good for all is *swadharma*.

There is great danger in ignoring *swadharma* and engaging in *paradharma* instead. *Paradharma* would translate to someone else's dharma, not one's own. If people could fulfil their responsibilities while being devoted to the welfare of all, how peaceful and harmonious would the family and society be? When we uphold *swadharma*, we work off the accumulated impressions (*samskaras*). Then, we align ourselves with the natural purpose of our lives rather than run tangentially. In summary, *swadharma* is the key to liberating ourselves from the impressions that grip us life after life.

## Yoga

Most people associate Yoga with exercise or postures (*yogasana*). However, Yoga is the fundamental science of achieving the goal of human life. Yoga means union. Yoga helps create unity within oneself by harmonising various parts or facets of the human system: body, mind and soul.

This harmony can then extend and reflect in our interactions with the world, for example, our family, community, and environment. Another higher step would be to unite or merge this integrated harmonised system with our higher essence, the Divine. Yoga is an all-encompassing integrative approach.

What or who can merge with the Divine: the gross body, the energetic body, the subtle body or the causal body? Oil and water do not mix, meaning only entities of the same essence can mix or merge. Only the causal body can merge with its own higher essence, which is to say, only the Soul (*Atman*) can merge with the Divine (*Paramatman*). This happens when distortions in consciousness are removed, and the sheaths around the Soul are purified.

The gross body, made up of food, dies and returns to nature. The subtle body mired by the karmic debt creates the opportunity for the next embodiment. However, when the subtle body is freed from the impurities, then the Soul, which is eternal and remains ever unsullied and pure, can merge with its original universal essence. Each constituent body plays a vital role in this endeavour. The gross body is the carrier of the soul in physicality to experience human life. The subtle body, which comes into existence through the interaction of the Soul with the gross body, has the potential for expansion and refinement to realise the Soul as the ultimate reality. Such a Jiva, who is self-realised, can then exist in the physical world while being divinised completely and freed from all bondage. That is true freedom.

Sage Patanjali described Yoga as: योगश्चित्तवृत्तिनिरोधः: meaning 'Yoga is the cessation of all modifications or distortions of consciousness.' The word *vritti* means 'waves, whirlpools or vortices'. Waves and whirlpools in water disturb the medium. Similarly, waves and eddies of thought disturb or distort the still lake of our consciousness. Distortion in consciousness prevents the expression of the true nature of the Soul.

What are the sheaths or coverings around the Soul? These are primarily:
1. Identity (*Ahankara*)
2. Consciousness (*Chitta*)
3. Intellect (*Buddhi*)
4. Mind (*Manas*)
5. Physical Body (*Sthula Sharir*)

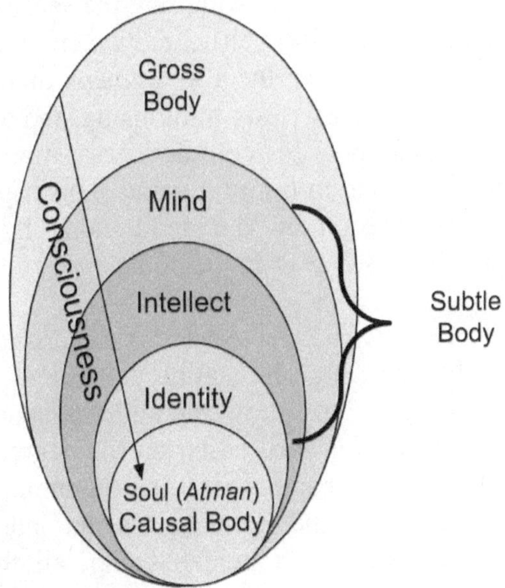


Consciousness is the degree of awareness or perception. If consciousness is pure, the perception is also clear to that extent. The higher the degree of awareness, the more elevated life is. Are we just the body living to fulfil its hunger, desires and sensual pleasures? Are we just the mind adhering to our achievements, thoughts, ideas, moods, passions, beliefs and opinions? Or are we experiencing ourselves as the Soul, centred in the heart, joyful and connected? Yoga is the process of becoming aware of the ever-subtler levels of our existence and continuously trying to refine our perception by gradually purifying our consciousness.

## Perception

What is perception? What is the process by which perception occurs? Perception happens almost instantaneously, involving all the senses, all the time. A yogi, however, has greater control over perception and its effect on consciousness. Yoga is the method or practice by which the yogi learns to withdraw the senses and the mind inward, away from its external movement. He also learns to exercise control over the involvement of his mind in its internal movements, thus minimising and finally ceasing the modifications of his consciousness. It requires diligent, sustained practice to train the mind. This happens naturally through meditation on the heart aided by transmission, which is discussed later in the book.

In the book *Raja Yoga*, Swami Vivekananda clearly and succinctly describes the entire process of perception in human beings. Perception and its corresponding reaction from the perceiver vary based on the degree of awareness or the purity of consciousness. In an animal, the reaction is almost immediate and instinctual, as the intellect and mind are undeveloped. In a human being, all the sheaths are involved in the process of perception. Refinement of the sheaths determines the quality of perception and reaction. Someone practising yoga can exercise restraint and control on perception and response.

As an example, let's consider that a person sees an object; the series of events or steps that take place in the process of perception are:

Step 1: An **Object** is seen. The object is an aspect of *Prakriti.* It reflects light, which is caught by the observer's eyes.

Step 2: The **Eyes** are external instruments for seeing. Like a camera, they catch reflected light, and the optical nerves convert the light signal into an electromagnetic impulse.

Step 3: The **Brain** is the organ of perception. The optic nerves of the eyes carry the message to the nerve centre in the brain, which decodes the signal.

Step 4: The **Mind** is the cognitive agency. It is attached to both the eyes and the brain. The mind assimilates the information received from the eyes and brain. The message is understood in the present context of time, place, relevance and memory.

Step 5: **Intellect** is the determinative faculty. The mind relays the entire information package to the intellect for appropriate reaction.

Step 6: **Ego or Identity** is the idea of ownership. Along with the reaction of the intellect comes the notion of egoism or door-ship.

Step 7: The **Soul** is the Seer or *Purusha.* Finally, the Soul gets the entire mixture of action and reaction filtered through the sheaths. It witnesses.

With yogic practices, we can perceive the stimulus (the sensed object, word or thought), the waves it creates on the lake of our consciousness, and the reaction caused, all as distinct processes. For an untrained person, these processes get mixed up; the reaction is almost immediate to the stimulus. Hence, he is devoid of the ability to discern or control it. However, with yoga, we can create a gap and learn to exercise restraint at each step of the process of perception. How does it help us? Instead of an uncontrolled reaction, we can have a restrained and measured response, which will help us avoid creating further impressions.

**States of Consciousness**

*Trigunas* define three distinct states of consciousness:
- Sat (Superconscious)
- Raj (Conscious)
- Tam (Subconscious)

Both superconscious and subconscious states are devoid of ego or sense of identity. The conscious state only involves intellect, rationality and door-ship (ego). How is that? Let's explore it further.

The subconscious is instinct-based, driven by previous impressions or conditioning. The inherent conditioning can be so intense that despite the rationality of the conscious mind, we are inadvertently led by the subconscious mind, and we wonder why we cannot change ourselves. Habits and tendencies dominate the subconscious mind. However, it can also be useful, as we can relegate new learnings, such as driving a car or repeated manual work, to the subconscious mind.

The conscious state is our everyday waking state, where we actively engage our minds to perceive, think, reason, and understand. It is in the present moment but can be conditioned by subconscious tendencies and habits. The superconscious state is higher inspiration devoid of individualism. It is common to all humans. It is unity consciousness.

Yoga aims to eliminate the auto-pilot mode of the impressions lodged in the subconscious and expand the current conscious state to a higher superconscious state. Yogic practices achieve this aim by cleaning the subconscious and creating one-pointedness at the conscious level. This one-pointed steady state in the practitioner is called *ekagrata* and is obtained by becoming heart-centered. An *ekagra* mind and intellect respond to the heart's call and are guided by the inspiration of superconsciousness.

# Ashtanga Yoga by Sage Patanjali

Sage Patanjali wrote the *Yoga Sutras,* which detail the eight steps of *Ashtanga Yoga.* These steps help prepare our body, mind and moral muscles for achieving *Samadhi,* the superconscious state.

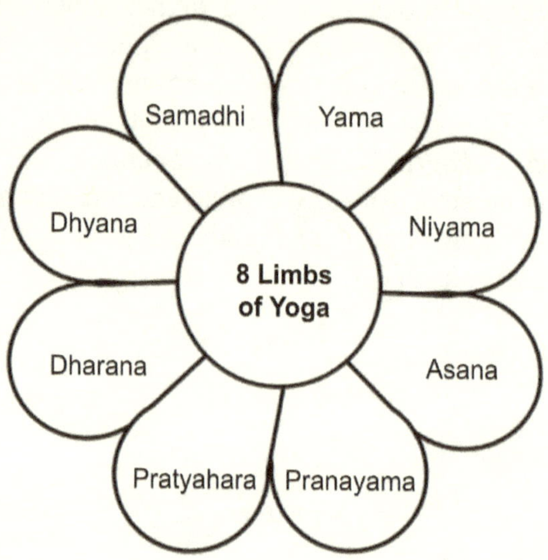


*Samadhi* has root words *sam,* meaning 'binding together or integration', and *adhi,* meaning 'the original state of being'. Hence, *Samadhi* means to acquire that original condition that prevailed at the time of our creation, which was pure, without any distortions. To understand the science behind the eight steps of *Ashtanga Yoga,* we need to know the meaning and benefits of each step. Here is a brief description:

1.  *Yama-* Yama refers to moral codes. Adopting good conduct and giving up negative tendencies is *Yama.* Basic goodness and purity of intention are foundational to the yogic approach. It has the following sub-aspects:

o *Ahimsa*: non-violence in thought and deed
o *Satya*: being truthful and honest
o *Asteya*: non-stealing, being non-covetous
o *Brahmacharya*: moderation of senses and faculties
o *Aparigraha*: being non-possessive

2. *Niyama*- The word *Niyama* means routine for elevated personal hygiene. This would include the entire gamut of lifestyle choices and attitudes conducive to the yogic goal. It has the following sub-aspects:

o *Saucha*: external and internal hygiene and purity
o *Santosh*: being content and in a state of acceptance
o *Tapas*: self-sacrifice and austerity
o *Swadhyaya*: self-study
o *Ishwar Pranidhana*: devotion

3. *Asana*- *Asana* means to sit. It involves holding the body in a steady sitting posture with proper alignment that is both comfortable and natural. Since the goal of Ashtanga Yoga is *Samadhi*, the most common sitting postures are *sukhasana* or *padmasana*. These sitting postures are such that the limbs are drawn inwards, gathered in preparation for drawing the mind inwards. Proper posture helps create a balanced and healthy body and helps to regulate the mind. It is scientifically proven that body language affects the state of mind of an individual. Thus, adopting a suitable yogic posture prepares the mind for practice.

4. *Pranayama*- Regulation of *prana* (the vital force) is *Pranayama*. Breath is the most prominent movement of *prana* in the human system. It rejuvenates the body and mind. When disturbed, we are advised to take deep breaths to regain balance. When breathing is practised

consciously,  the flow of *prana* is regularised, and we achieve greater balance in our physical and mental processes. In Ashtanga Yoga, as we sit in a suitable posture and observe our breathing, our senses naturally withdraw inward.

5. ***Pratyahara*-** *Pratyahara* involves withdrawing the senses inwardly and restraining their outward tendencies. It requires self-control and regulation of the senses by diverting them inward. This does not translate to self-denial or renunciation but rather a growing detachment from external influences. In this state, we witness events but do not allow them to disturb us. In our daily lives, we fulfil all household responsibilities while being devoted to the eternal Self within.

6. ***Dharana*-** Dharana is the practice of developing focus and the ability to pay unwavering attention. It involves collecting the mind at a single point and preferring only that idea over others.

7. ***Dhyana*-** *Dhyana* involves holding one's mind on the chosen object of meditation for a certain duration. It involves abiding in the essence of the object of meditation, going beyond thinking. Hence, selecting an appropriate object of meditation becomes critical. To achieve the ultimate goal of life, self-realisation, we need to choose the Self seated in the human heart as the object of meditation.

8. ***Samadhi*-** The Union with the original condition is *Samadhi*. With the sustained practice of *Dhyana, Samadhi* becomes a natural outcome. Being one or in an unbroken union with the chosen object of meditation as a direct experience is *Samadhi*.

Swami Vivekananda's commentary on Patanjali's Yoga Sutras describes how once *dharana*, *dhyana* and *samadhi* are established in a person, he can practice these three together as *samayama*. *Sam* means 'binding together or integration', and *yama* means 'practice or discipline'. When a yogi establishes *samayama* with any subject, he can gain complete knowledge and mastery over it. Hence, *samayama* is a tool for the Yogi to reveal knowledge about anything.

*"Words cannot convey the value of yoga. It has to be experienced."*

                                        *-BKS Iyengar*

# Heartfulness Meditation with Transmission

Meditation with Transmission is an evolutionary new approach to Ashtanga Yoga in the 21st century. Sage Patanjali gave the yoga sutras 2000 years ago, distilling the entire science of life through them. In current times, just like an evolving science, Ashtanga Yoga has again taken a leap by discovering newer methods and practices that are effective, efficacious and suited to the current times. This method is Meditation with Yogic Transmission or *Pranahuti*.

## What is Yogic Transmission or *Pranahuti*?

*Prana* is the vital energy or the life force, and *ahuti* means 'to give'; hence, *Pranahuti* is the giving of the very life force. Swami Vivekananda has described *Prana* as the **only** force in the world; it gives us life and animates nature, and all other forces like gravitation, magnetism, and light are material manifestations of the same Prana. It is also called *pranasya prana* or 'life of life'. Just as food is nourishment for the body and education is for the mind, *Pranahuti* is nourishment for the soul.

What is Prana? How can *Pranahuti* create change at the consciousness level? We know that change can only be affected from a higher level. Prana is the energy of the Source itself, called *Adi-Shakti*, which can remove impurities and elevate the consciousness of the seeker.

Thus, *Pranahuti* is the transmission of this vital, primal, original power of the Source itself. The Source is universal love; thus, Its power is ever-flowing pure love, too. Who can transmit this love? A yogi of such calibre who, having access to the Source, has become love himself. Therefore, it is relevant that Prana, a highly potent yet forceless force, is transmitted from heart to heart. The heart is the seat of the soul and a potential reservoir of love.

The yogic system of spiritual training that I have practised and trained under is called Sahaj Marg or Heartfulness, which is blessed with this opportunity of meditation with *pranahuti*. It is a matter of experiencing *pranahuti* first-hand rather than just conceptualising it. In this new method, we start the practice from the 6th, 7th and 8th steps of Ashtanga Yoga. We sit in meditation from the word go and receive *pranahuti*. Heartfulness guide Daaji has explained the rationale behind such a practice as follows:

> *"Heartfulness practices start from the 6th, 7th and 8th steps of Ashtanga Yoga. When we begin with Dharana and immerse ourselves in Dhyana, we go beyond the mind and attain Samadhi; then, we move from the centre of our being and touch the outermost frontier of our mind. The journey is from within to without, from inward to outward."*

> *"...The first five steps, Yama, Niyama, Asana, Pranayama, and Pratyahara, are from outside to inside. With Heartfulness practices, when we start from within and move outwards, we gradually recognise the establishment of the first five steps in us naturally."*
>
> *- Daaji*

With the mind regulated and heart at peace, we find the first five steps of Ashtanga Yoga *Yama, Niyama, Asana, Pranayama,* and *Pratyahara* gradually develop in us in the course of the practice. Shouldn't we use modern tools, be it in science, technology or yoga, for our growth rather than stay with the old ones? Heartfulness is a revolutionary new method that cuts short the entire journey of *Ashtanga yoga* and takes the practitioner to sublime levels of consciousness in a short time. Heartfulness presents this unprecedented opportunity for evolution in recent times with the help of Yogic Transmission or *Pranahuti.*

We already know we can change anything from a higher level, not the same level. In Yoga, we are dealing with the evolution of human consciousness and what is above consciousness. *Prana*, which comes from the Source, is above consciousness; it is the potential behind consciousness. Meditating on the heart with *pranahuti* purifies our subtle bodies, elevates our consciousness, and changes us from the inside out. Hence, it is the most unique method for self-transformation and self-realisation.

As per Daaji, this method of spiritual training existed in ancient times, 72 generations before the epic *Ramayana.* Over time, it got lost, as no more practitioners or trainers existed. However, it saw a revival in the early 19th century due to the presence of Yogis of such calibre who could tap into the Source to channel this highest-energy *Prana* (Adi-Shakti) for human evolution. Since then, this method has been kept alive as a lineage of spiritual Masters.

How can we calculate the 72 generations before the Ramayana? There is no consensus on Indian history, and many people interpret the yuga cycles as having vastly different time scales, creating confusion about the idea of time itself. For example, according to some references, the life span and rule of dynasties in antiquity could range anywhere between 100 and 1000 years! How can this be reconciled with our current time of one generation?

For simplicity and clarity, if we consider a 30-year gap between two generations, 72 generations would add up to 2160 years. The Ramayana epic occurred around 7000 years ago. Hence, we can calculate that meditation with *pranahuti* existed roughly 9,000 years ago. This is also the estimated origin of the Rig Veda, which mentions the grand river Saraswati flowing in the country's northwest region. Astro-archaeological mapping of the dried-up Saraswati riverbed places it on a similar timeline. This research can be found in Indian Earth Observation studies on Saraswati paleochannels by ISRO.

# Chapter 3: Yoga

## A Brief History of Yoga

Yoga is an ancient plan for self-development. In ancient times, Yoga and Vedic knowledge were passed down from teacher to disciple in a continuous tradition. In the post-Vedic period, the bhakti movement took root when the common population preferred worship and rituals over the practice of Yoga. However, various *Puranic* stories and festivals kept Vedic knowledge in the psyche of ordinary people. Yoga survived but was less prevalent amongst the masses as a living tradition.

Sage Patanjali compiled the knowledge of Ashtanga Yoga in the form of *sutras*. In Sanskrit, the word *sutra* means thread. Like pearls on a thread, each word in the *sutra* has a profound meaning waiting to be revealed to the practitioner with practice and growing understanding. Sage Patanjali elaborated on Raja Yoga, the king of yoga, a method of mind regulation to reach a sublime state of being.

Although the best estimates trace the origins of these *sutras* to the 2nd century CE, Yoga as a practice existed much before this time. The Rig Veda mentions Yoga, and Bhagavad Gita elaborates on it through its 18 chapters. The famous *Pashupati* stone seal from Indus Valley archaeological digs shows yoga posture. *Pashupati*, another name for Lord Shiva, is considered the originator of Yoga. It is challenging to locate the origins of Yoga, but with the available evidence, we can see that it is ancient and has been evolving. However, if we think that creation came from the One, and it goes back to the One, then Yoga, the idea of union with the One, came into existence as soon as creation occurred; however, practical methods might have developed later.

**Hatha Yoga**

Over the last millennium, new practices emerged called *Tantra*. The word *Tantra* means a method or technique. There are three primary *Tantra* texts which describe various yogic techniques:

1. ***Shiva Samhita***: Of unknown origins, this is a collection of verses by Lord Shiva addressed to Parvati. Lord Shiva is considered the *Adi-Guru* (the originator, the first Teacher) of Yoga. *Shiva Samhita* deals with a philosophical and ethical path to liberation. It describes the constitution of the Jiva and gives various techniques for the following:
   - *Pranayama*- breath regulation
   - *Mudras*- subtle psychic gestures
   - *Bandhas*- energy lock
   - *Kriyas*- cleaning processes
   - *Chakras*- energy points

2. ***Gheranda Samhita***: Written by sage Gheranda in the 17th century, this book describes the seven-fold path of yoga. In it, the body and mind are considered vessels for the Soul.
   - *Shatkarma*- 6 purification techniques
   - *Asanas*- 32 postures
   - *Mudras*- 25 hand gestures
   - *Pratyahara*- 5 techniques for gathering the mind inwards
   - *Pranayama*- 10 breathing techniques
   - *Dhyana*- perception technique
   - *Samadhi*- an experience of inner bliss

3. ***Hatha Yoga Pradipika***: Written by Swami Swatamarama in the 15th century CE, the book outlines techniques for performing *asana, pranayama, shatkarma, mudra,* and *bandha.*

The book's goal is to describe the physical disciplines of Hatha Yoga and then integrate them with the higher spiritual goals of Raja Yoga. It sees Hatha Yoga as a preliminary practice for Raja Yoga. The text tells us that achieving self-discipline is easier when we start with the physical and energetic body than trying to directly regulate the mind, as is done in Raja Yoga. Tantric texts deal primarily with the physical and energetic body, while Ashtanga yoga is based on Raja Yoga for regulating the mind through meditation to achieve *Samadhi*.

It is believed that Hatha Yoga practices or *Tantra* techniques came about to introduce Yoga to the general population so that all people could walk the Yogic path. For most people, starting with the physical aspect is more manageable than directly dealing with the mind. With the preparation provided by the well-defined practices of Hatha Yoga, all people could graduate to practice Raja Yoga (which deals with higher mental processes) and eventually reach the ultimate goal of self-realisation.

Many traditional Yoga schools have evolved and flourished in the last 100 years. Some examples are Satyananda Yoga, Iyengar Yoga, Patanjali Yogapitha, Vinyasa Yoga, and Heartfulness Yoga Academy. Many colleges and research centres offer yoga courses with options for postgraduate degrees and even PhD in yoga. Yoga is currently being practised for health and wellness worldwide in many different forms. Many more modern-day interpretations of yoga are also popular, as we see pop-up classes in every nook and corner of our society.

Eastern traditions such as Tao and Zen, which are paths for self-development, have profoundly impacted the culture of East Asia and the world. Taoism tells us to be in harmony with the natural flow of life without resistance by *Wu-Wei,* meaning 'effortless action'. Zen is an offshoot of *Mahayana Buddhism*, which talks about the practice of *Za-Zen*, a meditation to realise our true nature as a direct inner perception. New approaches like mindfulness, stillness, presence, inner silence and present-moment awareness have sprung from Yoga, Tao and Zen teachings. All have the goal of living a balanced life in harmony with nature.

As we have seen in the descending Yuga cycle, the consciousness levels of the human population dipped. We can see this even through the history of Yoga. First, people could practice meditation with *pranahuti*, but over time, it got lost. Although seekers would still be able to practice Raja yoga under the guidance of a teacher, this would be considered a niche pursuit that is only possible or practical for some of the population. Later, yoga branched into various techniques, as the Hatha Yoga texts elaborated. Over time, even Hatha Yoga lost its ultimate goal of union with the Absolute. Now, we see yoga as just an exercise to benefit the body.

With the revival of Raja Yoga with *Pranahuti*, humanity can now pursue the highest goal without limitations. Raja Yoga is for mind regulation, and Hatha Yoga techniques are for keeping the body fit and the energetic body in balance. What should one follow: Hatha Yoga or Raja Yoga? Why not combine both for the best results? A balanced approach is ideal. However, choosing what suits us best based on the goals we have set for ourselves is always better. Whatever we decide, a scientific approach to the practice, practical applicability of the learning, and a reverential attitude will go a long way in our path of yoga.

# Raja Yoga: Ancient Path Vs New Methods

Raja Yoga deals with the mind. In his commentary, Swami Vivekananda explains that the *sutras* describe precisely how the mind works. *Sutras* are the very first and complete treatise on human psychology. Ashtanga yoga gives eight steps that start from external facets of human life (behaviour and lifestyle) and go inwards (breath and mind regulation). In the following pages, we will learn how Heartfulness simplifies the entire approach of Raja Yoga. At the core, Heartfulness is an evolution of the same age-old philosophies of Samkhya and Yoga.

A spiritual seeker needs to understand what actions, choices, and attitudes help and what does not help in the path of Raja Yoga. Traditionally, the seeker had to demonstrate positive attributes to even start the practice under the guidance of a teacher. The traditional concept that defines these attributes is called *Saadhana Chatushtaya.*

## Saadhana Chatushtaya

The word *saadhana* refers to 'means and ways', and *chatushtaya* refers to 'four'. The set of four valuable practices and attributes that help us in our journey are as follows:

1. ***Viveka*** (Discrimination): Right understanding.
It is to discern right from wrong, knowing what helps and does not help achieve the goal.

2. ***Vairagya*** (Detachment): Renunciation of desires.
Renunciation is often misunderstood as giving up responsibilities. The correct interpretation is to give up desires or fruits of action while continuing to perform righteous and duty-bound actions (*swadharma*).

3. *Shat-Sampatti* (6 attainments): Virtues:
- *Shama*- Regulation of mind (by Ashtanga Yoga).
- *Dama*- Natural control of senses.
- *Upratti*- Self-withdrawal.
- *Titiksha*- Fortitude and total satisfaction.
- *Shraddha*- Faith and devotion.
- *Samadhaan*- Self-settled on the goal.

4. *Mumukshutva* (To seek liberation): Intense longing for the goal.

In short, the four-fold spiritual path encourages seekers to think correctly, develop the right understanding, take an honest approach to life, and focus on the goal. The six virtues result from sustained efforts to regulate the mind and senses.

In olden times, this preparedness was a **prerequisite** for the seeker to be eligible to acquire spiritual knowledge. Only those students who demonstrated positive, desirable attributes and were fortunate enough to find a teacher willing to accept them were initiated into the practice. In ancient times, the *Gurukula* system (similar to a boarding school where students lived with the teachers in the natural environment) was prevalent, and the students would gain knowledge and practical experience by being in the teacher's presence. Even today, many organisations in India offer training in yoga, and their systems are modified to suit the current times.

Learning spiritual knowledge and getting support in Yogic practice have been made very simple and freely accessible to all seekers with the help of a worldwide network of practitioners and volunteer trainers by Heartfulness. Modern technology is also helpful in creating such opportunities. Now, the only prerequisites are openness and willingness to be a spiritual scientist, to inquire, experiment, analyse, and come to conclusions based on one's experiences. Heartfulness meditation training is offered free of cost to all seekers worldwide. I am one such trainer who volunteers to pass on the benefits of a practice, which has greatly helped me for the past 25 years. Why is it free? What price can one place on *pranahuti* that comes from the Source itself? It is an excellent opportunity that is freely available to all.

In this hectic modern life, do we have the wherewithal to understand the four-fold path to spiritual practice and demonstrate the six virtues to become deserving of meditation? People are busy earning a livelihood, managing their households, fulfilling multiple responsibilities, and facing media distractions. Lockdowns, health scares, unstable economies, and military conflicts further complicate the situation. Despite such disturbances, we can create balance in our lives and harness our full potential.

Heartfulness is an efficacious Raja Yoga path to spiritual progress modified to suit the present times. It cuts across all the steps of the *sadhana chatushtya*, and we start straight with meditation. *Viveka* (discrimination), *vairagya* (detachment), *shat-sampatti* (six virtues) and *mumukshutva* (longing for realisation) develop in us naturally as a result of meditation with Yogic Transmission. In Heartfulness, *sadhana chatushtya* becomes a **natural outcome instead of a prerequisite**. We only need to follow the simple practice and observe the emergence of these virtues over time.

Heartfulness transforms the entire approach to spiritual practice and makes it easy and accessible for all humanity. The goal of life has become reachable within a short time.

However, as higher awareness develops in them through meditation, it is incumbent upon the practitioners to incorporate the other aspects of *Ashtanga Yoga* into their practice. We become more conscious of maintaining our health and hygiene. We become simple and in tune with nature. We seek to earn an honest living and uphold higher moral principles.

*Raja Yoga* encompasses *Karma, Bhakti* and *Jnana* paths.

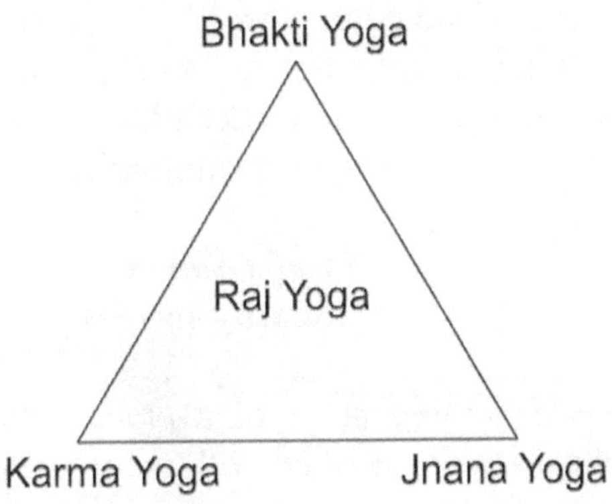


To explain it simply, in *Raja Yoga,* we meditate on the divine presence in the heart, which naturally leads to feelings of devotion (*bhakti*). This is the devotion to the formless essence within and, simultaneously, recognising that the same essence lives in all. We perform devoted, purposeful action (*karma*) in all spheres of our lives. With sustained practice, we gain experiential inner knowledge (*jnana*). Raj Yoga leads to a natural synthesis of the three paths, which are not mutually exclusive, as sometimes misunderstood.

# Evolution in Samadhi

Samadhi is the natural result of sustained meditation practice. Samadhi means to be the same as the original condition. What was our original condition? It was a state of union with the Source, our original home. Samadhi is the aim of Yoga, a state of unbroken union with the Source. However, it is attained in stages with continuous and devoted practice. How do we know if we are progressing? How do we recognise our present state of mind and heart in the context of the goal? Shri PY Deshpande's commentary on the Patanjali Yoga Sutras, *Authentic Yoga,* explains the various stages of samadhi. Let's look at some of the terms and their meanings and then summarise.

## *Sa-bija Samadhi*
## (Identity-based)

It is the beginning stage of a practitioner who finds his internal environment filled with many words, thoughts, and logic. Over time, he moves on to inner silence and then experiences pure joy and pure existence. But throughout this journey, the sense of 'I' remains. Hence, this type of Samadhi is called *Sa-bija Samadhi*; the Prefix '*sa*' refers to 'with', and the word '*bija*' means 'seed', the seed of 'I-am-ness'. Here are words, meanings and explanations to understand the different stages of *Sa-bija Samadhi*:

1. ***Sa-Vikalpa Samadhi:***
   - *Vikalpa* (Imagination, thought)- to delve into situations from the past and think of different results or imagine future scenarios.

   - *Sa-Vikalpa Samadhi-* is a meditative state in which thoughts are present but do not disturb. The meditator is aware of self and the world.

2. ***Sa-Vitarka Samadhi:***
- *Tarka* (Inferential reasoning)- to observe and make inferences. *Tarka* requires speech, language, words and their meaning.

- *Vitarka* (Logical reasoning)- to look at what is within and without and see all aspects.

- *Sa-Vitarka Samadhi*- is a meditative state in which the meditator uses logic, reason, comparison, and conclusions. After removing disturbing thoughts, the mediator applies his thinking.

3. ***Sa-Vichara Samadhi:***
- *Vichara* (Investigative intelligence)- to freely inquire into what is, an endless exploration into the essence of life and being.

- *Sa-Vichara Samadhi*- is a state of silence in which thinking can happen, but the mind is quiet. There are no unregulated thoughts and no need to apply thought.

4. ***Sa-Anand Samadhi:***
- *Anand* (Joy, bliss)- a sense of blissfulness.

- *Sa-Anand Samadhi*- is a state that is beyond the objective world, beyond the mind. One moves into a steady, settled state of tranquillity and joy.

5. ***Sa-Asmita Samadhi:***
- *Asmita* (Ego, Identity)- is a sense of pure I-am-ness devoid of all tensions.

- *Sa-Asmita Samadhi*- this state is beyond bliss, just pure awareness or Is-ness.

### *Nir-bija Samadhi*
### (Pure-seeing-based)

When the 'I' as the operating centre goes away, impressions (*samskaras*) drop off, and then pure seeing begins with no centre. This is a new state, a new type of Samadhi. The prefix '*nir*' refers to 'without', and the word '*bija*' is 'seed'. Hence, *Nir-bija Samadhi* is devoid of the sense of 'I-am-ness'. Here are words, meanings and explanations to understand the different stages of *Nir-bija Samadhi*:

**1. *Nir-Vitarka Samadhi:***
- *Nir-vitarka*- without words, logic, reason, or memory.

- *Nir-Vitarka Samadhi*- is that stage in meditation where words, meaning, and knowledge are suspended. The meditator gets in touch with the real essence without needing words, logic, reasoning and inquiry. It is pure perception.

**2. *Nir-Vichara Samadhi:***
- *Nir-vichara* - without thoughts.

- *Nir-Vichara Samadhi*- is that stage when the realm of subtle thoughts is transcended. Single-pointed focus or effortless concentration is developed.

**3. *Sahaj Samadhi:***
- *Kaivalya*- union, oneness

- *Kaivalya,* or *Sahaj Samadhi*- is the ultimate state of effortless union with complete awareness and expansion.

In summary, these stages of evolution in *samadhi* are the milestones that a meditator comes across. Initially, as the meditator observes his internal environment, he comes across unregulated thoughts and imaginings. With sustained practice, he develops an inner awareness to look at himself objectively and apply thought and reasoning. At this stage, the unregulated thoughts reduce considerably. Further on, the meditator abides in thoughtlessness, a kind of inner silence. Now, he moves into a state of steadiness with joy and peace beyond the mind. Further on, he experiences pure awareness beyond joy and bliss, but still, his sense of I remains. The next stage is beyond the sense of I, where there is pure seeing or perception without the idea of 'I am seeing'. Beyond this, there is an effortless single-pointed focus on the Divine. This leads to union with the Divine, called *Kaivalya* or *Sahaj Samadhi.*

Thus, returning to the original state of *Kaivalya* or *Sahaj Samadhi* is a very high attainment. It is described as a steady state in which the Jiva is one with Reality, yet it maintains its existence as an embodied Soul. Reaching such a state through Yoga and meditation requires diligent and sustained practice to refine consciousness. Meditating with *pranahuti allows* one to move through these stages faster, sometimes altogether skipping some and directly abiding in joyous absorption, going deeper with every meditation.

When we meditate with *pranahuti,* we immediately jump to the inner practices of Ashtanga Yoga and no longer need any prerequisites for our spiritual practice. We also move quickly through the initial stages of samadhi to arrive at a joyous absorption. As an analogy, meditation with *pranahuti* is like a supersonic jet compared to traditional practices, which rely heavily on self-effort and are slower, much like a bicycle.

Then, a question emerges: earlier, we could measure our growth through the evolution of *samadhi,* but now, how will we know our progress with Heartfulness practices? Heartfulness, as the name suggests, is a heart-based method of practice in which we perceive our growth as refined feelings and attitudes that emerge in us. These refined feelings propel us to take the right action. Part 3 of this book describes the journey of the heart, which traverses the entire **spectrum of feeling** states in greater detail.

What happens to our subtle bodies as our consciousness evolves? Each of the sheaths of the subtle body becomes refined, reaching its full potential. For example, the mind becomes regulated and still. Intellect comes under the influence of intuition and wisdom. The ego, the sense of I, becomes universal and all-inclusive. In such a purified subtle body, the degree of awareness, our consciousness reaches its zenith of knowing itself as the witness, the Soul, the Atman.

Having understood the yogic path and its evolution, let us look at potential pitfalls. The pitfalls are dangers or distractions on the way. If we do not tread with due diligence, awareness, and regularity of practice, then there is great danger of falling at any stage in the journey. Patanjali Yoga Sutras describe human psychology and its distortion in great detail. Daaji has provided an excellent commentary on the sutras, reinterpreting them in light of Raja Yoga with *pranahuti.*

# Yogic Psychology

In a collection of works titled *Yogic Psychology*, published in Heartfulness magazine in December 2019, Daaji gives the most lucid description of human psychology from the yogic perspective in the context of the modern world - a must-read for all yoga seekers.

The constitution of the human mind and its workings is the realm of psychology. However, Yoga is the holistic science of physical, mental and spiritual well-being. It describes the entire constitution of the *Jiva* and how each of its aspects can be refined and perfected to reach one's full potential. We have seen how human psychology comes under the cyclical influence of the *trigunas* and is changeable because of it. We need to understand and manage its various aspects to avoid pitfalls on our journey.

Let's take the analogy of the still lake as our consciousness. At first, the lake is still, and the water is clear; we can view the bottom of the lake. Due to thought waves on its surface, the still lake is disturbed. Multiple thought waves create interference patterns and whirlpools on the surface of this lake. Instead of identifying as the still lake, we mistakenly identify ourselves with these modifications and get affected by the increasing turbulence. This means the disturbance pulls our awareness away from the still centre.

Yogic Psychology describes these modifications in four distinct progressively worsening states. The first stage is the formation of tendencies, which further ingrain themselves to appear as afflictions. These afflictions, in turn, become debilitating habits, finally leading to disease. Mind over body.

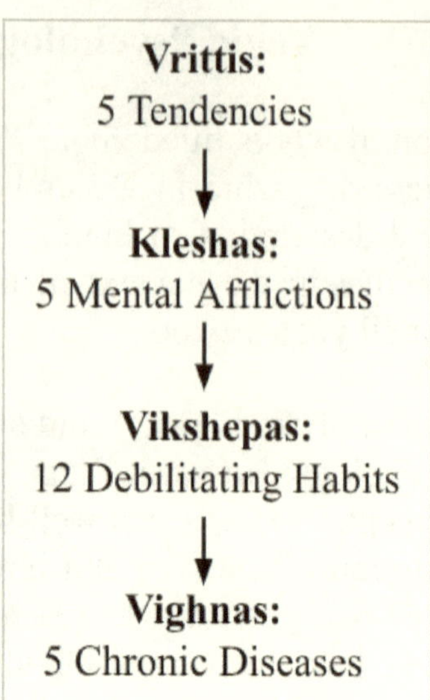


Simple yogic practices can restore balance and thus alleviate the disturbance. We can again become aware that 'I am the witnessing presence' and not the 'undulating modification'. Meditation can bring back this awareness of the still and witnessing consciousness by removing the tendencies and working towards acquiring positive habits.

Counselling can also help in some cases of mental affliction. In the advanced stage of chronic disease, distortion can reach such high levels that it might be too late to reverse it completely. However, the patient can still make positive gains with appropriate tools and strategies. Let's try to understand these modifications better and see what practices and attitudes can help us manage them.

## Vrittis

Vrittis are tendencies that create thought patterns and conditioning. These are:

1. ***Pramana*** (Means of right knowledge)
*Pramana*, meaning proof or means of knowledge, is a **positive** Vritti. It is a result of having a clear perception.

We can acquire the right knowledge by:

- Direct perception- One can get the right knowledge and evidence through direct perception. Become and know.

- Unbiased and rational observation- Use rationality, logic, and unbiased observation to determine the truth. This is devoid of any preconceived idea, dogma or superstition. Does it make sense? Is it true in my observation?

- Teachings of the wise and self-realised yogis- Does the evidence match the findings of previously realised teachers and yogis? All those who have walked on the path of truth have reached similar conclusions. Listen to the wise.

2. ***Viparyaya*** (False or wrong knowledge)
*Viparyaya* results from distorted perception. Anything that distorts perception can lead to false or wrong knowledge. For example, stress, anxiety, fear, anger, lack of sleep, and addiction to food, drugs, alcohol, or sensuousness can distort perception and lead to false knowledge. Avoid anything that has the potential to distort perception.

3. ***Vikalpa*** (Fantasy or Imagination)
Although imagination is necessary for creativity and innovation, *Vikalpa* refers to a kind of mental chatter or static noise in the background. It makes us believe things that have no basis in reality. Use your imagination creatively, but don't let the mind run riot.

4. ***Nidra*** (Sleep)

Sleep is necessary for rest and rejuvenation. Lack of sleep distorts our consciousness, reduces the clarity of perception and thinking, and makes us irritable, forgetful, and prone to mistakes. Adequate sleep helps detoxify the nervous system. Sleep well and at the right time.

5. ***Smriti*** (Memory)

Memory is essential for survival. However, memories associated with emotional events or trauma can debilitate us. Panic, phobia, and strong past likes and dislikes can colour our current perceptions, thus preventing us from making the right decisions. Resolve the past; don't let it live on in you.

Here, the key point is to be aware of our natural thought patterns and strive for balance with greater awareness. Too much or too little sleep, brooding over the past, engaging in constant mental chatter, and all kinds of addictions that cause distortions in consciousness are to be avoided. The best way is to adopt yogic practices, move with the natural circadian rhythm and maintain moderation in all activities to achieve clear perception. *Pramana,* or right knowledge, is a positive Vritti that helps us maintain balance and serves us well in our journey.

**Kleshas**

Kleshas are mental afflictions or colourings. These are:

1. ***Avidya*** (Ignorance)

*Avidya,* or ignorance in its fundamental meaning, refers to the lack of realisation of our true nature as a Soul. In its general sense, *Avidya* is a lack of awareness, the root cause of all mental afflictions. The purer the consciousness, the greater the awareness; hence, *Avidya* also refers to impurity in the consciousness.

Consciousness is impure and limited due to the presence of *samskaras,* which result from desires and ego. Desire refers to preferring one over the other, which stems from our likes and dislikes. The ego is the idea of ownership, the sense of 'I', which could be related to possessions, achievements, ideas or opinions. We can avoid forming new *samskaras* with yogic practices and eliminate the pre-existing ones. Hence, *Avidya* is dissolved by yogic practices. *Avidya* is the basis of the following 4 *Kleshas* as well.

### 2. *Asmita* (Egotism)

Egotism or a sense of separation develops when we identify with our body and mind but not the eternal Soul. This starts the process of forming *samskaras*, as we consider ourselves the doer of actions and thoughts, distinct from others. The ego gets refined as our consciousness is purified. As we meditate on our divine presence, we begin to identify with it more and more.

### 3. *Raga* (Attachment)

Identification with pleasurable experiences results in *Raga* or attachment. Yoga practices loosen the hold of attachment. As we meditate, we moderate our likes and dislikes, finally ceasing to favour.

### 4. *Dvesha* (Aversion)

Identification with or reaction to unpleasurable experiences results in *Dvesha* or aversion. Yoga practices loosen the hold of aversion. As we meditate, we moderate our likes and dislikes, finally ceasing to judge.

### 5. *Abhinivesha* (Fear of Death)

*Abhinivesha* refers to clinging to life or the survival instinct. This is an evolutionary impulse and also a result of *samskaras* of past lives. All fears, including fear of death, are removed by yogic practices. As we meditate on the heart and identify with the eternal Soul, fear of mortality naturally vanishes.

All mental afflictions (*Kleshas*) result from a lack of awareness. Heartfulness cleaning or rejuvenation is an incredibly beneficial practice for removing Kleshas. It directly removes the root cause of mental afflictions, which are impressions or *samskaras* lodged in our consciousness. With the help of cleaning, impressions are removed without the practitioner even becoming aware of them or facing their consequences (effects) to the full extent.

### Vikshepas

Vikshepas are debilitating habits and obstacles. These are:

1. *Vyadhi* (Disease, illness)

Diseases first appear as disturbances in the *Pranamaya Kosha* (vital energy body). Various energy healing modalities that balance the energetic body, work on this fundamental principle. Positive attitudes, joy, moderation, balanced speech, poise, gentleness and mind regulation help keep this *kosha* balanced and the physical body disease-free.

2. *Styana* (Mental laziness, dullness)

The natural state of purified consciousness is that of vitality, while *styana* leads to a waste of energy and subsequent loss of interest in performing actions. Act appropriately and on time.

3. *Samsaya* (Dilemma, indecision)

Doubt, or a state of confusion, arises when our consciousness is disturbed and we cannot connect to our innate wisdom for guidance. When in doubt, listen to your heart.

4. ***Pramada*** (Carelessness, negligence, haste)
Carelessness, haste, and indifference result when we do not put our hearts into action. When not in touch with the heart, we do not know what it wants; hence, we fail to do the task at hand. Pause, connect to your heart, meditate, practice due diligence, and find purpose in your actions.

5. ***Alasya*** (Laziness, sloth)
Giving up, not taking responsibility, hopelessness, and not finding purpose lead to *alasya*. Be responsible.

6. ***Aviratti*** (Lack of abstaining)
Overindulgence, sensual gratification or addiction can lead to distortions in consciousness where one cannot abstain or regulate one's desires, thoughts and emotions. Do not let addictions fester.

7. ***Bhranti-Darshana*** (False perception, delusion)
It is the opposite of *Viveka* or discernment. Losing the ability to discern leads to false perception, inaccurate interpretation, and delusion.

8. ***Alabdha-Bhumikatva*** (Failing to attain stages)
Being stagnant in the inner journey due to a lack of interest or determination to move forward. Reignite the spark and forge ahead.

9. ***Anavasthi-Tatvani*** (Inability to maintain the stage)
Being unstable at higher stages prevents us from proceeding further. Make your position firm at each higher stage by intensifying it and becoming one with it.

Daaji has added the following *Vikshepas* to the original list of Sage Patanjali, as they have only recently surfaced in the modern world. This is a true example of reinterpreting traditional knowledge in the current context.

## 10. **FOMO**

Fear of missing out or not being in the know. It makes us constantly seek online updates, as there is a persistent sense of missing out on the latest developments.

## 11. **Digital distraction**

It includes all social media, news, updates, games, and entertainment that occupy our time and minds without producing positive results.

## 12. **Guilt and shame**

Indulging in doom scrolling, net surfing, online gaming and other harmful content, despite knowing that it is wrong and immoral, leads to guilt and shame. Constant digital chatter, overindulgence in technology, too much screen time, random browsing, social media, and other negative digital influences create serious *vikshepas* in the consciousness. Being unable to free oneself from its tentacles could lead to internal guilt and shame, but most people deny this problem. Added to that are the harmful effects of radiation from modern digital technologies.

In summary, imbalanced tendencies can create mental afflictions, leading to debilitating habits. If left unchecked, these habits can create complications and chronic diseases. It is in our best interest to remove negative tendencies. Life can be healthy, fulfilling, creative, and joyous if we invest time and energy in maintaining our subtle bodies in good shape. Yoga offers a wide range of comprehensive and holistic wellness practices that can help everyone.

### Vighnas
Chronic diseases

1. ***Duhkha*** - Mental and physical pain
2. ***Daurmanasya*** - Despair and depression

3. ***Angam Ejayatva*-** Nervousness
4. ***Svasa*-** Irregular inhalation
5. ***Pravasa*-** Irregular exhalation

The modern world is afflicted with these *Vighnas,* which have reached chronic levels in certain societies. The use of painkillers, antidepressants, anti-anxiety, anti-stress medication, sleeping pills, illegal drugs, and alcohol is rampant. Moreover, the leading causes of distress in today's world are lifestyle diseases like heart failure, diabetes and cancer. The human population seems to have lost touch with inner reality and its connection to nature. It looks for externalised solutions to a problem rooted in the distorted consciousness. Regularising daily routines and sleep cycles, following simple yogic practices, and being in tune with nature can prevent or heal this distortion.

Afflictions distort consciousness, leading to a lack of clarity and imbalance in life. Each individual may have different afflictions to varying degrees. Yogic psychology stresses the importance of positive affirmative practices that alleviate distortion of consciousness. Dissecting the afflictions and treating them symptomatically with pharmaceutical drugs is of minimal benefit. Yoga is an antidote to distorted perception, but the seeker's body and mind must be capable enough to to practice it. People with pre-existing severe debilitating physical or mental diseases who cannot practice yoga may require medical treatment to stabilise their condition. Yoga is not an emergency treatment but a conscious and sustained effort undertaken diligently as a preventative health and wellness tool.

# Solutions
## Heartfulness Yogic Practices

Swami Vivekananda has described how every force in the universe is **Prana**, from the infinitesimally small to the infinitely large. The forces holding the particles and planets in their orbits, forces of nature, the energy that sustains all life, the power that governs and runs the universe, and the life force in our hearts are different forms of the same *prana*. It is the most subtle, divine and highly potent force-less force at its highest level. A Yogi who has reached this level of subtlety can access this energy from the Source and give it a direction with his intention. Another name for Prana is *Adi-Shakti*, the power of the Source.

Heartfulness is based on the ancient method of Raja Yoga and is aided by Transmission (**Pranahuti**). When we meditate with *pranahuti*, our consciousness is progressively purified, and the practitioner develops an effortless focus on the heart. This naturally creates simplicity, centeredness and peacefulness. The practitioner only needs to meditate and be receptive to *prana* being transmitted to the heart. Meditation with *pranahuti* presents an excellent opportunity to pull ourselves out of this quicksand of distorted consciousness. The call is to purify our consciousness, connect to the heart, raise our vibration and realise our true selves. This is the spiritual renaissance, the dawn of a new era where we can live peacefully, in tune with nature, and recognise our potential as divine beings. Heartfulness proposes simple practices: Relaxation, Meditation, Cleaning and Prayer.

**Relaxation**

Relaxation is a simple technique to calm our body and mind and relax in the present moment. Relaxation gives us the experience of being in tune with our body; it draws our attention inward and helps us be at ease. Anyone can try the relaxation technique and feel its impact on the body and mind instantaneously. Relaxation can ease muscle and nerve tension, calm the mind, and improve sleep. The relaxation technique is also useful when preparing to meditate. It helps us ease into meditation when we take a few minutes to centre ourselves.

## Meditation

We meditate on the heart, as it is the core of our being. The object of meditation is the divine presence or light in the heart. Just an idea of divine light is enough; we need not visualise any form of light. Since divine light is an abstract idea we meditate on, the physical heart helps us fix a general location to focus our attention. As we meditate, drawing our attention inward, we become aware of our internal environment.

We may encounter thoughts, feelings, ideas, images, experiences, or memories that might repeatedly pull our attention away from our object of meditation. We gently bring our attention back to the heart. With some practice, we achieve a certain level of steadiness in meditation and the resultant regulation of the mind. A certified trainer can aid the seeker with guided meditations.

## Cleaning

Cleaning is a willful effort to cleanse our internal environment effectively yet simply. The objective is to remove the impressions or *samskaras* lodged in our consciousness that give rise to thoughts and disturbances during meditation. Effective cleaning removes these impressions, changing our inner landscape for the better. Cleaning can be done in the evening at the end of a day's work. A certified trainer can guide the seeker through the method of cleaning.

**Prayer**

Prayer is a way to connect and communicate with the divine presence within. True prayer does not demand anything from the divine but only expresses devotion. It helps the practitioner reaffirm the highest goal. In humility, a yogi prays for the welfare and spiritual upliftment of himself and all humanity.

These simple practices aided by *pranahuti* promise the seeker the highest attainment, union with the divine. This is achievable with diligent and persistent practice. We see tangible progress when we engage in the practice and carefully record our observations as we change and grow.

**Resources**

Heartfulness offers many resources to aid one's practice. The free HeartfulnessApp, with its many audio guides, helps seekers go deeper into the practice. Download the application from https://www.heartfulnessapp.org.

The bestsellers *The Heartfulness Way, Designing Destiny, The Wisdom Bridge* and *Spiritual Anatomy*, written by Daaji, the Heartfulness global guide, describe the practices and their benefits in practical daily life. The president of India conferred Daaji with the *Padma Bhushan* award, and he has received multiple honours from various organisations worldwide for his services to humanity.

Heartfulness also offers free workshops for schools, colleges, universities, technical institutes, corporates, governmental and non-governmental organisations, village panchayats, and all other groups of people. These life-skills workshops are designed to suit the requirements of the institutions while catering to the basic human need for mental and spiritual balance through meditation, aided by transmission.

Heartfulness has a global presence, with thousands of trainers, practitioners, and centres. For more information, visit www.heartfulness.org. You can find trainers and centres at www.heartspots.heartfulness.org. The masterclasses explaining the practices are available at www.heartfulness.org/global/masterclass.

The simplicity of this method hides its efficacy. As a practitioner and a trainer in this way, I have benefitted immensely. A significant degree of inner calmness, balance and stability has emerged, which has helped me live peacefully with conscious choices.

# Part 2

# Scientific Discoveries
(Rational Thought and Observation)

# Chapter 4
# Ancient Greek Philosophy

## Origins of Western Philosophy

In Part 1 of the book, we examined the evolving yogic perspective on the science of life. In Part 2, we will review the evolution of Western philosophy and modern science to see if we can draw any parallels between the two approaches.

For Europe and the larger Western world, the fundamental ideas of philosophy, art and knowledge are derived from the great Greek scholars of the classical era circa 500 BCE-200 BCE. The classical Greek period ended with the Roman conquest of Greece in 146 BCE. Greek knowledge was passed on to the Romans, and then it spread further into Europe. Following the fall of the Roman empire, 1000 years of a non-rational period dominated by religious orthodoxy ensued, which denied free thought and enforced dogmatic belief. Today, the awakened Western mind calls this period the 'dark ages'. A social and cultural renaissance in the 14th and 15th centuries CE became the turning point when new ideas based on liberty, humanism, rational thought and democracy took root in Europe.

Even today, Greek and Roman thought dominates Europe in all areas of human life. For example, the governance and jurisprudence laws worldwide are Roman, while the philosophy and the sciences that emerged from it were originally Greek discoveries. Western philosophy and modern sciences are a gift of Greek culture. The current theories of existentialism, humanism, functionalism, and materialism also emanate from Greek foundations. Even modern scientific and mathematical technical terminology and vocabulary are from Greek and Latin. English has borrowed heavily from these languages to build its scientific vocabulary.

Language plays an essential role in learning and expression. However, words' meaning and contextual usage change over time, leading to misunderstandings and inaccurate interpretations. Due to the ever-changing language landscape and vocabulary, language itself is considered a barrier to true knowledge. However, due to their ease of usage and blending, Greek words have provided an excellent foundation for the practical need for language in pursuing science.

Notably, Sanskrit has not changed over long periods following rigid sound-root-word-meaning relationships. Interestingly, it has also found practical utility in the modern world. Sanskrit grammar is well-defined and intensely logical and is now used for AI machine learning. In Sanskrit, the meaning of root words has remained the same; hence, the interpretation has also remained unchanged. Despite this consistency in language, the ancient texts only point towards the direct realisation of existential truths rather than an intellectual understanding of words. Words only serve as pointers or milestones on the way, nothing more than that.

The origins of Western philosophy and sciences are traced to Greece, circa 600 BCE. In that era, Greek people were polytheistic and had a pantheon of gods and goddesses representing powers of nature, much like ancient India. The beginnings of Greek philosophy coincide with the birth of Prince Siddhartha in 625 BCE in India, who later became Gautama the Buddha. Budhha's teachings were a revolution or renaissance in India, as he spoke against religious orthodoxy and favoured a yogic path to nirvana.

We can see how much older the ancient Indian texts of Vedas and Upanishads are compared to the origins of Western philosophy. Modern historians do not want to recognise this fact and try to fit the timeline of Indian texts to suit their historical narratives. The now-debunked theory of the Aryan invasion of India is a concrete example of this deliberate distortion.

The Vedic era in India was ancient and influenced all cultures worldwide. Even seemingly isolated ancient cultures had identical nature worship practices and folktales. Greek mythology is also similar to Indian folktales. Homer's famous book, *Odyssey,* is an allegorical tale of a soul's journey back to the Source. Although multiple interpretations exist, the story gives us a glimpse into the polytheistic nature of Greek culture and society. We even have popular characters, novels, and movies inspired by polytheistic Greek culture.

**Prominent Philosophers of Greece**

Philosophy is based on the concept of **Wonder**. When a philosopher observes the world, he wonders about it, and questions emerge. Free inquiry and rational thought are its foundations, just as curiosity is a natural human trait. Although people might have different intellectual capacities, each person is unique and has inalienable rights. Ethics places all humans at the same level. Thus, the seeds of humanism arose in Greek society, and it moved towards a more equitable and just outlook.

Ancient Greece saw many religious reformers, philosophers, poets, and mathematicians who later became the stalwarts of Western thought in many fields, such as science, philosophy, mathematics, and humanism. Let's examine the works of some of these brilliant minds and see if we can find any links to Vedic ideas.

Disclaimer: This is a brief study focusing on the salient points of Greek philosophy in the context of this book. The entire scope and evolution of Greek philosophy, which deals with various subjects, will require a much greater discussion, which is outside the scope of this book.

### Pythagoras (570- 500 BC)
'All is Number'

Pythagoras was a mystic who lived a simple life in tune with nature, followed vegetarianism and immersed himself and his followers in mystical mathematics and music to understand the universe. There was a cultural and knowledge exchange between various regions of the world during the time of Pythagoras, and he was well aware of Egyptian, Sumerian and Indian knowledge systems, among others. Like an ancient Indian *Gurukulam*, where students would live with their teacher and learn by his example, Pythagoras also had a school where the prerequisite to learning was self-discipline by silence. Years of silence and contemplation prepared the students' minds to absorb the higher knowledge that Pythagoras held in high regard.

*"Learn silence. With the quiet serenity of a meditative mind, listen, absorb, transcribe, and transform."*

Pythagorean school viewed learning as a 3 step immersive experience of knowledge, understanding and wisdom. The content of this kind of classical education had four main components, which are:

1. **Number** - *All is Number*. This dictum proclaimed a mathematical order of the world. We can define all phenomena numerologically. Each number has a specific meaning.

2. **Geometry** - Pythagoras considered geometry as 'number in space and form'. He saw shape and form as a divine blueprint, a number fixed in space by a particular shape.

3. **Music, Vibration or Harmony** - Pythagoras saw music as 'a number in time', defined by a change in ratio and proportion over time. He spoke about three types of music:

   - Instrumental music and of all objects.
   - Music of the human body and all living systems.
   - Music of cosmic bodies, all planets and stars.

   He said that music could heal all disturbances in the human energy field. He considered instrumental music as just a faint echo of the music of the heavens. He adored the Sun and other heavenly bodies as deities.

4. **Cosmology** - Pythagoras considered cosmology as a number in space and time, a number in constant motion over time. Hence, he considered numbers as the basis of existence: form, vibration, and the universe.

*"Each celestial body, in fact, every atom, produces a particular sound on account of its movement, its rhythm or vibration. All these sounds and vibrations form a universal harmony in which each element, while having its own function and character, contributes to the whole."*

Pythagoras believed in the eternal law of nature, which states that all beings are divine and have an equal right to peaceful coexistence. He also thought that the soul is transferred into another body after death. He was considered a mystic who combined ideas of religion, science, and philosophy in a grand synthesis.

To an onlooker, Pythagoras's teachings seem mathematical and devoid of divine reference. However, he pointed towards the underlying divine reality by explaining the universe's mechanics through numbers and vibration. Pythagoras also emphasised heightening perceptions to experience higher vibrational reality beyond the limitations of the senses. Knowing the creative potential of one's mind is akin to knowing the creator.

Pythagorean ideas are similar to those of the Vedas, which also refer to sound, form and astrology. His emphasis on refining the perception through silence is a Vedic concept, too. In the Indian context, *Vedic Ganita* or mathematics is a vast treatise encompassing numbers, place-value, decimals, fractions, differentials, geometry, patterns and astrological calculations of cyclic time and distances.

**Socrates** (470- 399 BC)
'Knowledge is Virtue'

Socrates is considered the wisest man born in Europe. His legacy is the greatest heritage of Europe. Ironically, he was persecuted and killed. Due to his revolutionary ideas against corruption and his puritanical views on morality, he was sentenced to death by poisoning. It is said that he did not try to escape the prison despite an opportunity. Instead, he chose to die to uphold the tradition of truth. Socrates did not leave any written work. His student Plato produced *Dialogues,* which explained Socrates' ideas. Some of his ideas are as follows:

**Epistemology** is the method of gaining knowledge. Socrates gave the famous dialectical method, which involves wondering and questioning. Hence, Socrates is credited with developing systematic thinking to gain knowledge.

Socrates propounded the importance of **Concepts** in knowledge. He said concepts, not percepts, are universal and objective. Percepts are sense-based and subjective. Socrates also gave the inductive method for gaining knowledge, which states that based on repeated observations and reasoning, one can arrive at the universal idea or the concept behind anything. Knowledge is rational, not sense-based. Only ideas and concepts are real, not particular objects. Senses can misguide us as they are limited. All objects are just imperfect copies of one universal idea or concept.

Socrates also brought objectivity to **Ethics**. He stated that moral codes are universal and equally applicable to all. Knowledge is the highest virtue, and the power of discrimination, right thinking, and conduct comes from knowledge only. Like his predecessor, Pythagoras, Socrates believed in the soul's immortality. Socrates' most significant contribution was seeding the ideas of constant pursuit of conceptual knowledge, equality, and universal applicability of morals in the Western world, a concept closer to *Dharma* in the Vedic context.

## **Plato** (428- 348 BC)
### 'Essence of Knowledge is Self-knowledge'

The most outstanding disciple of Socrates, Plato, collected the ideas of his teacher and presented them to the world in the form of *Dialogues*. Seeing how Socrates was sentenced to death due to his puritanical views on morality and truth, Plato tried redefining knowledge and virtue. He said a human being does not only act based on his knowledge and understanding; his inner motivations and emotions also influence his actions. Although one might know how to behave reasonably, he might fail due to his inherent tendencies. Hence, apart from knowledge, one should have higher intentions and create balance in oneself. Plato said that the only knowledge worth having is knowledge of the soul; all else is just transient knowledge. Plato wrote on many subjects but is best known for the 5 Platonic solids named after him.

Synthesising all previous views of his predecessors, Plato gave his ideas on Metaphysics. He said that Oneness is the basis of knowledge, not multiplicity. Ideas or concepts never fade, never die. Ideas or definitions can survive beyond objective reality. In the end, what remains is the only permanent thing, and such a metaphysical entity can be the sole objective of knowledge.

What is the **Idea**? As per Plato, an idea is the ground where the quality and attributes of an object lie, but ideas are independent. Like a universal mould, they are eternal. The idea is demiurge (demi-god), the moulds through which creation can happen. Ideas are not of this physical world but transcendental, beyond the senses. Ideas are the essence of objects. Ideas are non-spatial and non-temporal, i.e., beyond space and time. Ideas are not things; they are thoughts, but not particular thoughts either; they are generalised thoughts existing outside any individual mind.

An idea is original; the world is a reflection or an imperfect copy of that original idea. Ideas are immutable, while the sense-based world is changeable. The foundation of modern unified theory is the search for that One Idea, the basis of all creation. Astonishingly, Plato's metaphysics resembles the Vedic description of Brahma and its three bodies: causal, subtle and gross.

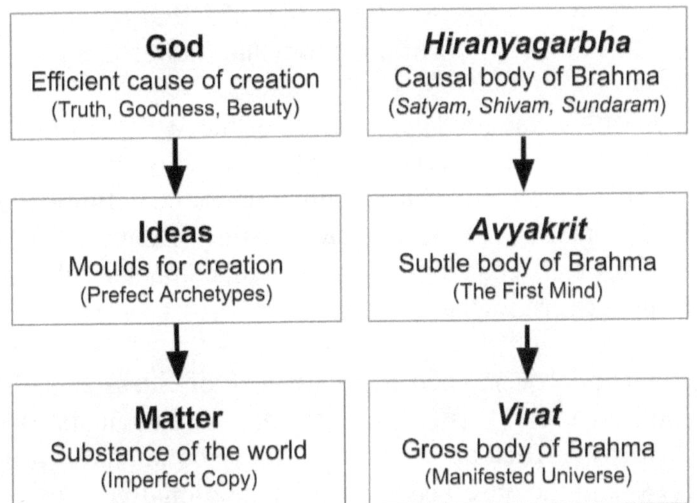



Further, Plato considered the soul the cause of motion in the world, called the vital force (or *Prana* in Sanskrit). The soul is immortal and eternal. It manages the entire administration of the body and mind. Without this vital power, the body cannot be alive.

Plato spoke about two types of souls: wise and unwise. Wise souls have discriminating power; they express love and seek beauty, while the unwise ones lack these qualities. Depending upon the tendencies of the soul, it faces a similar fate. The soul is immortal, and it reincarnates repeatedly. This kind of soul classification is also seen in Vedic philosophy as *daivic* or *asuric* souls. In the Indian context, the soul's trajectory is defined by the theory of *samskaras,* or impressions, which causes the Jiva to act in a certain way. These impressions can control us as if we were on an auto-pilot, or we can change them with yogic practices and redesign our destinies. Hence, in India, the Soul is considered ever pure; however, each Jiva has multiple coverings and distortions that give it a distinct personality.

# **Aristotle** (384- 322 BC)
## 'World is Form and Matter'

Aristotle, the intellectual giant of the Western world, wrote 400 books on every subject of the day. Even today, his works contain relevant terminologies and definitions for the appropriate use of language in any subject. One of his significant contributions is the fundamental rules or laws that govern logical reasoning.

Aristotle questioned Plato's theory of 'ideas as archetypes of creation'. Instead of creating an imaginary world of 'ideas', Aristotle said that Plato should have sought to explain the observed phenomenon rationally.

In the context of this study, let us delve deeper into the Aristotelian description of life and processes. Aristotle divides the world into organic and inorganic worlds in *Aristotle's Psychology (De anima and Parva naturalia)*. Per him, the soul is the animating principle in all organic life. All living beings possess the capacity to think, sense and move. The movement could be external (walking, eating, talking) or internal (assimilation, growth, decay). Since Aristotle takes the soul as life itself, he regards psychology primarily from the point of view of biology and not as a mental or psychic phenomenon as we understand it today.

Aristotle also sees nature as a continuous phenomenon of inanimate matter moving to higher animate life. He considers moving, sensing and thinking as attributes of the soul itself. He reasons that the growing complexity in animal life compared to plant life is due to the complexity of the animal soul, as animals have a greater capacity to move and sense. Humans can also think or reason; hence, the human soul is the most complex. In the opinion of Aristotle, the soul is the unity in which the principles of life, i.e., movement, sense-perception and thinking, are embedded.

Aristotle describes the world primarily as **Form and Matter**; form is the actuality, or the soul and matter is the potentiality. The potential matter transforms into various organic structures or organisms. In other words, the formative principle that is constantly active to cause this transformation of passive matter to an animate organism is the soul. If the form wasn't there, we might just be a lump of clay or loose grains of sand.

Aristotle observed that anything that moves is a composite of soul and body. The soul is the efficient and formal cause, as all movement and activity are due to the soul only, while the body is the material substrate. The soul is not the body but is inseparable from the body. The soul is in every part of the body. He explains how parts of some plants can be grafted, and certain body parts grow back in some insects. As the organism becomes complex, this life principle (soul) gets centralised, although it is still active throughout the body. For humans, the heart is considered the centre of the being, hence, the seat of the soul. He further explains how any damage to the heart can be fatal, how the heart bears the brunt of emotional disturbances, and how the heart is the first organ to be formed in an embryo; as the heart starts to pulsate, it gives the movement of life to the organism.

Aristotle coined **Central Common Sense** to denote a faculty that can take all sense perceptions and give a holistic meaning to the sensed object. For example, a flower can be fragrant, red in colour, with soft petals, having a specific shape and form; all this sensed information, when analysed by the central common sense, identifies the flower as a rose and creates an experience of it. Common sense has a different meaning in current times, as it refers to a common knowledge that everyone possesses, lacking which someone can be deemed foolish or not street smart. Aristotle used 'common sense' to point toward a 'central sense' that corroborates information from all the senses, like the mind or brain we recognise today. He stated that one of the functions of this central sense is **Perception**. Perception can be external (5 sense organs) and internal (feelings, thoughts and memories). External sensing can stir up the inner world, for example, how an odour resurfaces the memory of the mother's cooking with its associated feelings. Once the data is stored, we do not need to use all our senses to perceive an object; one sense is enough, or just the associated word is enough to bring up its memory. Sensing deposits information to the **Memory**.

Another function of this central common sense is knowing about perception, being **Conscious**. We see the object, we know the object, and we are aware of its meaning and relevance. Although the senses gather data, they do not make observations. Another function of this central common sense is **Observation** and **Judgement**.

Aristotle calls **Sleep, Imagination, Memory and Dreams** *disturbances in the constant flow of consciousness*; hence, these are also considered functions of this central common sense. Sleep is a state where consciousness is not present. Imagination is the power to hold the idea of a sensed object removed from the vicinity. Then, just a word or past association is enough to bring it up in our thoughts from memory. Imagination is an impression of an object or idea we can entertain. How about things that do not yet exist? How will we imagine those? Abstract imagination is also based on the foundation of what exists, an idea projected further. Dreams are a product of experiences had while awake, which come up as a play of consciousness while asleep. Dreams could also arise from our inner world of feelings and memories or due to illness and discomfort. Our central common sense, which usually distinguishes between fact and fantasy, is absent during sleep; we become prone to dreams beyond our judgment's oversight.

Aristotle defines **Will** as any action towards the good. At its lowest form, it is an impulse, where no conscious choice is exercised, and at its highest, it is a rational desire to do good. **Reason** is yet another function of central common sense. It operates in two distinct fields, namely, knowledge and morality. **Morality** is the right end, while reason is the prudent means to that end.

Let's summarise the Aristotelian model of human composition: Just as the body and senses are tethered to the soul, this central common sense is a definite faculty of the same soul or life. As described by Aristotle, central common sense is observable, and there is evidence of it to varying degrees in different human beings. However, Aristotle wondered about the soul itself, asking many questions as he was unsure about the fundamental nature of the soul: What is the soul made of? Is it a potentiality or itself caused? Is it quantity or quality? Is the soul divisible? Can it exist apart from the body? Can there be a single true definition of the soul?

We can find parallels between the Aristotelian model of human composition and the Yogic description of a human being. Both talk about casual, subtle and gross elements. Interestingly, Aristotle's common sense is another word for intellect, and what he describes as 'disturbances in the constant flow of consciousness' are the *Vrittis*. However, Aristotle's description seems quite elementary compared to the exquisite details given in Yogic Psychology. The Aristotelian model appears to be motivated more by physical evolution rather than the evolution of consciousness itself.

In the 3rd century BCE, a new stream of Greek philosophers called Neo-Platonists revived symbolism, mysticism and monotheistic ideas by amalgamating Pythagorean, Platonic, Indian and other metaphysical views. However, due to a lack of clear, rational thought, it could not take the shape of a coherent new philosophy in the world. The world still considers Pythagoras, Socrates, Plato, and Aristotle to be the foremost thought leaders in the Western world, and their work is referenced as foundational even today. Although Neoplatonist ideas failed to put forward a complete philosophy, they brought together the Western and Eastern approaches, thus creating a bridge.

The Western world has produced great thinkers and philosophers who were stalwarts in their fields. In the last 200 years, brilliant Western minds have created modern science and technology. Although many great mathematicians, scientists, and artists have come from other cultures, the cutting edge of modern science is still a Western front. However, in recent decades, Asian countries have also taken a significant leap in scientific research and development.

# Ancient Indian Science

In the Indian context, we can say that Yogis from the Vedic era were pioneers too. *Vedas*, *Upa-Vedas* and *Vedangas* encompass philosophy, language, medicine, economics, astrology, archery, mathematics, architecture, music and arts. There were great personalities like Chanakya, Aryabhata and Ramanuja in the more recent historical context. We are witnessing a renewed interest in their work amongst the current generation.

It is futile at this stage to discuss where the idea originated. Can we instead just call it a human heritage? It is better to avoid tribalism of the intellectual kind and consider all knowledge common to all humanity. Isn't it ironic that the promoters of globalisation do not allow such a free flow of knowledge and technology through modern intellectual property rights regulations? Nevertheless, it is worthwhile to look at the evidence available to credit the ancient Indians for their contributions to sciences before the existence of these laws. The study is to understand the Indian civilisation that valued scientific temper and freely shared it with the world, considering the whole world as one family.

As we keep going deeper, we realise that the ancients did not take credit for the work, as it was *Shruti*, meaning 'heard', not produced by them. Hence, ancient Indian texts and their knowledge systems are considered divine in origin; therefore, it is for all humanity. As Indians, we must first value, follow, and imbibe it before we can share it with others confidently. As explained in Part 1 of this book, Vedic or Yogic knowledge is not an intellectual pursuit alone; it requires a certain readiness of lifestyle and attitudes. As an analogy, this sacred knowledge is not about having the best bow and arrow or knowing the archery techniques but about self-mastery.

In his well-researched book titled *Ancient Hindu Science*, author Alok Kumar goes into great detail about the Indian culture that is inherently scientific. He highlights the notable documented contributions by Indians towards advancements in science with extensive, detailed references. He explains how, from ancient times, all branches of knowledge flourished in India, namely geography, metallurgy, mathematics, astronomy, astrology, cosmology, economics, processing of different types of natural resources, shipbuilding, tool making, textile, sculpting, philosophy, art, music, dance, drama, poetry, etc.

There is documented evidence of sharing this knowledge pool along the ancient trade routes. Various Chinese and Arabic scholars and historians travelled to India and translated this wealth of knowledge to take back to their homelands. They also wrote about the culture and life in India. These records predate the classical Greek era. Of course, inspiration, discoveries, and inventions happen in any open, progressive society, and in ancient times, India was known as the land of seekers and wise people. Students from around the world who came to study in large universities and libraries, to the scale of Takshashila and Nalanda, testify to this fact. The Arabic translations of Indian books were carried to Europe and further translated into Latin and other European languages.

Taking reference from these records and the information available in the archives of many universities, author Alok Kumar painstakingly gathered data that pays homage to some of the prominent inventions by ancient Indians. In addition to the foundational *Shruti* and *Smriti* texts, some other famous scientific works are *Charak Samhita,*

*Shusruta Samhita, Ganitapada, Arayabhatiya, Nyaya-sutra, Sulbha-Sutras, Arthshastra, Vaisheshika-sutra, Surya Siddhanta, Sutra-sthanam,* and more.

Some modern scientific ideas that find their origins in these texts are listed below:

**Mathematics**: The foundations of modern mathematics and digital computing are based on ancient Indian science.

1. **Zero and the place value system:** Ancient India developed the world's current mathematical system based on zero (*shunya*). The *Rig Veda* mentions the binary system used by modern computing.

2. **Fibonacci Sequence:** Fibonacci learnt mathematics from Indian scholars and, realising its soundness, wrote a book titled *Liber Abaci* to popularise it in the West. The so-called Fibonacci sequence, currently defined as a natural growth pattern, appears as the science of poetic meter in Sanskrit hymns.

3. **Number Operations:** Square root operations, algebra, the sum of series, quadratic equations, geometry, the value of pi, Pythagorean theorem, and trigonometry are a few recorded examples of concepts that originated in India.

4. **Astronomy**: Indian astronomical texts describe the solar system, eclipses, constellations, orbits, rotation, geocentricity, calendar making, and time calculation. The Hindu cosmological time scales are vast, and the concept of Yuga as cycles of time and consciousness still baffles us.

5. **Physics**: Extensive ideas on space, time, matter, mass, atom, gravitation, and tides are a part of the Vedic treatises.

6. **Chemistry**: There are records of mining, metallurgy, and fermentation. Author Alok Kumar gives multiple examples, such as non-rusting iron pillars and steel, that are still present today.

7. **Biology**: Indians catalogued diverse flora and fauna, the human body and its functioning, diseases and their treatment, and surgery. In ancient India, biology was more than a study of the classification of plants and animals or how the body works. Ecology, vegetarianism and sacredness went hand in hand with biology. The traditions of considering rivers, *tulsi* plants, and cows as sacred are examples of the culture forming a symbiotic relationship with nature, which it regarded as sentient.

8. **Medicine**: The land of India has had a conducive climate for diverse flora and fauna. The records show a rich library of medicines with trained practitioners and hospital set-ups. *Ayurveda* is taught and practised to date.

9. **Psychology:** Yoga encompasses the entire science of wellness, taking care of the body, mind, and soul. No other psychological theory and application is as complete, comprehensive, and practical as Yoga. Yoga is an evolving science; its modern developments by Heartfulness are also freely available to all seekers.

It would be wonderful if today's youth could pick up these books and delve deeper into the concepts. We need to remember our ancient roots and our true nature.

# A Comparative Study of the Indian and Western Philosophical Outlooks

## *Darshana* Vs Philosophy

The Sanskrit word *darshana* refers to 'seeing' or direct perception, which is beyond knowledge yet contains all knowledge. Its corresponding mistranslation in English is 'philosophy', which refers to the love of wisdom. It is an endless quest for knowledge through intellectual pursuits, finding the concept behind phenomena and defining the principles. Only an educated intellectual with an excellent grasp of language, meaning, and reasoning can indulge in philosophy. That is a core difference between the Eastern and the Western approaches.

In India, even a layperson, a farmer, an engineer, or a scholar can have *darshana* based on their own experience. While *darshana* might lead to knowledge, it goes beyond that and refers to direct perception and understanding, the experience of *becoming*. In India, the goal of life is *moksha,* or liberation from the cycles of life and death, for which knowledge is not a prerequisite. It requires a life lived with devotion, sacrifice, and purposeful action.

However, both approaches are not mutually exclusive. We can engage in the joyous pursuits of the inner and outer worlds according to our capacity.

## Becoming Vs Knowing

Veda is derived from the root word *vid,* meaning knowledge, but it does not refer to only an intellectual pursuit. Since Indian culture is based on Vedas, which talk about one's true identity as a soul, people inherently identify themselves as eternal souls. Irrespective of the level of education, language proficiency, or social or financial status, people can achieve the goal of life through the pursuit of yogic practices. No special education or intellectual rigour is needed; it asks for a sincere commitment to a purposeful life that is well lived. There are many examples of people, such as sages, kings, warriors, poets, and ordinary people from all walks of life, who are dedicated to self-realisation, irrespective of their worldly pursuits.

## Self-realisation Vs Wonder

Indian Vedic thought is seeded on the existence of the soul as the prime mover. Yoga shows ways and means to extricate the soul from physical bondage, as physicality is the leading cause of misery, sorrow, sickness, old age and death. Western philosophy wonders about the world and asks probing questions to understand the nature of the universe. The quest to find answers leads to the creation of new fields of science. Various science streams study outer material nature, while inner nature comes under psychology. Interestingly, the Greek word *psyche* originally meant soul, but later became identified with consciousness, and finally as mind only. Currently, Merriam-Webster dictionary defines it as the science of mind and behaviour.

The field of consciousness is not mainstream in Western science, and psychology is considered a study of mind and behaviour only. The concepts of soul and consciousness are relegated to dogmatic religions beyond the scope of reason.

## Yogi Vs Mathematician or Thinker

Yogis produced ancient Indian texts from a higher perceptual state, where they could directly grasp the nature of reality as an inner experience. Greek scholars were primarily excellent mathematicians and philosophers who laid the foundation of emerging sciences. Modern scientists have continued on the same path to understanding natural phenomena, finding patterns, and defining the basic substance and laws of the physical world. These laws could then be applied to solve the practical problems of material life. This approach, however, left out the problem of spiritual life altogether.

## Devotion Vs Concept

Yogis are scientific, and they also express their devotion to the Divine in myriad ways. Knowledge can always be helpful as a tool, but the real yogi is born in the heart. The heart is the seat of the divine, and its language is love. One who is in pursuit of divinity grows in love for all creation. He is in a state of surrender (*sharnagati*), completely accepting all that is, having resolved his karmic debt.

All the bodies or sheaths of the yogi are in perfect balance. He is strong physically, his mind is still, his intellect is refined, and he effortlessly focuses on the divine presence in the heart, wholly identified with it. He has now become an instrument of the divine will. For the yogi, the divine is not a concept to be understood but a presence felt in the heart.

## Anonymity Vs Intellectual Property Rights

Since ancient texts are of divine origin and exist as vibrations, anyone can perceive their essence. Modern philosophy and science are private intellectual pursuits, and copyright laws protect their discoveries.

## Teacher-Disciple Relationship

*Guru-Shishya parampara,* or the tradition of the Teacher-Disciple relationship, is the cornerstone of yogic knowledge and spiritual heritage. It is the most respectful, sacred, reverential, and divine relationship. The teacher is called *Guru*, the remover of darkness or ignorance. Without a *Guru*, all higher pursuits are impossible.

In the Western tradition, the student synthesises the ideas of previous teachers to create a new philosophy. The student is seen as completing the teacher's unfinished work. In the yogic context, the pursuit is self-realisation, and the real *Guru* is the one who has realised himself. The student does not attempt to contradict or improve on his *Guru's* work; he follows the path shown by the *Guru* to unite with the Divine.

Today, we need a grand synthesis of these two approaches: an inner approach to self-mastery and an outer approach to understanding natural phenomena for a better material life. This requires an Eastern heart and a Western mind.

> *"One ounce of practice is worth a thousand pounds of theory."*
>
> — *Swami Vivekananda*

# Chapter 5
# Number and Geometry

## Geometry: Understanding Shape and Form

Fundamentals of geometry, currently taught in schools worldwide, are based primarily on Greek discoveries. Euclid, Pythagoras and Plato are some famous mathematicians and thinkers. However, number, form and shape are universal languages without cultural connotations. People of all ages and cultures have observed natural phenomena and counted, measured, mapped, and drawn what they saw. Forms and shapes have fascinated everyone, with each culture expressing it uniquely. Geometry has further led to astrology, architecture, cartography, engineering and more. Ancients couldn't have created great architectural wonders without numbers and geometry. Geometry is an ancient science.

Pythagoras (570 - 495 BC) was a famous and highly respected Ionian Greek mathematician who gave the well-known Pythagorean theorem. His work is about numbers, shapes, proportions, harmonics and cosmology. In the Pythagorean view, the universe is an ordered unit. The universe begins from the middle and expands outward around a central point; hence, it has a spherical nature. Pythagoras did not see mathematics as only numbers and computation but practised mystical mathematics and considered everything of divine origins, with numbers being its representation. Pythagoras established the Pythagorean school to go deeper into the mysteries of the natural world. In this chapter, we look at the basics of Pythagorean geometry as a common universal language. Let's start with the most basic fundamental geometric unit of a point in space, as we have studied in school.

## 1D: Point and a Line

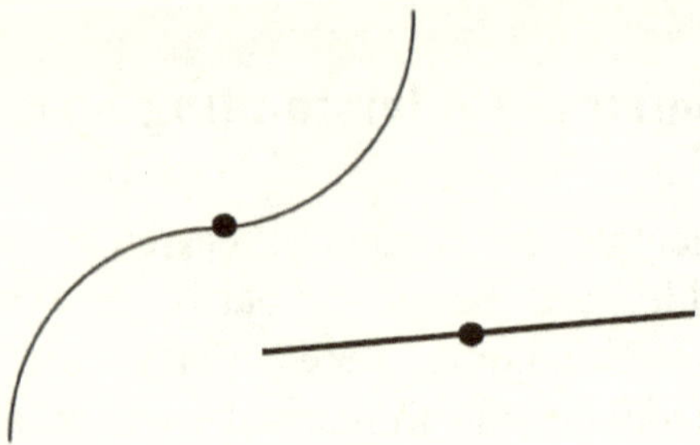

A point is a location in space anywhere. The line is the directionality that emerges from a point. It can be straight or curved. A fixed line has two reference points.

## 2D: Regular Polygons

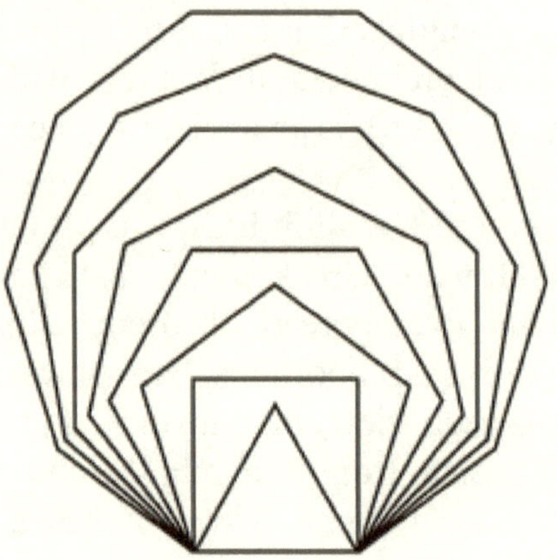

2D shapes are enclosed areas. Regular polygons are a geometry of enclosed space and have fixed properties. The triangle is the minimum or basic polygon. As the number of sides is increased infinitely in the regular polygons, we finally reach closer and closer to a circle. The circle comes from infinity, while other shapes have to polish their edges infinitely to get there!

# 3D Platonic Solids

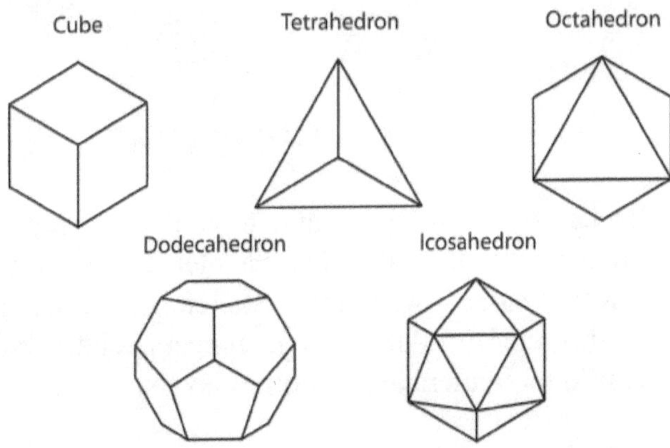



Platonic solids, also called the perfect solids, are named after Plato (428- 348 BC), the famous Greek mathematician and philosopher who followed the Pythagorean school. Plato described these solids as regular convex polyhedra. The faces are congruent regular polygons, with the same number of faces meeting at each vertex. There are precisely five solids that meet this criterion. These have specific irrefutable properties. Any change in these properties renders the shape unstable.

The platonic solids are named based on the number of faces they have. They represent the five elements in Nature. All platonic solids can nest inside each other and transition or transmute from one to the other by compression or expansion. They can fit inside a square (cube) and a circle (sphere). They can also pair up as complementary duals, i.e., changing from one to the other by interchanging faces with vertices. Further, all Platonic solids can be built from closely packed spheres.

*The cube and the sphere and their intersections are the basis of all forms in our experience.*

-Walter Russel

## Cube or Hexahedron

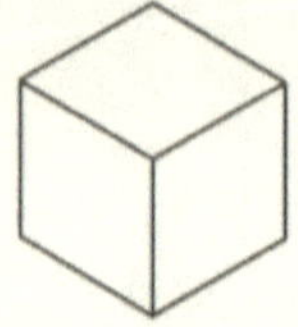 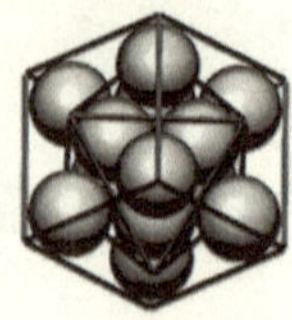

Cube has 6 square faces and 8 vertices. It represents the Earth element. It is the densest element. It gives solidity and form; stone, mountains, skeletons, wood, and metal have this quality. Although it appears relatively stable, it has rapid movement at subatomic levels.

## Octahedron

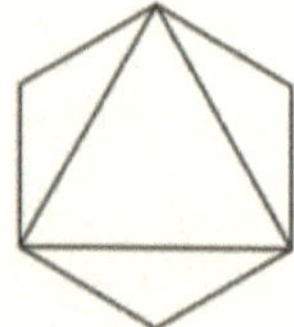 

Octahedron has 8 triangular faces and 6 vertices. It represents the Air element. It is the element of movement; it transports ideas, inspiration, pollen and even germs around the planet and within our bodies. It is in constant flux. Both cube and octahedron have flux-like qualities. Air appears to move and change rapidly, while Earth seems to move slowly, but both are in a continuous churn. Heavier elements, like the iron core of the Earth and heavier gases in the air, settle down while lighter ones rise. Both are stratified.

## Dodecahedron

A dodecahedron has 12 pentagonal faces and 20 vertices. It

represents Ether or Akash, commonly called Space. Ether is the basic primordial substance everywhere and within us but cannot be detected by senses or instruments. The other four elements manifest within the energetic container of the ether.

**Icosahedron**

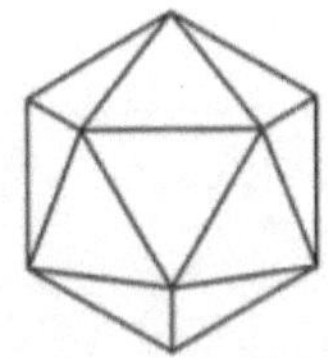 

The icosahedron has 20 equilateral triangular faces and 12 vertices. It represents Water, the universal solvent. It defines fluidity and wetness; some of its domains are rivers, oceans, blood, and mucous.

Dodecahedron and Icosahedron both have a fluid-like quality. Just as we have vortices in water creating whirlpools and hurricanes, we have vortices in the ether manifesting light and matter.

**Tetrahedron**

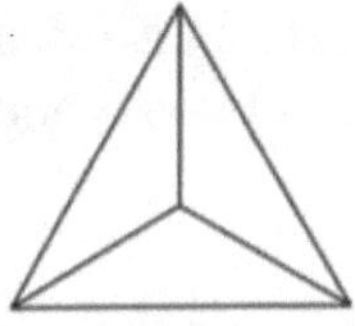 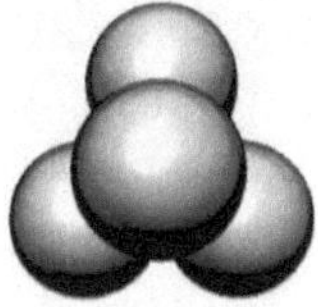

The Tetrahedron is self-dual and has 4 triangular faces and 4 vertices. **Fire** is the element that gives heat, light, and warmth. It is also responsible for digestion and combustion.

**Archimedean Solids**

Archimedes was another Greek mathematician and inventor of the 3rd century BC. The 13 Archimedean solids can be created by truncating, twisting, and manipulating the edges and sides of the primary 5 Platonic solids. Platonic solids have only one type of regular polygon, while Archimedean solids can have more than 1 type of polygon.

One of the 13 Archimedean Solids is the Cuboctahedron, which has triangles and rectangles.

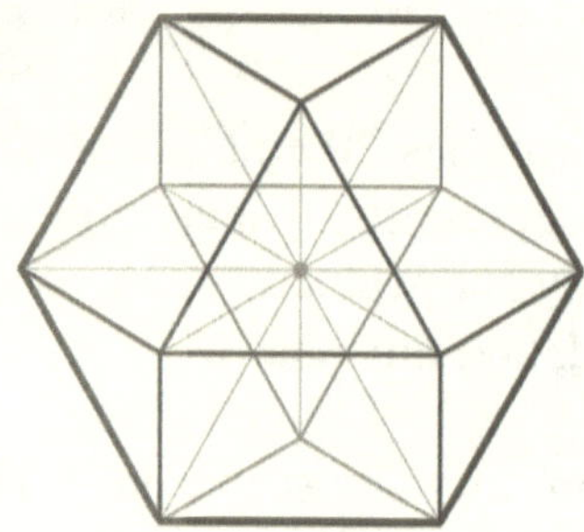

In a cuboctahedron, the distance between the centre and the vertex equals the edge length; hence, it is termed 'vector equilibrium' by the famous American scholar Buckminster Fuller (1895-1983). He demonstrated how the cuboctahedron can transform into other platonic solids. It can rotate both ways: clockwise and counterclockwise when compressed.

The cuboctahedron is a unique polyhedron, as it is the most stable shape. It has 14 faces made of of 8 triangles and 6 squares. It has 12 vertices and 24 edges. The cuboctahedron is the basis of the 3D Flower of Life pattern (discussed later in this chapter).

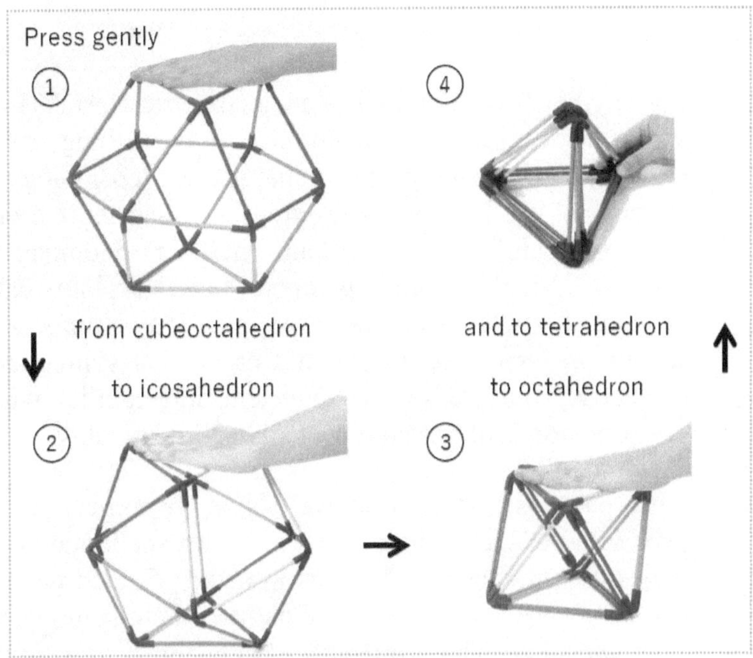


Source: Buckminster Fuller's Jitterbug Geometry

The five basic elements of nature (air, water, fire, ether, and earth) are energy forms of varying compression; the higher the compression, the greater the energy. Compression concentrates energy, while expansion dissipates it. A dodecahedron representing ether, and a cube representing earth is not seen in the image above. However, these can be visualised as nesting perfectly within their duals, the icosahedron and octahedron, respectively.

*Where there is matter, there is geometry. Geometry is the archetype of the beauty of the world.*
- Johannes Kepler

# Numbers and Sacred Geometry

For Pythagoras, numbers and geometric forms had a spiritual meaning. He saw numbers in everything and saw mathematical relationships in nature, art, cosmology and music. As per him, numbers are all around us; the entire creation manifests due to pure number, geometry and process. Numbers and geometry can explain natural growth, form, music, and even creation. Numbers and shapes are symbolic. One could argue that symbolism is subjective, but we see its universal applicability when a phenomenon is observed repeatedly and irrefutably.

Also, patterns emerge when we look at phenomena with the eyes of a devoted seeker, and we are left spellbound by the majesty of numbers and forms in nature. Sacred geometry can be viewed as divine mathematics, where symbols have deep meaning. The word *sacred* here refers to a timeless and permanent code of creation. The numbers and forms are like source codes, taking us back to our origins. Sacred geometry shapes can be drawn without any particular measurement, although a compass is required to make perfect circles. In sacred geometry, all shapes are interrelated and are derived from a pattern of overlapping circles. A greater understanding and connectedness emerge when one starts to draw out these shapes.

Sacred geometry can explain how patterns form in nature. It is also related to spiritual symbolism and architecture. With greater immersion, one can see how it points toward a basic universal design that expresses itself on all scales, from an atom to the galaxy; it is the grid or the blueprint for creation itself. The sacred geometry drawings are not just 2D shapes but are seen as symbolic energy manifestations ranging from a simple to a greater degree of design complexity.

# Numbers and Shapes

## Monad or *Advaita*

A circle has an invisible centre everywhere with infinite circumference. It represents a sphere in 2 dimensions.

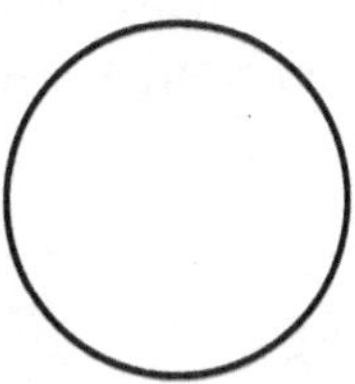

In different cultures, it symbolises Unity, Timelessness, Expansion, Omnipresence, All-That-Is, Source, Singularity, Nothingness, Stillness, Inertia, Potential, *Nirguna* Absolute, Infinity, Eternity, Divinity, Love, Wisdom.

## Dyad or *Dvaita*

By joining the centres of the two circles, we get a line. From there, all regular polygons are born. The Potential casts a reflection of itself and thus becomes two. It appears as two but is still one, creating the illusion of separation: Principle-Power, Yin-Yang, Positive-Negative. The two parts seek completion in the union. There is polarity in all systems in nature, including our body structure. It creates complementarity and relatedness.

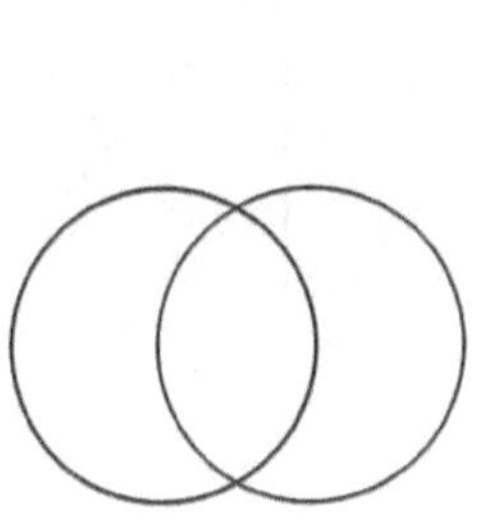

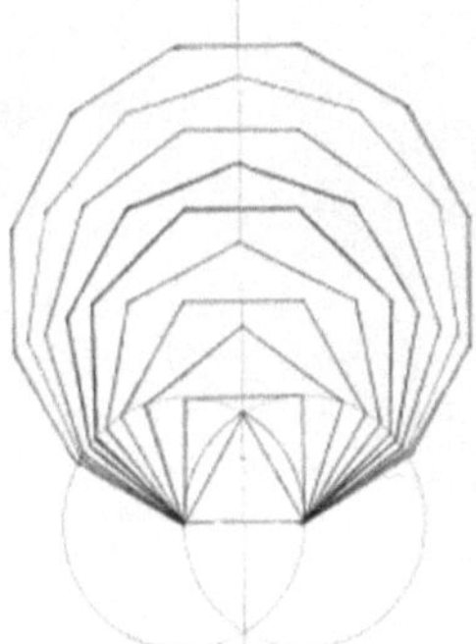

## Triquetra or *Tribhuj*

Sanskrit has many words indicating triple attributes: *Trigunas, Tridoshas, Triloka, Trikala, Trishula,* and *Trinetra*. Two give rise to the third. The triangle represents stability, harmony, responsibility, and a relationship based on mutual respect and recognition: AUM, *Brahma Vishnu Mahesh, Sat Raj Tam,* Word Sound Vibration, Sound Light Form and Mind Body Soul are some of its connotations.

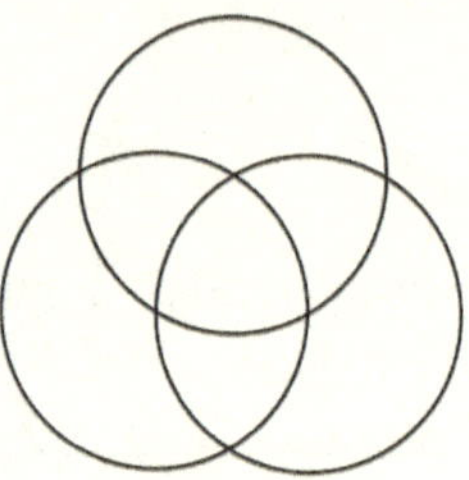 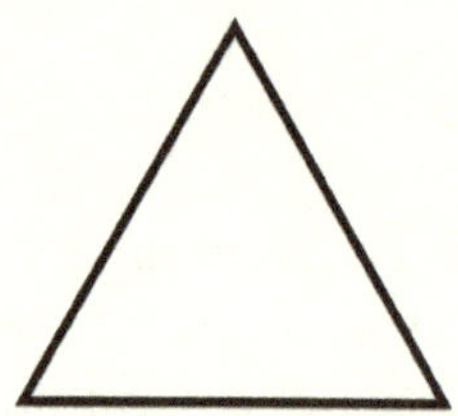

## Tetrad or *Chatuburj*

The number 4 is all about the created system. It also represents Time, Volume, Measure and Order. A few examples are seasons, directions, parts of a day, phases of the moon, *Varnas (Brahmana, Kshatriya, Vaishya, Shudra), Varnashramas (Brahmacharya, Grihastha, Vanaprastha, Sanyasa), Purusharthas* or goals of life (*Dharma, Artha, Kama, Moksha*). These concepts are a result of the natural order created for organised living.

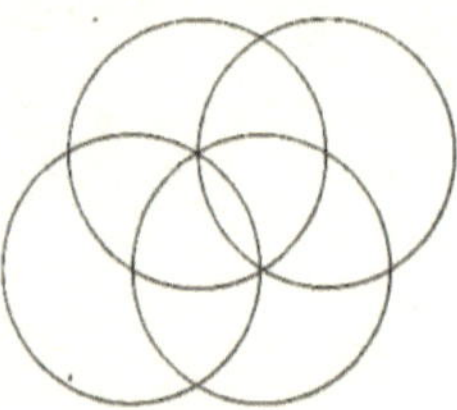 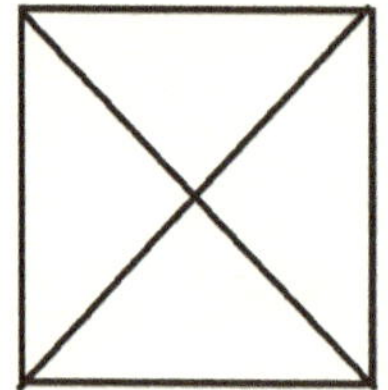

## Pentad or *Panchakona*

5 represents pentagonal symmetry in nature. All biological life, including humans, shows pentagonal symmetry. Pentad is related to life, humanity, health, and vitality, *as well as panchabhutas, panchendriyas, and karmendriyas.*

 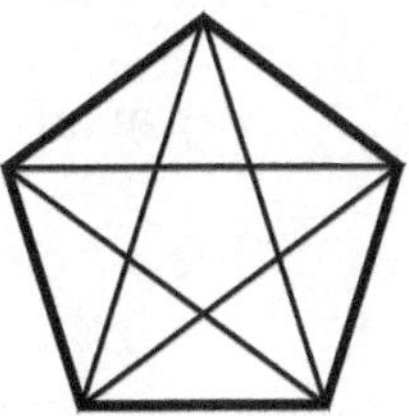

## Hexad or *Shatkona*

Hexad is the structure of nature and life. The hexagon tessellates, and it creates fluid geometry like water. Water, the elixir of life, has hexagonal crystals, as shown by Dr Masaru Emoto in his incredible book *The Healing Power of Water.* The images show how water responds to information by observing changes in water crystals exposed to different stimuli. With water comes life. Water is the medium for consciousness to emerge in matter, creating life's movement. Evolutionary theories also state that life forms appeared in water first. Hexagon represents the universe, efficiency, function, fluidity, and structure of life.

 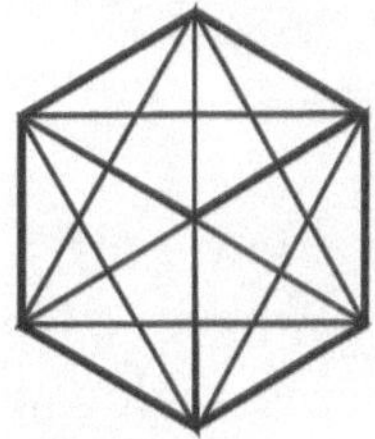

By adding the seventh circle in the middle of the hexad, we get the Seed of Life pattern. Visualising one more circle at the back makes it a 3D egg-of-life pattern of eight spheres.

Seed of Life

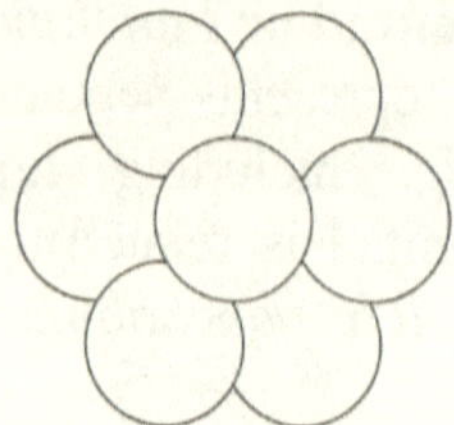

Egg of Life

Seed of life (7 circles), when repeated, creates the Flower of life (19 circles). Take away six circles from the Flower of Life to see the Fruit of Life. It is the blueprint of the manifestation of all matter, including the five elements.

The Flower of Life represents consciousness, continuity, self-propagation, interconnectedness and life as a seamless whole. It is a fundamental pattern of the Universe, the blueprint that unfolds manifestation. Even the molecular and atomic grids are laid out in this pattern.

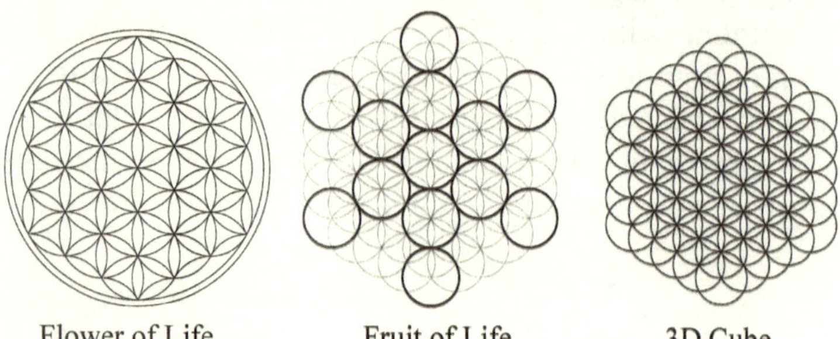

Flower of Life          Fruit of Life          3D Cube

The Flower of Life is also the root of all mathematical proportions, platonic solids, musical systems, energy patterns, light and everything else. It has been found in almost all ancient cultures worldwide, irrespective of the prevailing beliefs or practices. It is not just a 2D geometric pattern but an invisible 3D hologram in the background.

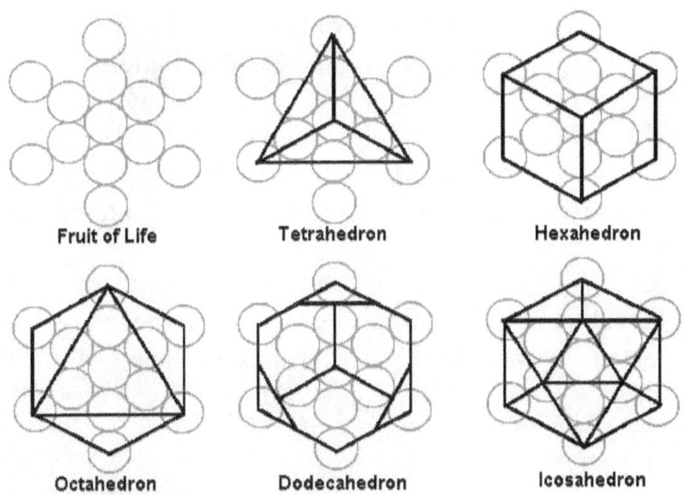



All the Platonic solids nest in the Flower of Life 3D Cube, and they can transmute from one to the other. These geometric forms are different energy manifestations in nature.

*"Geometry is knowledge of the eternally existent."*
-Pythagoras

# Sacred Geometry of Life
## The Biological Genesis Pattern

On observation of the human embryo cell division, amazing patterns appear, some food for thought. Is there any relevance to these 3D shapes? Here is an interpretation:

Cell division during the first stage of embryonic development is called cleavage or segmentation. Mitosis occurs within the zygote during this stage to form the new embryo.

**1-Cell**:

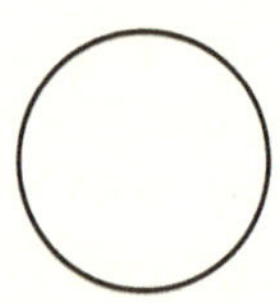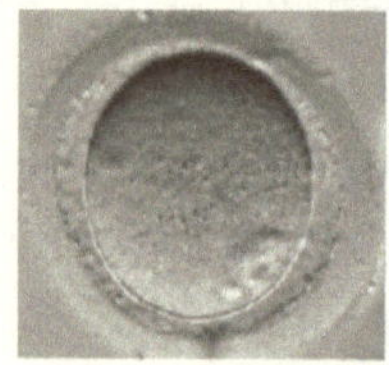

**2-Cells**: Cell division is the doubling of cells at each step.

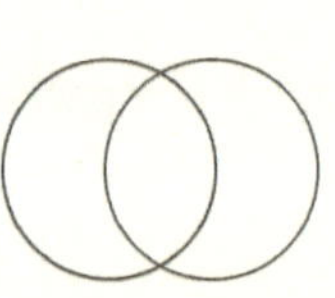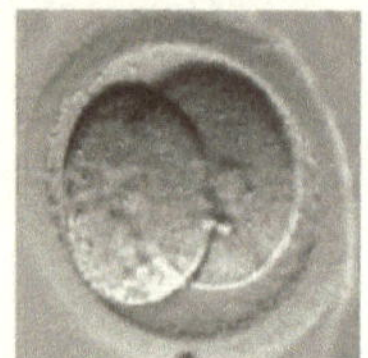

**4-Cells**: The 4-cell structure can be visualised as the self-dual 3D tetrahedron.

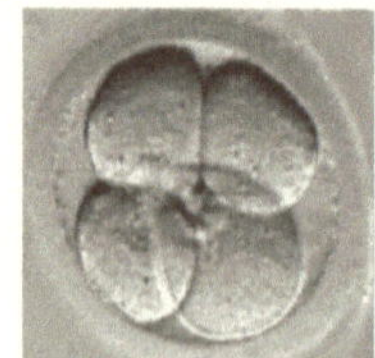

**8-Cells**: Connecting the centres of these 8 cells forms a star tetrahedron.

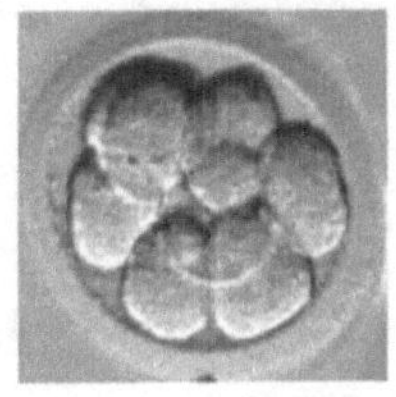

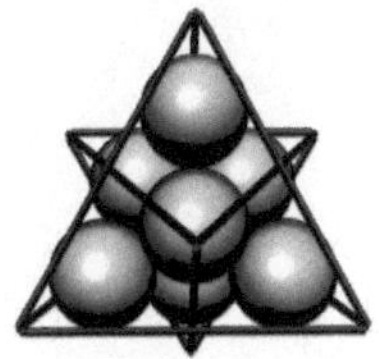

**16-Cells**: The stage at 16 cells is called a zygote. These 16 cells make a larger cube or a star tetrahedron.

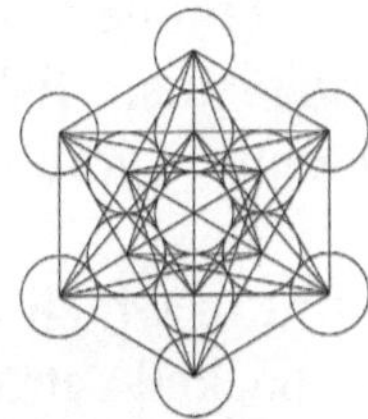

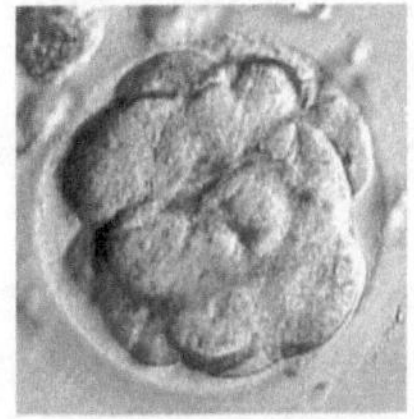

**32-Cells**: The stage from 16 to 64 cells is called Morula. In this stage, the embryo is a compact mass of cells. The 32 cells make a dodecahedron or its dual icosahedron.

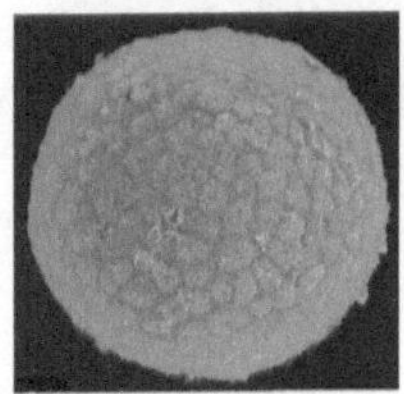

**Blastula stage:** At this stage, compactness is lost, and an internal cavity filled with fluid appears. Later, a line of symmetry appears and creates the two sides of the body and all its organs.

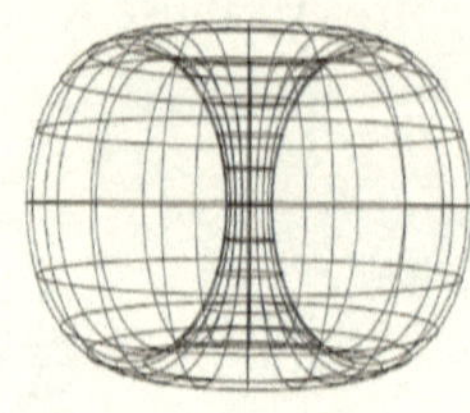 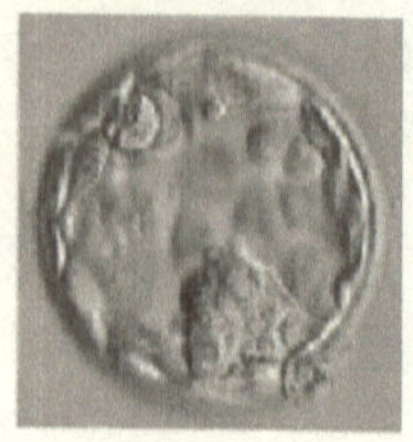

All mammalian embryos undergo a similar development cycle. In the early stages of cellular division, as shown in the steps above, the regular geometric solids represent the mineral or elemental stage of evolutionary development. Following this elemental stage, the human embryo passes through all the preceding evolutionary phases, including those of single-celled organisms, fish, reptiles, and mammals. DNA encodes the entire evolutionary history.

Regular solids are the blueprint in which the cells organise themselves as a closely packed structure, where a maximum number of cells are in contact with other cells. Apart from the regular solid structure in the table above, other regular platonic solids appear in cell division at different levels; for example, 6 cells organise as an octahedron, 12 cells organise as an icosahedron, 13 cells arrange as a cuboctahedron, 14 cells organise as a cube and its dual octahedron.

*"Learn how to see. Realise that everything connects to everything else."*

*-Leonardo da Vinci*

# Special Irrational Numbers
## (Fundamental Constants in Nature)

**Pi ($\pi$)**

Pi is the ratio of a circle's circumference to its radius. Circumference = $2\pi r$, r is the radius. Pi is an irrational number approximating the second decimal point with great accuracy. The origin of Pi is unknown; however, ancient architecture suggests that it was known and used a long time ago.

$$\pi = 3.14159265359\ldots$$

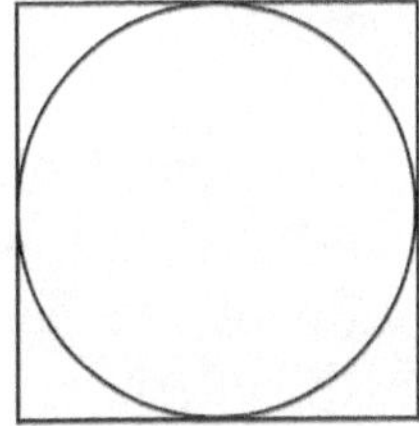

**Golden Ratio Phi ($\Phi$)**

The Golden ratio, represented by Phi ($\Phi$), is the ratio that divides any line, plane or volume in such a way that the ratio of the smaller portion to the bigger portion is the same as the ratio of the bigger portion and the whole. The name of the Greek sculptor Phidias is used to symbolise Phi ($\Phi$).

$$\frac{\text{Golden}}{\text{Ratio}} = \frac{a+b}{a} = \frac{a}{b} = 1.61803 \text{ (approx)}$$

The Line segments can represent the golden ratio or even growing squares. When a curved line joins these squares, it makes a golden spiral.

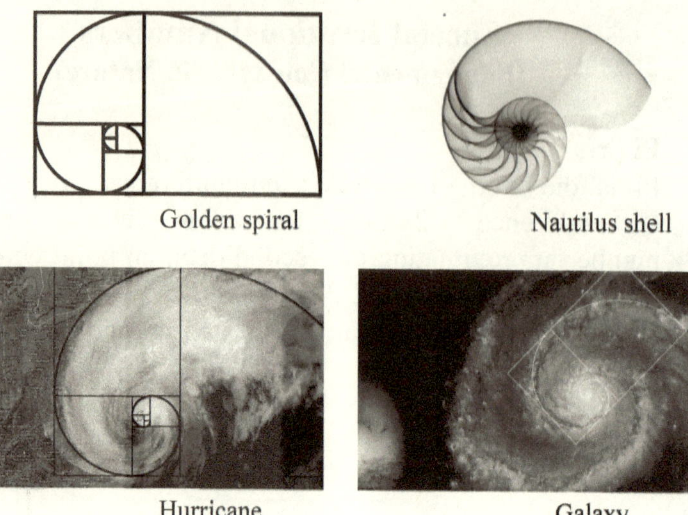



In a growing system, the Golden ratio represents the relationship between 'part' and 'whole'. At each step of the progression, the ratio of the part and the whole are the same. Natural growth patterns follow the Golden ratio. All phenomena, both micro and macro, follow the Golden ratio. The formula for calculating the value of Phi is:

$$\Phi = (1 + \sqrt{5}) / 2$$

The following formula calculates the integer powers of Phi:

$$\Phi^{(n+1)} = 1 + \Phi^n$$

Example: $\Phi^2 = 1 + \Phi$, where n equals 1

Since Phi ($\Phi$) is the formula for the self-replicating proportion between part and whole, it is infinite; it has no beginning and end. It is a unique ratio. All ratios generally need three measures, but the Golden ratio is the only one that requires only two measures. Greek mathematician Euclid wrote about the Phi in his book *Elementals,* but it is believed to predate him.

## Golden Angle

The golden ratio's corresponding angle is the golden angle, which is 137.5°. When the circumference of a circle is divided according to the golden ratio, the angle produced is the golden angle. The most common example of a golden angle is the seed arrangement in a sunflower. The golden ratio and angle optimise form and space for the best opportunity for growth and perpetuation of life.

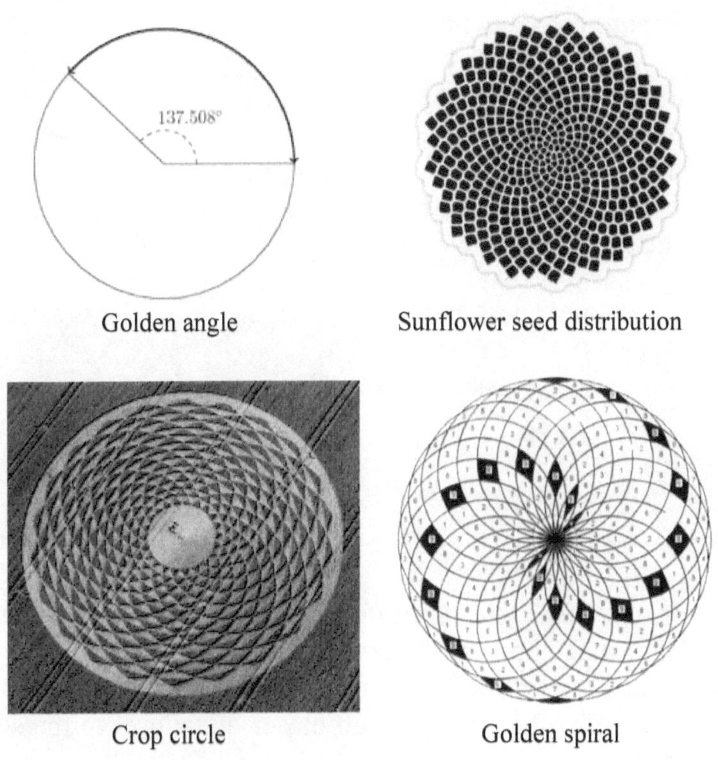

Golden angle

Sunflower seed distribution

Crop circle

Golden spiral

## Relationship between $\pi$ and $\Phi$

6/5 is the ratio that equates $\pi$ and $\Phi$:

$$6/5 \times \Phi^2 = 1.2 \times 2.618 = 3.1416 = \pi$$

Phi (Φ) is associated with the formation, growth and transformation of the physical, natural and conscious world.  Phi is the spiralling journey or ever-increasing perfection towards the source.

Pi (π) represents the beginning, direction of growth, and ending or re-absorption of the entire creation into its absolute source.  Pi is the Source, or Oneness.

**Fibonacci sequence**

$$1,1,2,3,5,8,13, 21, 34\ldots$$

The Fibonacci sequence continues as the sum of the preceding two numbers. As the numbers keep increasing, the ratio reaches closer to $\Phi = 1.61803398875\ldots$

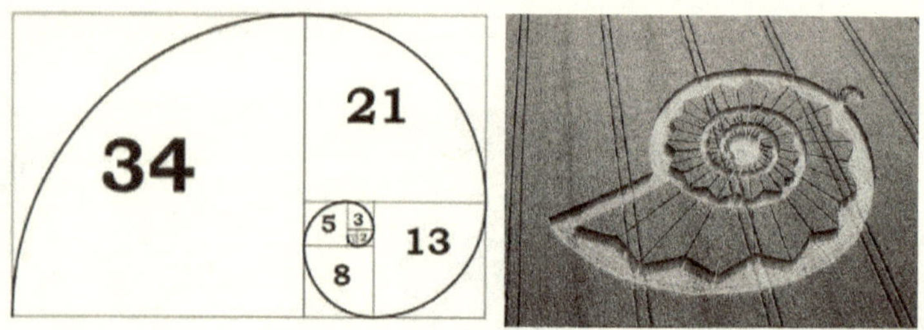


Φ is the most irrational number and cannot be approximated appropriately at any decimal point. All natural growth follows this sequence. It is as if all systems keep growing, trying to go closer and closer to the source code Φ.

*"According to the law of Nature, everything tends to go back to the source"- Babuji.*

# Patterns In Nature

**Spirals**:

 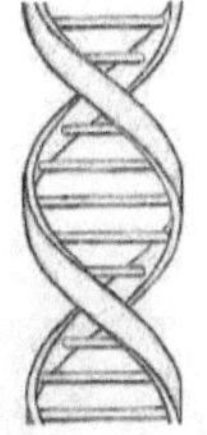 

Spirals follow the golden ratio. Some examples are shells, hurricanes, galaxies, DNA, orbits and vortices.

**Fractal branching**:

 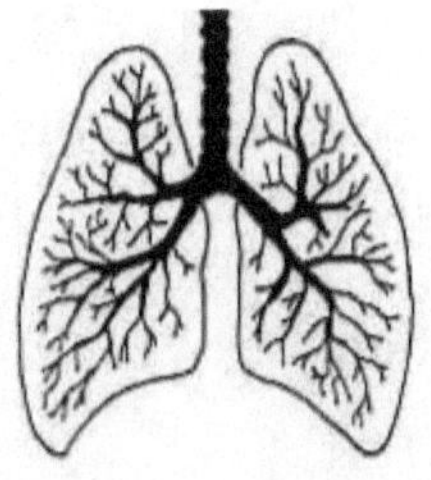 

Fractals are never-ending, complex, self-replicating patterns. A single geometric pattern repeats many times at different magnitudes. Fractals follow the Fibonacci sequence. Some examples are lightning, river tributaries, trees, neural networks, blood vessels, crystallised ice, Romanesco broccoli, silver crystals, and *nadis* (energy pathways).

**Labyrinth**:

  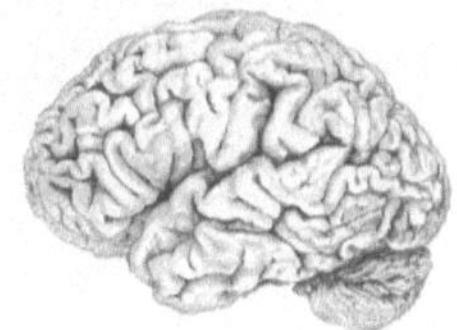

A labyrinth is a maze with a single path leading to the centre. It is a tightly packed layered structure. Some common examples are corals, mushrooms, cabbage, and the human brain.

**Cellular patterns**:

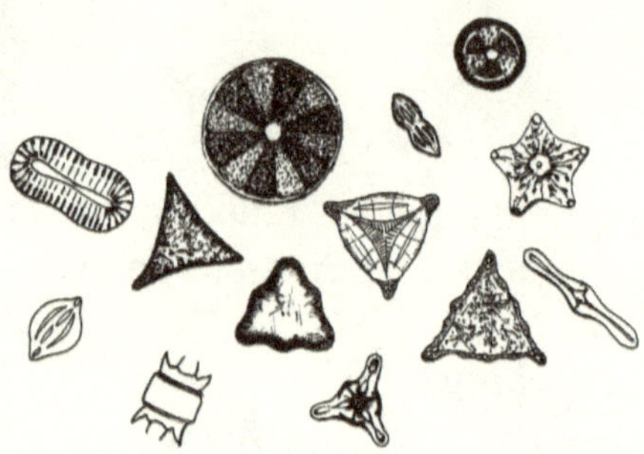

There are myriad cellular patterns in plankton, diatoms, and single-celled organisms. The multitudes of geometric patterns in these organisms are defined by their unique purpose and function.

Through numbers and shapes, we can see how nature creates and what the fundamental ratios and proportions are for growth. These are irrefutable constants. Natural intelligence at work follows simple concepts of self-similarity in all its patterns and expressions. Similar principles are found in sound, light, and matter, which we will explore in greater detail in the next chapter.

*"Life is a great tapestry. The individual is an insignificant thread in an immense and miraculous pattern."*

*-Albert Einstein*

# Fractality

Fractality is the concept of 'change in scale without any change in ratio'. In other words, fractality is going towards infinity at both ends of the spectrum - expansion and contraction, where the part remains the same as the whole. The inside is the same as the outside; there is no difference. In other words, there is unity in form and design at all levels. In simple terms, a fractal is a shape or an object that, when broken down, has each part as a reduced-size duplicate of the whole. The image below is an example of growing fractality in these shapes.

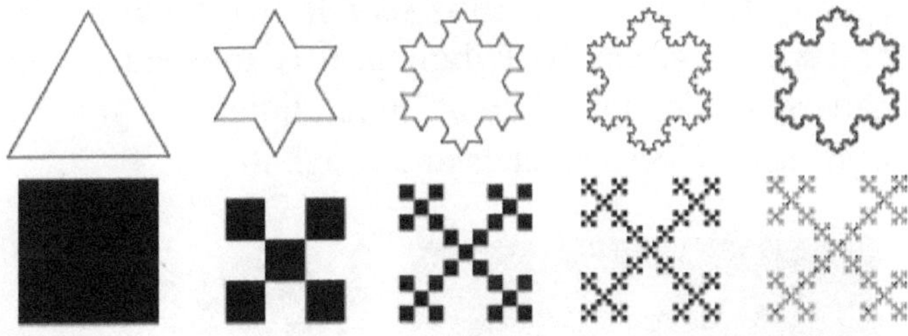

Fractals appear similar at various scales, as illustrated in successive magnifications of the famous Mandelbrot set.

When we zoom in on a fractal pattern, we see an infinite expansion of the base design to unimaginable scales from any vantage point. This is also the method by which the universe creates self-replicating systems.

The human body's structure of lungs, neurons, and blood vessels are all fractal patterns. These structures show natural growth by branching out in self-similar ways. Tree branches and roots grow as fractal patterns.

Another example of fractality is the Lichtenberg pattern, named after German physicist Georg Christoph Lichtenberg, who discovered and studied them in the 18th century CE. This pattern is seen in live lightning bolts and on surfaces struck by lightning. It is an electrical discharge pattern made on different solid, liquid or gas media by passing an electrical current through it.

Natural Lightening

Wood-burning by electrical current

*"A fractal is a way of seeing infinity."*
*- Benoit Mandelbrot*

# Golden Ratio and Fractality in Shapes

Now that we have explored Pythagorean shapes and sacred geometry let us go deeper into the mysterious measurements of these geometric shapes. Both Pythagoreans and, later, Plato looked at shape, form, geometry, growth and creation as sacred and, through these subject lenses, could explain both the manifested and the unmanifest world.

The key to understanding this is the golden ratio $\Phi$. We all know the famous Pythagorean theorem, which states the relationship between the lengths of a right-angled triangle. Pythagoras also studied and defined shapes and fractality using the golden ratio.

## Golden Triangle

A golden triangle is an isosceles triangle with angles of 72, 72 and 36 degrees. The ratio of the side ' a ' to base ' b ' is equal to $\Phi$. The golden ratio can further divide or expand the golden triangle, creating a series of nesting golden triangles. When joined, they make a golden spiral.

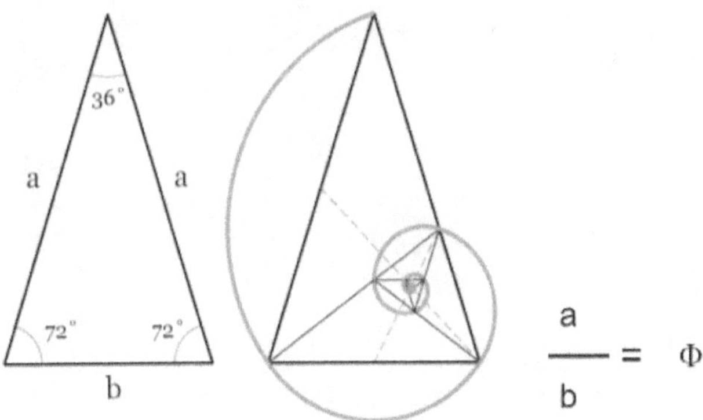

## Golden Rectangle

In a golden rectangle, the ratio of the short side 'a' to the long side 'b' equals the ratio of the long side 'b' to the sum of both sides 'a+b', which in turn equals Φ. We get a golden spiral if we plot and join a series of golden rectangles.

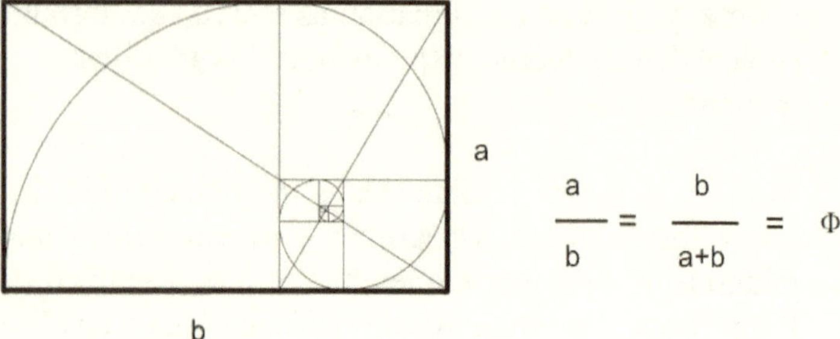



$$\frac{a}{b} = \frac{b}{a+b} = \Phi$$

## Golden Pentagon

In a regular pentagon, each angle equals 108 degrees; however, the diagonals form an isosceles triangle. If the side length is 1, then its diagonal is Φ. Again, such nested golden triangles will create a spiral.

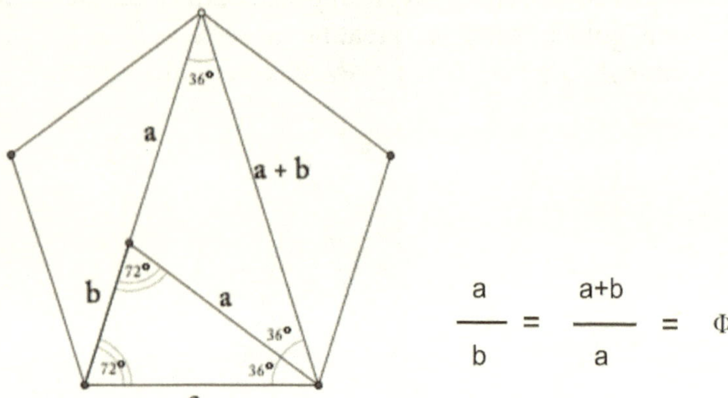



$$\frac{a}{b} = \frac{a+b}{a} = \Phi$$

## Golden Pentagram

Joining the vertices of a pentagon gives us a pentagram, a five-pointed star shape. The golden pentagram has isosceles triangles at the star points and multiple integer powers of the Φ.

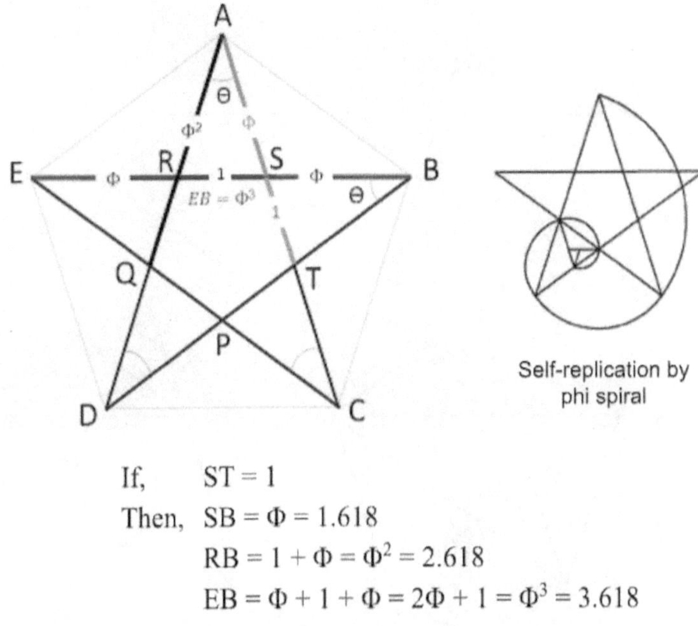


If,     ST = 1
Then,   SB = Φ = 1.618
        RB = 1 + Φ = Φ² = 2.618
        EB = Φ + 1 + Φ = 2Φ + 1 = Φ³ = 3.618

## Fractality in a Pentagram

Pythagoreans considered the pentagram a sacred symbol representing the five elements.

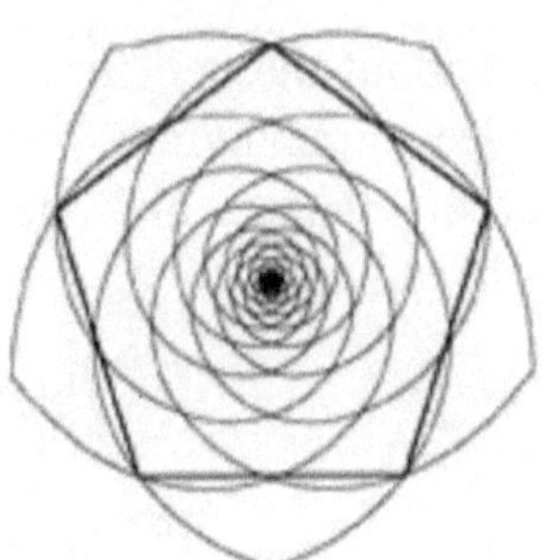

10 nested phi spirals in a pentagon

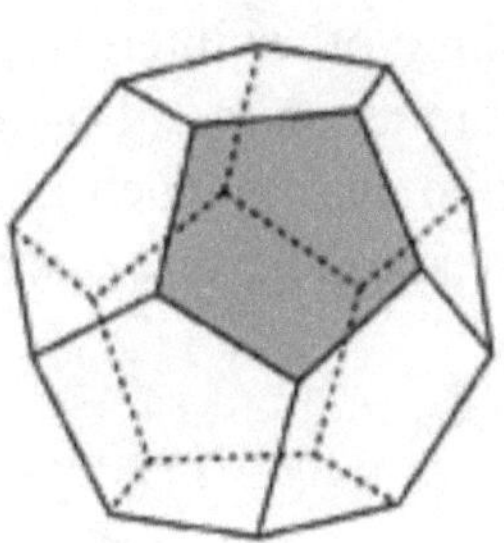

12 pentagons in a dodecahedron

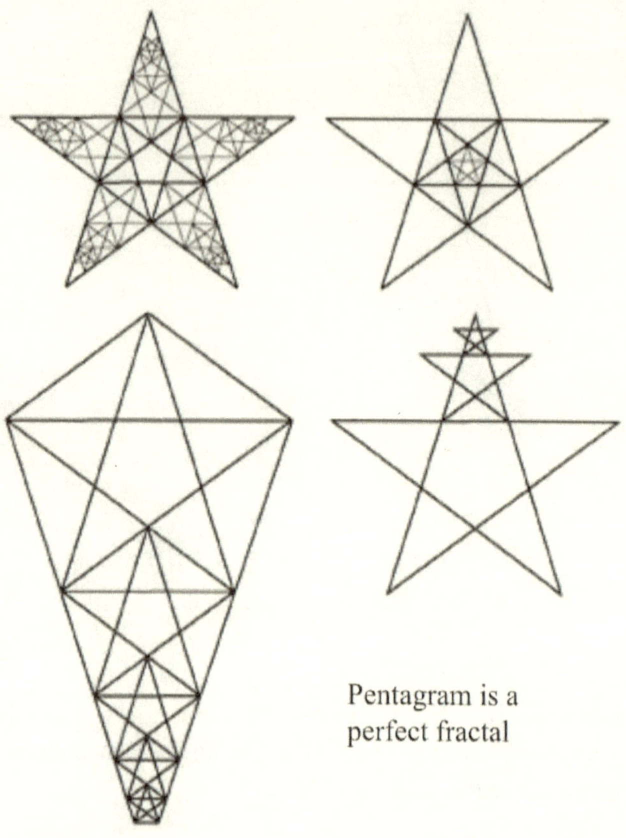

Pentagram is a
perfect fractal

Some other interesting facts about the pentagram make it a unique shape. For example, a pentagram has isosceles triangles at each star corner. It can also be made by overlapping three isosceles triangles.

Interestingly, the water molecule ($H_2O$) also has the same isosceles triangle geometry. Water molecules create the fluid hexagonal lattice.

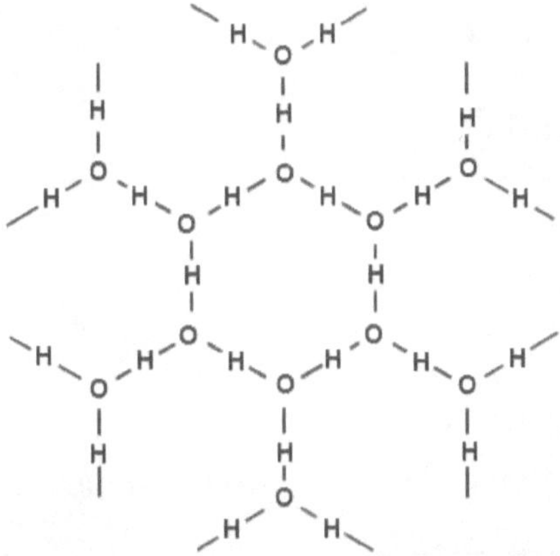

Dr. Emoto's experiments have produced beautiful pictures of water crystals. His research shows that water can receive and transmit information, like a tuning antenna.

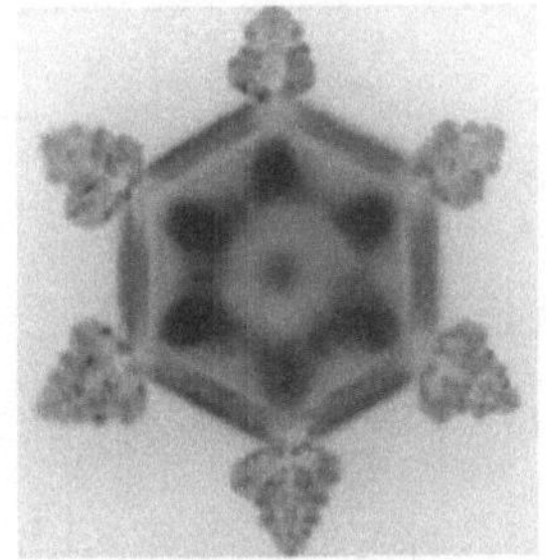

Image source: Dr Masaru Emoto

Flower of Life

Homoeopathy also works on the same principles. With high levels of dilution, even when the slightest trace of the molecules of the dissolved substance (medicine) is not detected, the water still holds the medicine's information. It works at subtle levels on the body to remove the root cause of the ailment. In summary, the golden ratio or phi is the only structured way of expanding or contracting creation, like a divine blueprint of forms and grids, defined by a universal intelligence for self-organisation. Geometry was considered sacred by the Greeks and other cultures. We are still fascinated by its sheer perfection, beauty and logic.

# Sacred Geometry in the DNA

## Golden ratio in DNA

The double helix of the DNA spiral follows the exact Phi ratio.

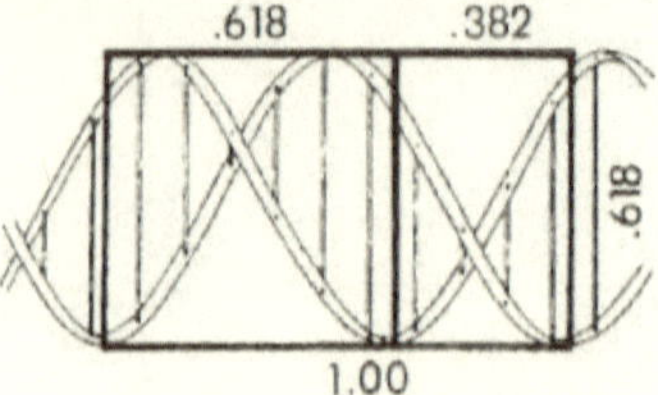


## Dodecahedrons in DNA

Cross section of DNA as two overlapping dodecahedrons.

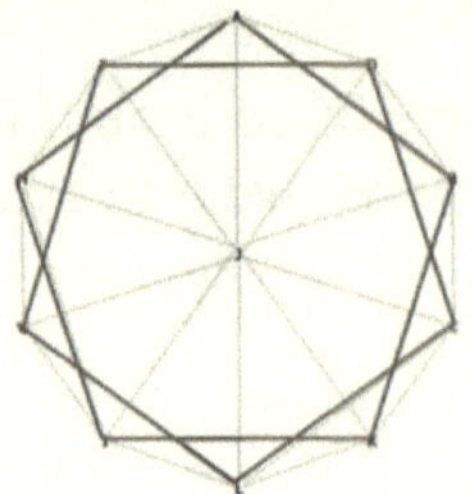

Source: Dr Robert Langridge

## Pentagons and Hexagons in the DNA structure
## (5 & 6 geometry)

Not only is the DNA double helix a spiral with a 5 & 6 geometry, but the chemical structure of DNA formed by oxygen, nitrogen, and hydrogen atoms also has a 5 & 6 geometry. The four bases (ATCG) bond to form the double helix of DNA.

With more and more information packed into it, the DNA's wrapping, twisting and crinkling increases. The estimated total length of DNA in just one cell is about 2 meters, and there are trillions of cells in the human body. All the evolutionary data from the beginning of time is stored and passed on from generation to generation over countless millennia. As shown by the genesis pattern and embryology, the data has records of the evolution from mineral to single cell, plant, animal life, and human life. We are the entire record of evolution so far.

Carbon, Hydrogen, Oxygen, and Nitrogen make up the structure of amino acids, which in turn create proteins. Proteins are the building blocks of physical structure. Metals combine with amino acids to make essential molecules of life; for example, iron combines with C-H-O-N to make haemoglobin for animals, and magnesium makes chlorophyll for plants.

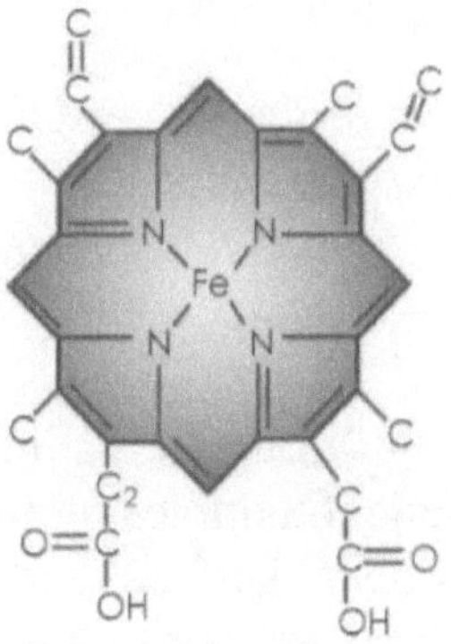

Hemoglobin

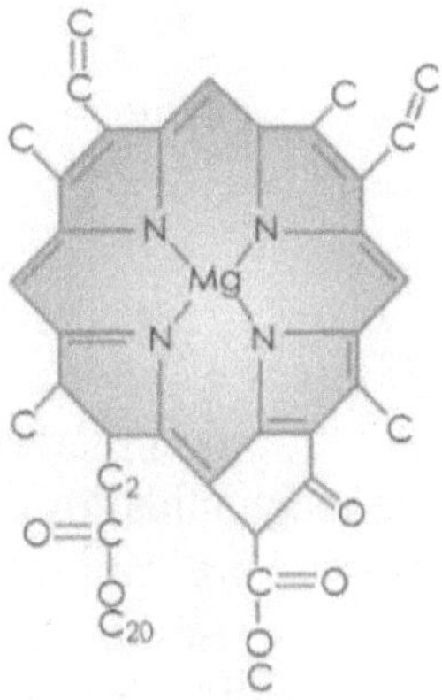

Chlorophyll

There are many examples to fill an entire library as subject matter experts are furthering the research into these fascinating subjects. However, only some examples have been showcased here as evidence to arrive at the fundamental concepts that self-similarity, fractality and perfect geometry are built into the universal design at all levels of creation.

# Chapter 6
# Physics

## Wave Mechanics and Resonance

At the time of Pythagoras and Plato, wave mechanics was not yet a science, yet they understood that all matter had a specific music, a vibration. The vibration of the entire universe was called 'the music of the heavens'. Since then, modern science has progressed in understanding the phenomena of waves and fields. In this section, let us delve into the contemporary science of sound waves and resonance and find parallels in the practical Yogic science of self.

> *If you want to find the secrets of the universe, think in terms of energy, frequency, and vibration.*
>
> *-Nikola Tesla*

**What is a Wave?**
A wave is a disturbance passing through a medium. It can be mechanical or electromagnetic. Examples of mechanical waves are ripples on the water's surface and tectonic activity. Sound is also a mechanical longitudinal wave in the air, which means that when we speak, the vocal cords vibrate and disturb the air, creating contraction and expansion. Air molecules carry or transmit the wave by their longitudinal to-and-fro motion. Waves in water and tectonic activity can be seen, but sound waves are not.

Despite being longitudinal, a sound wave is illustrated as a transverse wave diagram to be able to measure it or show its properties. The contraction point becomes the peak, and the expansion point becomes the trough, as demonstrated in the following figure:

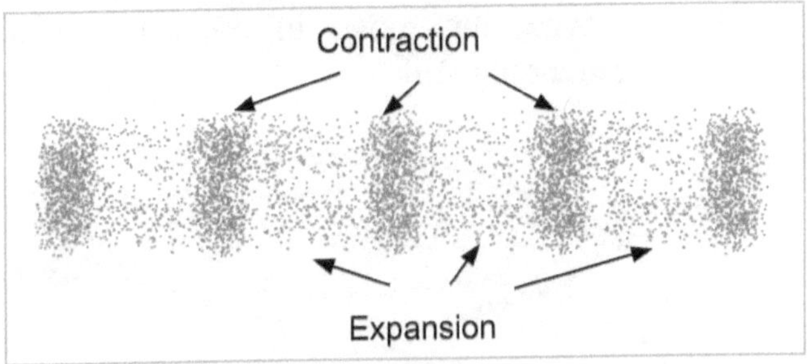


Sound wave as a longitudinal contraction and expansion in air

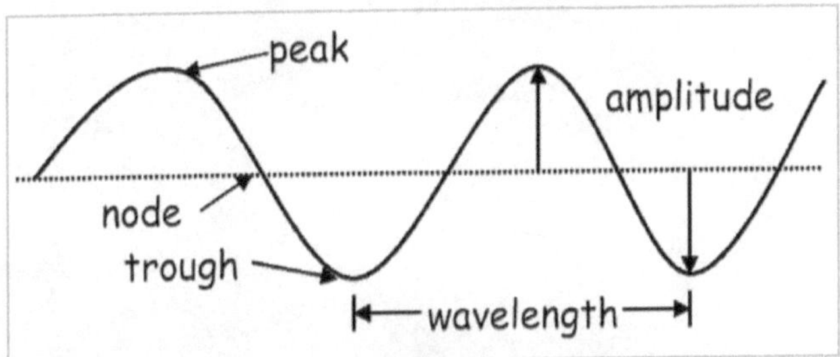


Sound wave as a transverse wave diagram

Like the visible interference patterns created by interacting ripples on the surface of water, sound and light waves also create interference patterns that instruments can detect.

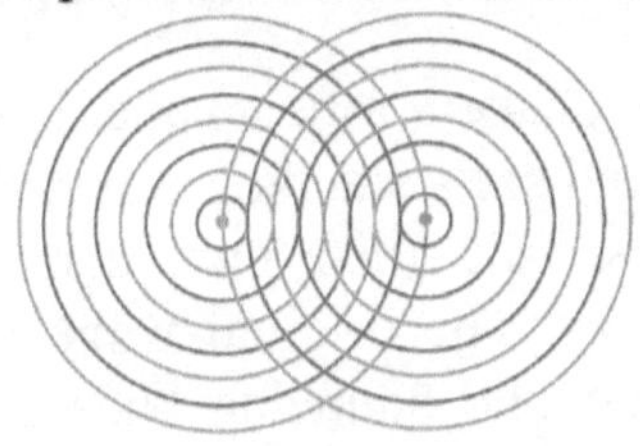

Light is an example of an electromagnetic wave. It is a transverse wave in which its two components (electrical and magnetic) oscillate perpendicular to the direction of propagation. Electromagnetic waves are discussed in detail later.

**What is a Standing Wave?**

Standing waves are produced by the interference of two travelling waves that move in opposite directions but appear to be standing still.

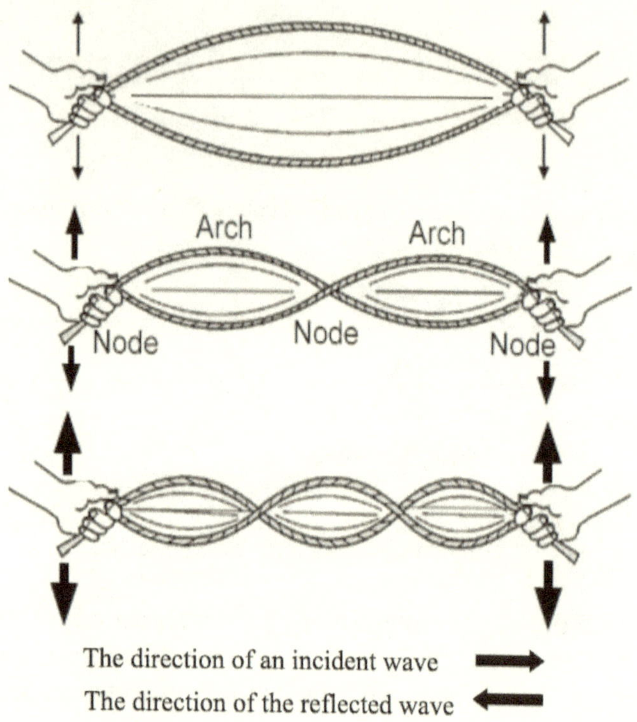



The direction of an incident wave ⟶

The direction of the reflected wave ⟵

If we were to shake a rope up and down between two fixed ends, we would see a standing wave, as in the image below. Sound waves, like this rope, also interfere and create standing waves. The original wave is called the incident wave, and the one bouncing back is the reflected wave. Sound waves can interfere destructively or constructively. An example of this phenomenon would be waves in the ocean; sometimes, they add up to create a massive wave, and sometimes, they fizzle out.

In destructive interference, the resultant wave has reduced amplitude or is nullified.

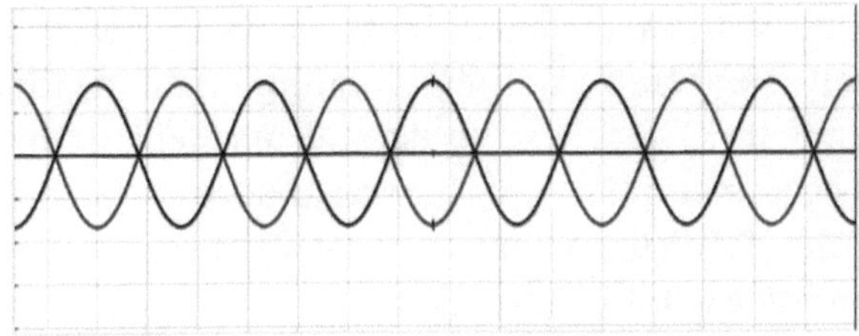

Destructive interference

In constructive interference, the resultant wave has a higher amplitude, which increases the combined amplitude at anti-nodes or peaks.

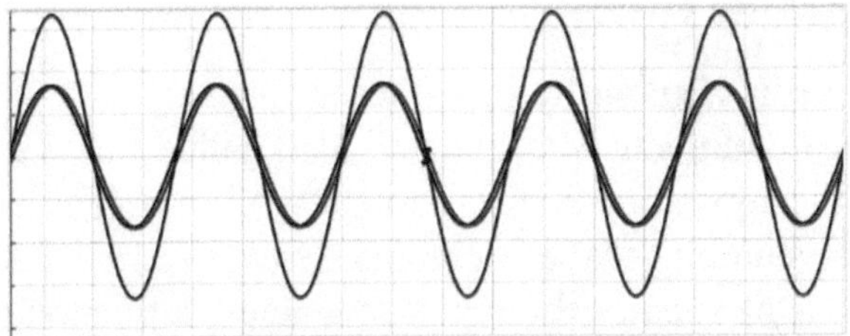

Constructive interference

## What is Resonance?

An object struck with some force demonstrates its characteristic vibration, a natural frequency at which it vibrates. That is the object's resonant frequency, its fundamental base frequency. Frequency is one complete cycle of the waveform. The object's resonant frequency depends on its base material and its shape. It does not matter how hard or soft we strike the object; what matters is the rhythm of the strike. The force of a hit on the object can change the wave's amplitude but not its frequency, which means it can get louder or softer, but its 'tone' stays the same.

All musical instruments, whether strung or piped, are tuned to their resonant frequencies. Whenever a musician plays an instrument, its resonant frequency is set in motion.

Sound can break hard objects such as glass. This occurs when the vibration of the vibrating medium (for example, a tuning fork) reaches the natural resonant frequency of the glass. As a result of the resonance between them, the amplitude of the vibrating glass increases. This increase in amplitude shatters the glass.

Resonance is when a nearby external vibrating system forces another system to vibrate at a higher amplitude. This happens at specific frequencies called resonant modes. Tuning forks and singing bowls are some other examples of resonance in action.

## What is Harmonic Resonance?
The fundamental frequency, also called the first harmonic, is the lowest resonant frequency of an object, at which the first standing wave is created. However, resonance can also occur at specific higher frequencies, a phenomenon called harmonic resonance.

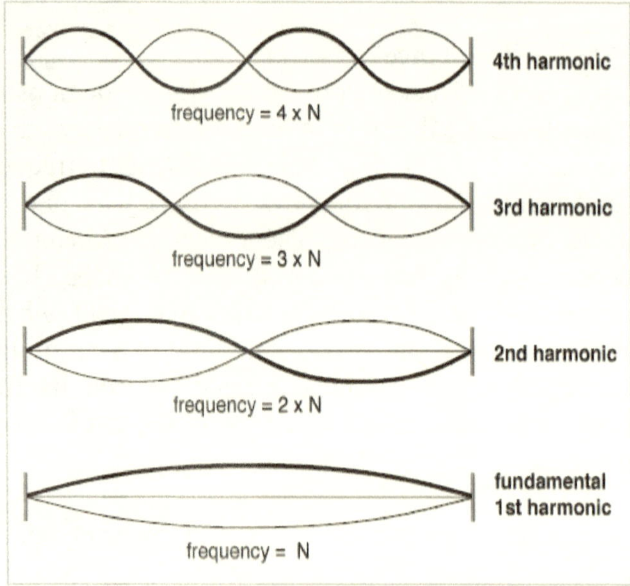

As we get standing waves at shorter and shorter wavelengths, resonance is reached at higher and higher frequencies. The diagram above shows that the first base standing wave is formed at the fundamental harmonic frequency N. Subsequent harmonics are created at shorter and shorter wavelengths. At all these frequencies, where standing waves are created, resonance is reached.

## Cymatics

Cymatics is a field of study that examines how sound creates form. Cymatics works on the principle of resonance. When a medium is vibrated with the resonant mode frequencies, we can see its effect in the medium as it reorganises itself in response to the vibration. Cymatics makes a sound 'visible'. We cannot see sound, but when a material medium resonates with a particular sound frequency, it allows us to see the manifested form of the sound wave. The intricate patterns created by various sound frequencies are awe-inspiring.

Interestingly, the geometric patterns created by sound in the material medium resemble many of the patterns found in nature, such as the shell pattern on a tortoise, the fur patterns on animal bodies, or even sacred geometry. The sound patterns become increasingly complex as the frequency increases and resonance occurs at higher harmonics. To understand cymatics, one must grasp the fundamental phenomenon of waves and how they interact.

The resonance depends on the medium and the base on which it is kept. For example, the medium could be sand, and the base could be a metallic plate on which the sand is kept. Resonance can be seen in two-dimensional surfaces as well as in three-dimensional volumes. Experiments have been done with sand, salt, water and fire as media, resulting in the most beautiful geometry of sound. The visuals based on different sound vibrations show shapes and flow patterns. The matter is either held together in a particular shape or moves along well-defined patterns of circulatory movements with clockwise and counterclockwise rotations. A large amount of data and images of cymatics research have been gathered and are available online for further study.

The following image is made with salt on a black base plate. Wherever there are salt particles, it is an antinode in the interference wave pattern, and wherever there is a void, there is a node. It is interesting to note the striking similarity between the cymatic images and the *Kolam Rangoli* designs that have been made in households in India since ancient times. Kolam designs represent a broad spectrum of resonance geometry that women have traditionally made in India.

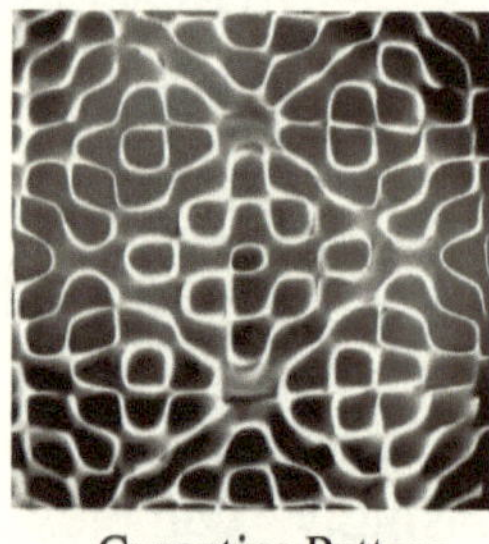

Cymatics Pattern

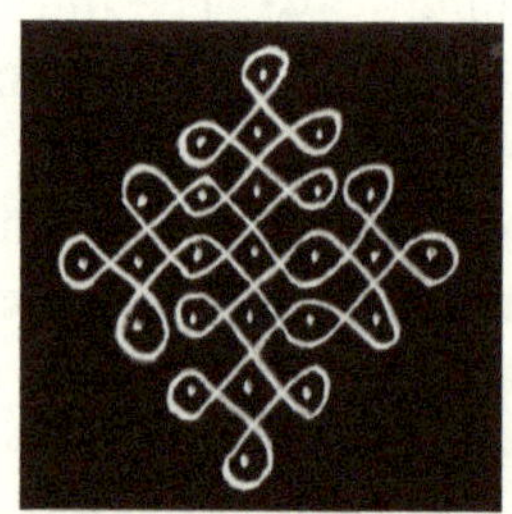

Kolam Rangoli

Kolam patterns are unusual examples of the expression of geometric and mystical ideas in an ancient living culture. The cornerstone of Kolam designs is the intricacy of colourful designs that are in perfect proportion and balance.

Computer models for cymatics have been developed, and the results are intriguing. At higher frequencies, the pattern becomes increasingly intricate. The images show how nature creates form: patterns of animal fur and skin, tortoise shells, water crystals, sunflowers, etc. Most of the geometric patterns observed in nature can be seen in cymatics. Nature creates with sound, which makes us wonder about the fundamental sound, *Shabda* or AUM, that upholds the entire creation.

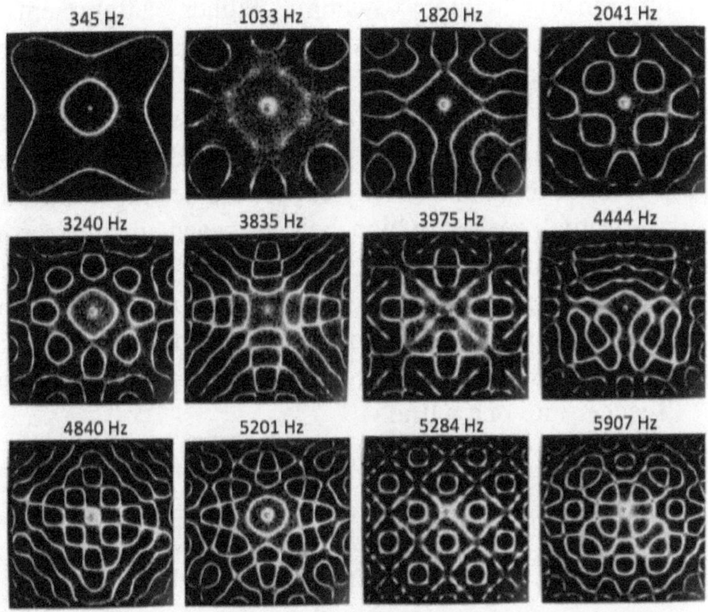



Image Source: Resonance Experiment! Brusspup on Youtube

## Resonance in Thought Waves

Thought waves also create resonance. That is why we say like attracts like, or birds of the same feather flock together. This is the reason for the importance laid on keeping good company. We come under the direct influence of the thoughts of those we associate with. There are many ideas and thoughts in the world; we need to ask what attracts us and what we resonate with. Are there any original thoughts, or are we just picking up vibrations from around us? As long as we have not restrained the outward tendency of the mind and senses, we are not immune to external influence.

As an analogy, raising ourselves to higher ground will prevent us from getting wet in flood waters. Choose to resonate with higher vibrational thoughts rather than lower appetites.

In Indian culture, the *Guru* or the Teacher is the dispeller of ignorance, without whom higher attainments are impossible. We are advised to test the Teacher before accepting his teachings. Test him for his ethics, morals, etiquette, sense of duty, knowledge, impartiality, commitment, and selflessness. Reverence, devotion and surrender to such a noble Teacher are desirable attributes of a spiritual seeker, which help to reach greater resonance and osmosis with the Teacher. Search for such a Teacher becomes very critical in spiritual pursuit. A desire to seek truth, follow logic, listen to the wisdom of the heart and offer a sincere prayer are the best ways to invite such a Teacher into one's life.

# Magnetism and Electricity

In Part 1 of the book, we explored the Vedic view of creation and the Yogic science of self. In Part 2, so far, we have seen the ideas of a few eminent Greek thinkers who contemplated numbers, geometry, sound, and archetypical ideas as blueprints for creation. It is no surprise that both views are strikingly similar. Is it because both civilisations bore curious scientists and seekers? Was the Greek civilisation influenced by the older Indian and Egyptian sciences and practices? Since modern history and science are Europe-centric, all previous contributions are not credited to original sources. However, we want to look at all views and synthesise a common heritage of ideas.

The scientific method is all about observation, proposing a hypothesis, conducting experiments, recording results, checking for repeatability of results and asking how and why. A scientist wants to discover the governing principle behind the observation. A Yogi does the same with his inner experiences. In this section, let's dive deep into the natural phenomena of light and magnetism. For thousands of years, the magnetic properties of metals were a magical phenomenon. In the 6th century BCE, there is evidence that the Greek philosopher Thales referred to the magnetic properties of the naturally occurring iron called loadstone. This study starts with a detailed look at what makes a lump of iron become a magnet and exert force outside its physical form. How does it do that? What is magnetism? What are the unseen forces at play in a magnet?

## Magnet

A magnet is an object that has polarisation. All atoms (or domains) inside the magnet align themselves in one direction, becoming coherent. The Merriam-Webster dictionary describes the meaning of the word coherent as logically or aesthetically ordered or integrated, consistent, having clarity or intelligibility, understandable, and having a quality of holding together.

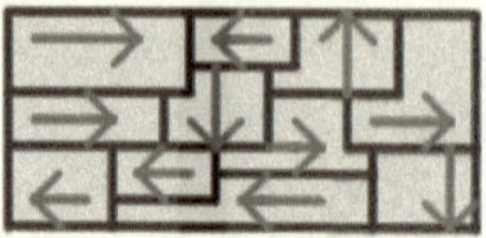

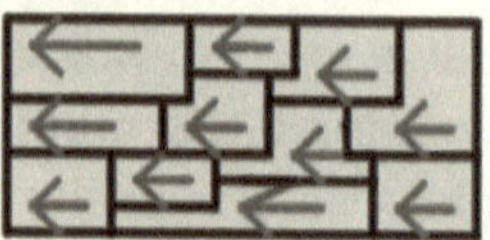

Random/ Incoherent arrangement    Polarized/ Coherent arrangement

This alignment of domains inside the metal turns it into a magnet. Now, the magnet can affect other objects coming into its magnetic field. The magnetic field extends outside of the magnetised object. We have observed the iron filings gathering along the magnetic field for a simple bar magnet, thus showing the field influence.

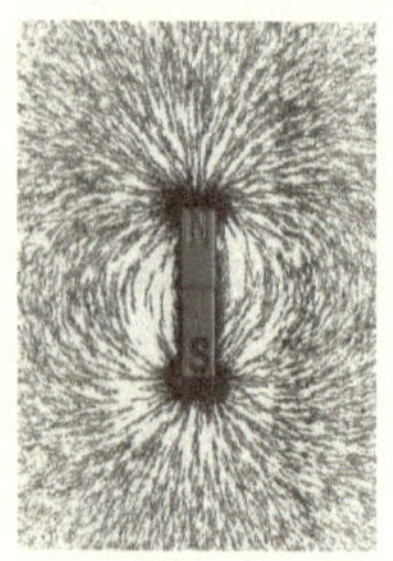
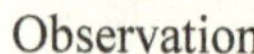

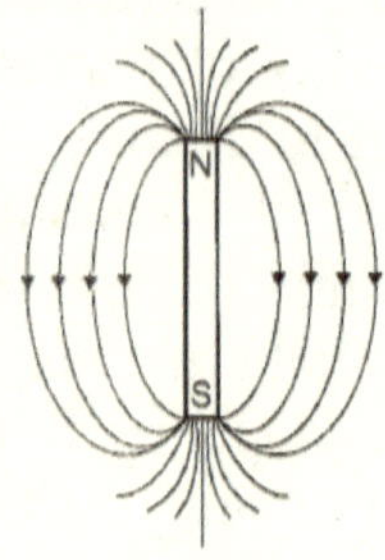

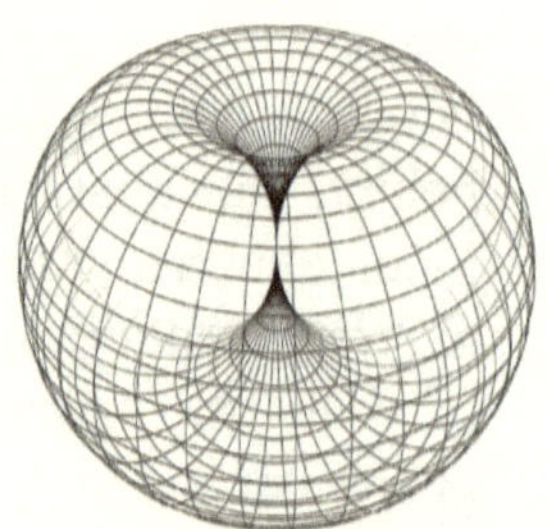

Observation          2D Field Drawing          3D Field Geometry

School students often perform this typical iron filing experiment to learn about magnetism. Based on their observations, they surmise that the magnet attracts iron at the poles, and the arrangement of iron filings shows the magnetic field lines. However, this is an **inaccurate and incomplete** explanation of magnetism. To understand this phenomenon, we first need to understand electromagnets.

**Electro-Magnet**

With the discovery of electro-magnetism, modern science took great leaps in harnessing its potential to develop amazing technology. Our current modern world is based on the principles of electromagnetism. Generators, motors, transformers, electric bells, induction cookers, particle accelerators, loudspeakers and MRI machines use electromagnets. Interestingly, we have figured out the application of magnetism but have yet to define it accurately. In the early 19th century, James Clerk Maxwell gave the unified theory of electromagnetism by synthesising and adding to the work of his many predecessors. The theory says a magnetic field is formed when an electric current passes through a solenoid (coiled metal wire), as shown in the figure below.

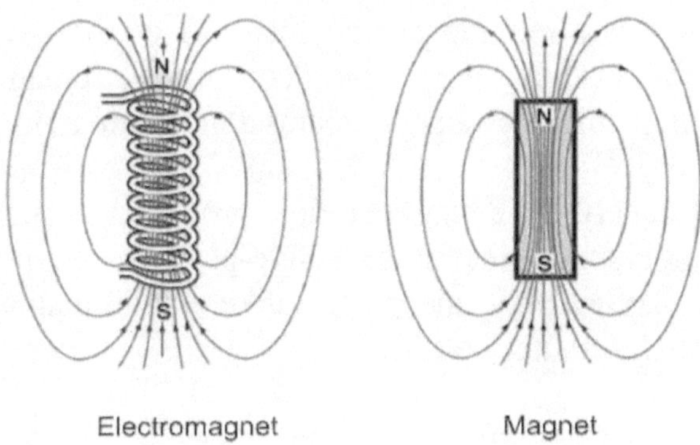


Electromagnet          Magnet

The difference between a regular solid magnet and an electromagnet is that an electromagnet displays magnetism only when current passes through it, while an ordinary magnet is permanently magnetised. The electric current passing through the coils temporarily causes polarisation, thus creating an electromagnet.

Hence, following the principles of electromagnetism, it has been observed that two current-carrying wires behave as electromagnets. In the book *Electrical Discharges, Waves and Impulses*, 20th-century scientist Steinmetz explained the dynamics of these wires. When the current flows in the same direction, the wires repel each other, and when it flows in opposite directions, the wires come closer.

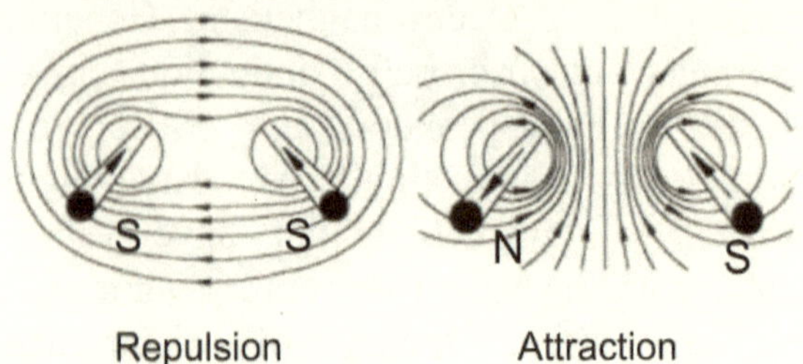



Repulsion        Attraction

At any given cross-sectional point, the two wires behave as poles of two magnets. Steinmetz further explains that we need to look at a point charge to understand the field dynamics of a magnet. What is a point charge? A point charge is a moving charge seen in the cross-section of the current-carrying wire. The theory of electromagnetism tells us that a moving charge creates a magnetic field.

Let's analyse the magnetic field produced by such a moving point charge. Since it is a single-point charge, it is unipolar, i.e., having only one pole, unlike a solid magnet with two poles (north and south).

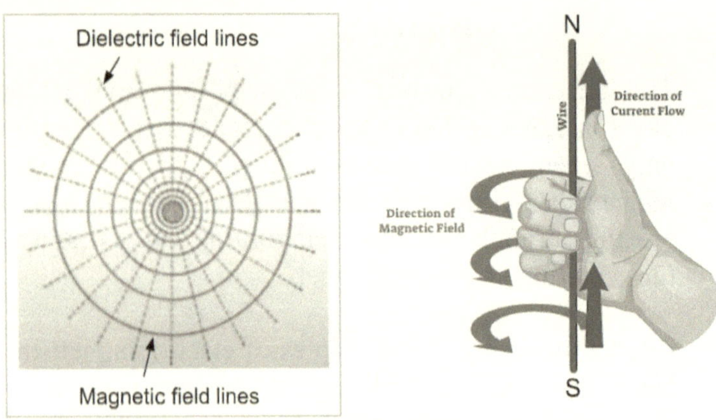

A moving charge can behave as either a north or south pole depending upon the direction of the current flow, as defined by Fleming's right-hand thumb rule.

The point charge, as depicted in the figure, is unipolar; we are looking at the cross-section of the wire from one end. As seen in the diagram, the point charge creates not one but two fields: a **Magnetic Field** depicted as circular rings around the wire and a **Dielectric Field** shown by dotted radial lines. The magnetic field is repulsive, while the dielectric field exerts an inward gravitative pull towards the magnet. The properties and attributes of these two fields are tabulated below:

| Dielectric | Magnetic |
| --- | --- |
| Terminates at a point | Spreads out from a point |
| Radial | Concentric circles |
| Straight lines | Curves |
| Inward tension | Outward pressure |
| Compression | Expansion |
| Centripetal | Centrifugal |
| Unites | Separates |
| Attracts | Repels |
| Cause of Inertia and Acceleration | Cause of Force and Motion |
| Potential | Kinetic |
| Charge | Discharge |

Since these two fields are conjugate, i.e., paired, they always exist together. The loss or discharge of the dielectric potential causes the magnetic field.

These two fields are perpendicular and opposite to each other. These are the conjugate force fields produced by a point charge. The same conjugate fields exist in solid magnets, but we have failed to observe and identify them accurately. Recent experiments conducted by various researchers in this field using devices like the Ferrocell have shown these conjugate fields very clearly and accurately.

Now, let's look at two parallel current-carrying wires When the current flows in the same direction in the two wires, they repel each other. The wires attract each other when the current flows in the opposite direction. The following shows the fields produced by two wires carrying current in opposite directions, thus behaving like the two poles of a magnet.

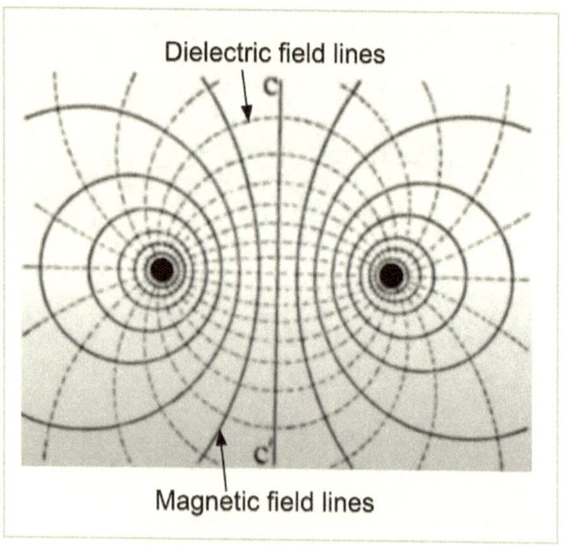

Interestingly, the conjugate-field image is also the stereographic projection of Earth's longitude and latitude lines, with two magnetic poles. Like the dielectric field lines, the longitudes radiate between the two poles. The latitudes create parallels that run east to west around the Earth, along the equator. In the case of magnets, the magnetic lines generate a pressure gradient between two poles of the magnet.

An optical device called the Ferrocell, invented by Timm Vanderelli, has visually shown the presence of these conjugate fields. It is a simple device which can display magnetic fields in real time as a 3D holographic image. It consists of a thin film of ferrofluid and mineral oil between two sheets of glass, sealed and illuminated by LED lights. When a magnet is placed on it, the field appears as an illuminated holographic image. We can now define magnetism accurately as consisting of two fields: a *magnetic field,* which creates outward pressure and causes repulsion, and a *dielectric* or *gravitational field,* which creates inward tension and attraction. Experiments conducted on different types of magnets with magnetism viewing films, ferrofluids and Ferrocells by many researchers show these conjugate fields in a magnet. Anyone can make such a magnetism-viewing device at home or buy a simple Ferrocell online and try these experiments.

In a solid magnet that is bipolar, like two current-carrying wires, the iron fillings arrange themselves around the magnet, causing attraction. Hence, the first image shows the *Dielectric Field* or *Gravitational Field* lines radiating between the poles. The second image is the same magnet seen under the Ferrocell, showing the *Magnetic Field* lines. The magnetic field lines create a pressure gradient with a neutral plane called the Bloch wall at the magnet's centre.

When we merge or overlap these two pictures, we get the composite view of the conjugate forces acting simultaneously. This composite view is the 3D geometry of the torus.

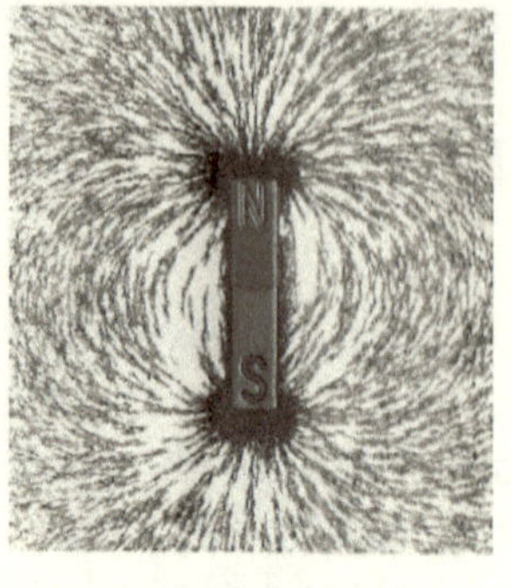

Dielectric

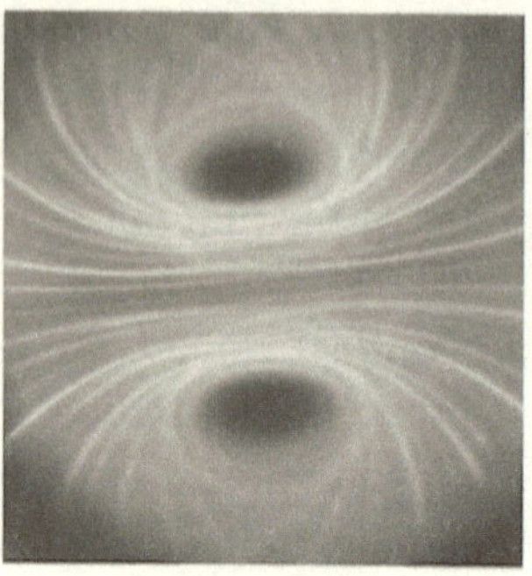

Magnetic

Why and how opposite poles attract or like poles repel has thus been explained by these two conjugate forces.

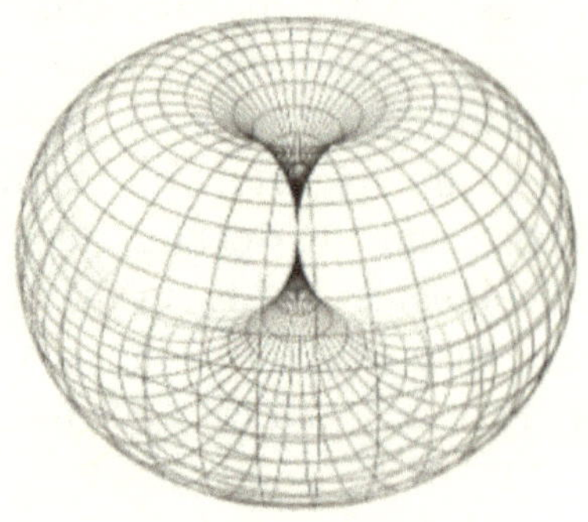

3D conjugate fields
represented by the Torus

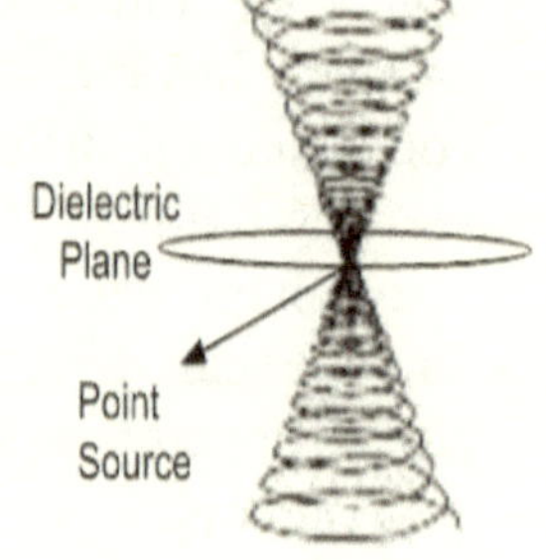


Hyperboloid or a vortex
showing the dielectric field

Gravity unites or attracts, while magnetism separates or repels. Increasing the inward tension brings things together, and increasing the outward pressure pushes them apart. When viewed as a 3D geometry, the magnet creates a torus with two poles at the end of the hyperboloid.

What powers the magnet? The magnet's entire power to create this conjugate field dynamics lies at its **centre,** called the point source or singularity. This centre is non-cartesian, meaning it has no coordinates or location in our 3D space. If we were to cut a magnet in the middle to locate this point, we would not find it. One magnet would now have become two smaller magnets with a point source in the middle of each piece. What is this non-cartesian point source? Let's explore this further.

When viewed under the magnetic viewing film, all magnets show the presence of a middle plane where no magnetism exists. This is called the dielectric inertial plane or the Bloch wall. The two poles of the magnet and the dielectric plane in the middle create the torus of this conjugate field geometry. The magnetic field is the outward spatial geometry of the flowing torus, while the dielectric field is the inverse geometry called the hyperboloid (hourglass shape). The dual forces of nature are the foundational forces which are also the cause of electricity and gravity. The toroidal field theory proposes such a unification of all natural forces. This conjugate field geometry of the toroid explains all natural phenomena from an atom to a galaxy. As above, so below. We have seen in Part 1 how creation from the Source and its manifestation also has the same torus geometry.

The inward spiral of the dielectric field creates a vortex on both ends. The dielectric inertial plane, or the Bloch wall, is the plane of the least pressure, which is why all orbits are planar. A planet does not have to make any effort to orbit in the dielectric plane of the larger body, as it is in the least pressure zone in the entire torus.

All matter is in perpetual motion to balance or void the effect of these two fields of the inward pull of dielectric potential and the outward push of magnetism. Due to this force dynamics, it is safe to say that the Moon is effortlessly and weightlessly stuck in orbit around the Earth, the Earth around the Sun, and so on. Likewise, the entire universe spins and moves to offset or balance these dual fields. The orbit is the plane where these two fields balance out, or in other words, when pressure mediation is reached between the rotating bodies.

The toroidal field theory further explains how the torus is the blueprint by which nature forms energy into matter. Everything has a toric field, from massive galaxies to one single atom, the Earth, a human heart, or an apple. The toric field manifests as the physical particle. It is the subtle, energetic cause behind the manifestation of matter.

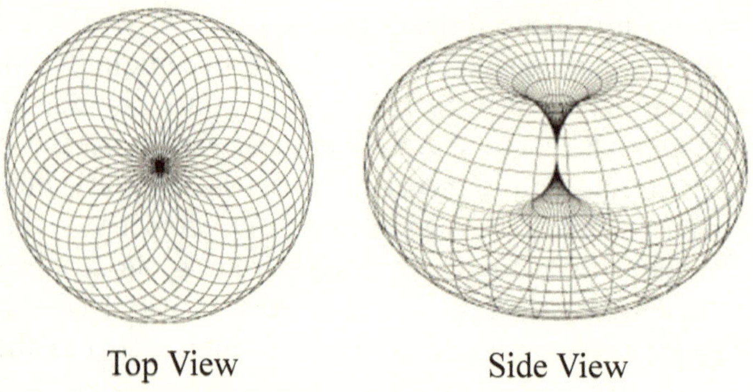


Magnetic resonance imaging or MRI performed on a single atom shows this result:

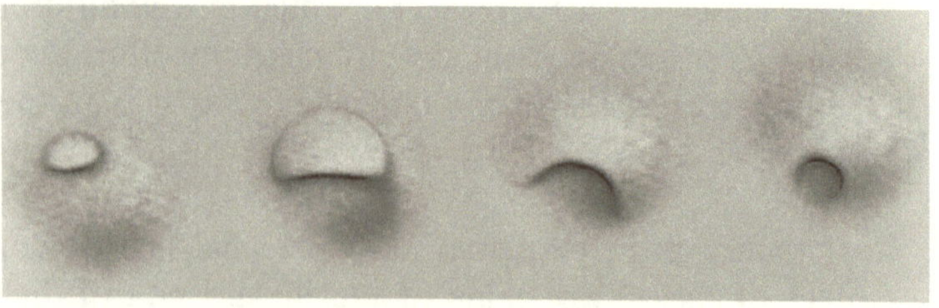

It is a moving, pulsating toroid in action. Matter, or an atom, is a polarised entity that holds its shape as a unique identity. We see this torus geometry in many cultures, myths, and mystic traditions. The magnetic field under the Ferrocell appears as a 3D holographic image showing how light behaves in the magnetic field. The shape or geometry of the hologram does not change if the light source or type of magnet is altered. With a single light source, one can see how the magnetic field bends or distorts the light, creating beautiful geometry. This points to fields and potential rather than particles.

Torus geometry in 2D

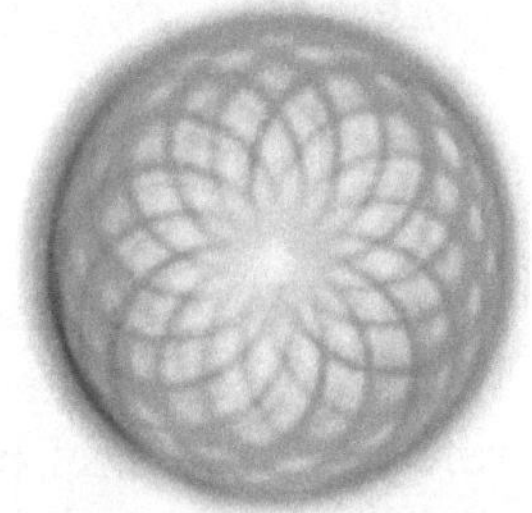

Magnetic field (Ferrocell)

Since the classical Greek era, modern science has been searching for the fundamental substance of the universe. This search has led to subatomic particles as the basic building blocks of matter. What is beyond the subatomic particles? Do modern particle physicists account for the field of potentiality? Isn't it interesting that in Yoga, we look for this field of potentiality as an inner experience by being in union with it?

Vedic science says that creation comprises five elements, from which we can see and experience four: air, water, fire and earth. The elusive ether is everywhere, but it escapes our instruments, as everything is in ether and is made up of ether. There is no emptiness in the physical world; even seemingly empty space is teeming with ether, which is the source of all energy and matter in the physical world. Ether is pure potential that responds to consciousness or information. It is the very field of manifested and potential existence.

*"What we have called matter is energy, whose vibration has been so lowered as to be perceptible to the senses. There is no matter."*

- Albert Einstein

*"For ages, man has thought of matter as being substance. Posterity must learn to think of matter as motion only."*

- Walter Russell

## Human Heart's Magnetic Field

In 2015, HeartMath Institute published its research on 'the role of the human heart in human performance'. It shows that the human heart has a powerful magnetic field that can be detected several feet away from the body. The pulsations of the human heart are toric. In the middle of this torus, we can safely imagine an inertial non-cartesian point (also called void or nothingness by the yogis) that powers it.

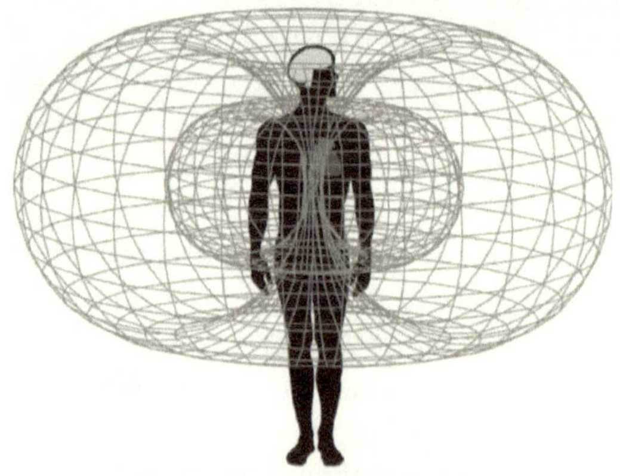

Image Source: HeartMath Institute

The physical world has certain inherent **dualities**: hot/cold, wet/dry, up/down, left/right, light/dark, day/night, good/bad, god/evil, you/I, this/that, right/wrong, hungry/full, healthy/unwell, etc. We choose one way or another based on our impressions or conditioning. Yoga aims to rise above judgemental choice-making and reach the level of choiceless witnessing awareness. We need to manage these dualities to live a balanced, positive, purposeful life.

Our consciousness is **polarised** between the individual self and the Source. We can integrate the polarity to return to the Source or Oneness. Yoga defines this return journey as removing multiple channels in our thinking and action and aligning ourselves with only one channel: our highest potential, the Divine. In simple words, aligning ourselves with our Soul's purpose with a single-pointed focus is the way to dissolve the polarity.

Let's look at the scientific concept of **Coherence** to understand how to channel our energies.

## Coherence

### Coherence in Magnets

As we have seen earlier, how domains inside the magnet align themselves in one direction; that is, they become coherent. What is the difference between a magnet and a non-magnet? In terms of quantity or material, there is no change. The composition and magnitude of the material remain the same after magnetisation. So what changed? It is a qualitative change in the material. All individual magnetic fields of the domains are nullified in an iron piece, but in a magnet, all fields are aligned. The magnetised material now creates a coherent magnetic field.

Since we know that a magnet has conjugate fields, it is correct to say that a powerful dielectric field also exists in the magnet. The dielectric field originates from the very centre of the magnet, and loss of the same dielectric potential causes the magnetic field.

Due to the dielectric field at the very centre of the magnet, the magnet has now become a singularity or a point source. All its power is due to this centre point. Will we get to the centre if we cut the magnet into two halves? As discussed before, the answer is no. Cutting a magnet in two will create two separate centres in the smaller pieces. Likewise, when two magnets join, a new plane of inertia and a new centre is formed between them, voiding the previous ones. So, this dielectric centre of the magnet is beyond the 3D location; in other words, it is non-cartesian. It does not lie in our 3D space but beyond it. We cannot say where, as our 'where' is located in our 3D reality. For example, locational words do not have any meaning at the singularity in a black hole.

## Coherency Vs Capacitance

Coherency in a system makes it aligned, integrated, united, and harmonised, making it very effective and efficient. Increasing a system's capacitance makes it more energetic and powerful. A magnet can be created by rubbing a small iron piece against a strong magnet, making the iron piece coherent. A magnet can be made more powerful by increasing its capacitance by infusing electric charge, thus increasing polarity.

As an analogy, an integrated person is coherent, in whom all functions are optimised and efficient. But if we had an entire community of such persons, what would be the capacity of such a population? It would have greater capacitance and hence increased power to create desired outcomes. It would be united, aligned and able to make an egregore, a cascading effect greater than the sum of individuals.

We have seen such unity at physical levels in teamwork, where individuals work together towards a common goal. What would result when each person has optimised their full potential and become coherent within themselves, and then they resonate with others in the team in perfect harmony? Increased coherency and capacitance together in any system make it powerful and potent.

**Coherence in Lasers**

LASER stands for Light Amplification by Stimulated Emission of Radiation. Laser light is focused; it does not spread over large distances. Scientists have bounced laser light off the moon's surface to calculate its distance from Earth. Incoherent and dissipated light, like fire or an incandescent bulb, has many different wavelengths and looks scattered. Laser light is monochromatic, i.e., it has a single output wavelength. Laser light wavelengths are coherent, which means they are in phase with one another.

Laser light is also directional; it has a pinhole exit or spatial filter. Laser light is amplified by multiple lenses, which makes it very powerful. In simple terms, laser light has a frequency filter, a pinhole aperture and amplification lenses. There is a world of difference between an incandescent bulb's power and a laser's. A laser has so much power that it can be hazardous at higher wattages. Simple lasers are in a multitude of technologies that we use today; they are used to read bar codes, run appliances, conduct surgeries, etc. Lasers can point, mark, signal, print, cut, etch, burn, decorate, and more.

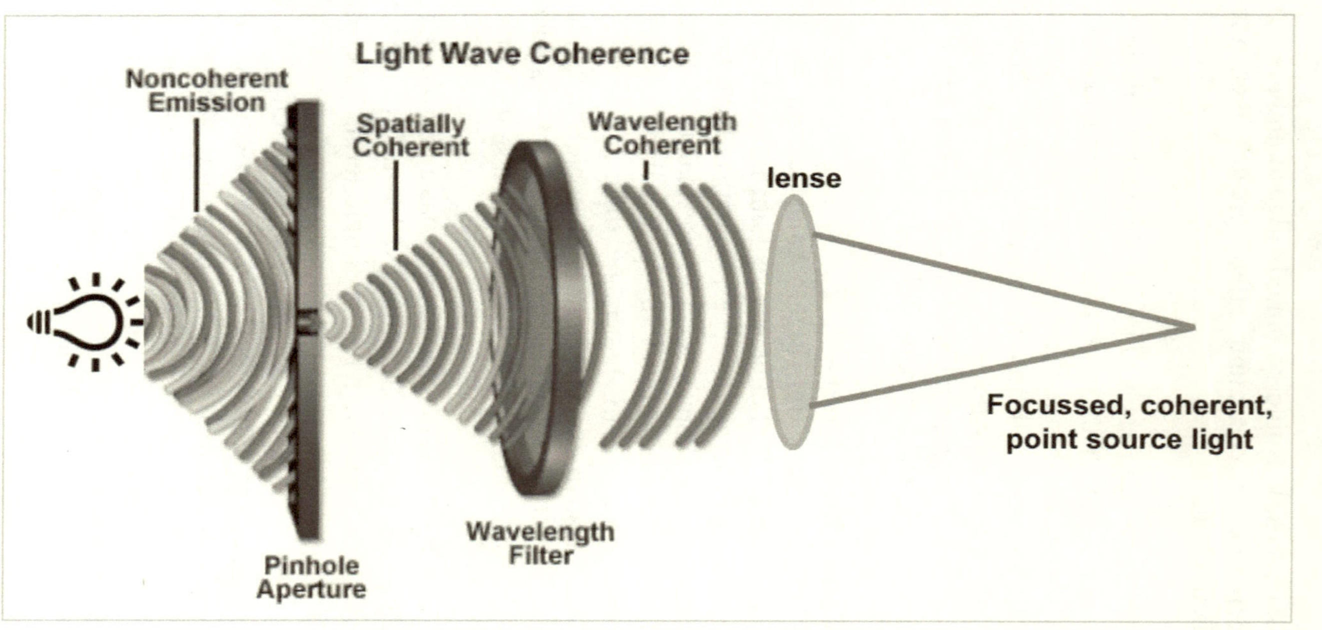

Light Wave Coherence
Noncoherent Emission
Spatially Coherent
Wavelength Coherent
lense
Focussed, coherent, point source light
Wavelength Filter
Pinhole Aperture

The secret to the laser's power is coherence, single-pointed focus, and amplification. In short, lasers act as concentrated point sources of light.

| Light Bulb | Laser |
| --- | --- |
| Incoherent | Coherent |
| Multiple wavelengths | Single wavelength |
| Multi-directional | Uni-directional |
| Dissipation all around | Have a spatial filter |
| Not focussed | Focussed and amplified |

**Coherence in Brain Waves:**
Can our brain waves become coherent, too? Brainwave research shows impressive results with meditation. Meditation with Transmission makes the brain waves coherent and changes their frequency, slowing them down to a state where energy is conserved.

Brain waves are electrical currents that show brain activity. The frequency of brain waves, measured in Hertz (Hz), depends on the state of the brain. There are five main types of brain waves, whose frequency range is as follows:

- Gamma      40 Hz to 100 Hz (Highest)
- Beta      12 Hz to 40 Hz (High)
- Alpha      8 Hz to 12 Hz (Moderate)
- Theta      4 Hz to 8 Hz (Slow)
- Delta      0 Hz to 4 Hz (Slowest)

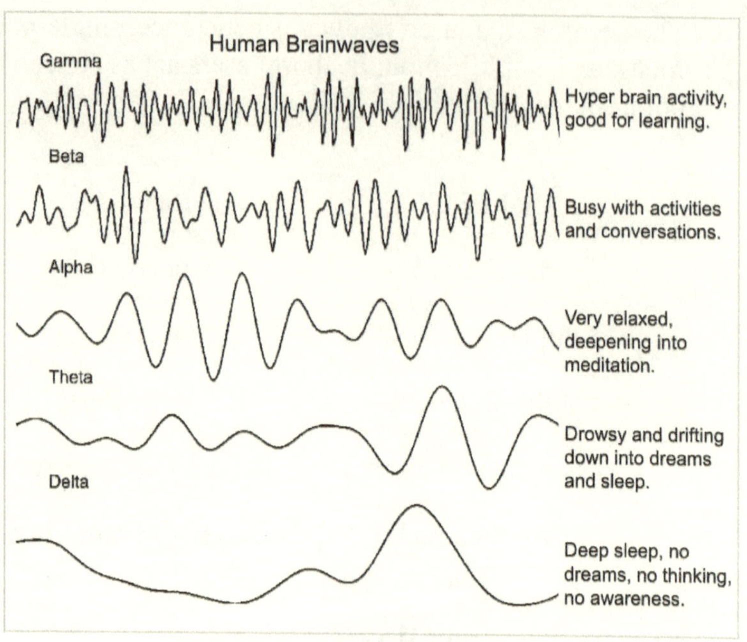


Source: www.heartfulnessmagazine.com

We can avoid being a scatterbrain, someone whose thoughts are incoherent, lacking focus, and being pulled in multiple directions by his unregulated mind. Correct maintenance and proper utilisation of the mind make us efficient and effective.

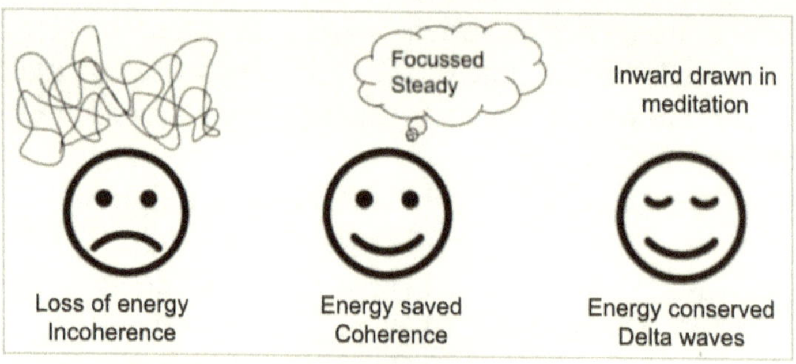


With meditation, we can go beyond coherency to energy conservation. We can tune our minds to the activity at hand.

If we need to engage in learning, we can train our minds to stay at the optimum frequency for learning. Likewise, we can train our minds to experience deep, relaxing delta waves through meditation.

**Schumann Resonance and Human Brain Waves**
Earth's atmosphere has electromagnetic waves of different wavelengths, man-made and natural. Man-made electromagnetic waves include radio, light, telecommunications, microwaves, and sonar. Natural electromagnetic waves include those caused by lightning discharges and cosmic radiation. Earth also emits electromagnetic pulses that radiate from its centre outwards towards the ionosphere.

In the 1950s, German physicist Dr Schumann discovered this frequency to be around 7.83Hz; hence, Schumann Resonance was named after him. This frequency is also considered the Earth's natural heartbeat rhythm to which all biological life, including the human brain, is tuned. A 7.83Hz frequency is the human brain's alpha/theta brainwave frequency. Over the last 40 years, Schumann Resonance frequency has been steadily increasing, and there are some spikes observed caused due to Earth's changing magnetic field or atmospheric changes. Being in tune with nature would mean resonating with the Earth's natural heartbeat as it helps sustain and heal all biological life. An out-of-sync person can experience compromised physical and mental health.

**Coherence in Heart Rate:**
The human heart is an amazing organ that beats rhythmically throughout life. Its natural pacemaker conducts the cardiac system by sending out an electromagnetic signal at a regular frequency. The signal initiates the heartbeat and determines the heart rate. The

pacemaker controls the heart muscles to coordinate the pumping action. The pressure changes in the blood vessels due to the pumping action are felt as a pulse. An adult's pulse rate is roughly 60-100 beats per minute.

The heart also makes sound waves. The heart sound frequency is generally between 20 to 500 Hz at the lower end of the audible spectrum. We must put our hands or ears on someone's chest to gauge the heartbeat. These are some of the physical measurements of the heart's movement. The movements of the heart and its measurements are no doubt intriguing, but even more interesting is the heart's relation to our emotions and thoughts. The heart rate with positive emotions is coherent. Our experience shows that when our emotions are stable and balanced, we experience calmness, connection and clarity, and the heart beats rhythmically. However, the heart tends to beat erratically due to negative emotions such as anger and fear, and our breath becomes short, shallow and irregular. Yogic psychology defines irregular breathing as a dis-ease (*Vighna*).

The effects of our thoughts and beliefs go much beyond the heart rate. In the book '*Biology of Belief*', author Dr Bruce Lipton shows us how biology responds to our beliefs. We become what we believe. Our beliefs create our corresponding thoughts and emotional states, which trigger our glands to release associated hormones in the body. This chemical environment in the body produces the stimulus to which the human genes respond. Gene expression is a possibility depending upon the environmental stimuli; this phenomenon is called epigenetics. Environmental stimuli primarily constitute our beliefs, thoughts, ideas, feelings and emotions. In addition, physical inputs like exercise, nutrition or geography also play an important but secondary role.

What happens when we meditate on the heart? We take the life force in the heart as the object of meditation. As we practice, we begin to regulate the tendencies of the mind, creating balance, and we feel a softening of the heart. We feel universal love as a natural result of the practice, which is the most coherent feeling, producing immense peace and joy. In the Yogic language, this feeling of universal love is called *ananda* or bliss. Hence, developing positive emotions and keeping our hearts light is recommended. Also suggested is a sustained practice of meditation to experience deep, relaxing delta brain waves. When calm, the mind can be engaged at will towards directed thinking and action as needed. When not required, it is at rest, conserving energy.

Heartfulness Research Institute conducted research with both new and experienced meditators to see the effect of Transmission on their brain waves. It was found that irrespective of how many hours of meditation someone had clocked or not, as soon as they commenced Heartfulness meditation, the delta waves appeared within a few minutes of starting the meditation. This is the profound effect of transmission on the human system, which is freely available to all seekers. It is an experience rather than a conceptual understanding or belief. Transmission heals and creates integration in the system from the deepest levels. Research has been conducted on how meditation impacts mental health, the sleep cycle, and overall well-being. For more details on various published research papers, visit https://www.heartfulnessinstitute.org/research.

**Coherence in a Human Being:**
A magnet and a laser are point source objects, i.e., integrated, coherent systems. They generate coherent fields that are powerful and can do seemingly magical things. Magnets can move items at a distance and manifest energy.

Lasers can do precise, unbelievable work. Both magnets and lasers have concentrated energy because incoherency has been removed from them, and all continents work in unison. It is similar to the sayings 'strength in numbers' or 'unity is strength'.

What about a human being? A human being can become a point source with Yoga. Yoga creates integration within and helps us rise to higher vibrational states with resonance.

| Levels | Incoherent | Coherent |
|---|---|---|
| Mind | Unregulated thoughts. | Regulated thoughts. A mind capable of concentration. |
| Heart | Restless heart with many desires. | Peaceful, loving content heart. |
| Identity | Multiple self-identifications. | Identified with the Self, centered on the Being. |
| Senses | Unregulated senses pulling in all directions. | Senses withdrawn inward. |
| Action | Multiple channels of action. | All actions aligned towards one goal. |

A human being can become coherent at many levels of his subtle body: A calm and regulated mind capable of single-pointed focus can work extremely efficiently. A light heart, devoid of incoherency caused by impressions, feels peaceful and at ease. It is in a natural state of joy. The individual consciousness expands to the universal level, while at the physical level, it still experiences a separate embodied existence. Thus, the subtle body of the human being is refined and brought to its optimal state. A human being can become a point source, in whom all the channels of expression are divinely oriented. Such a realised person can manifest and transmit the highest energy of love. Hence, a Yogi practices to become a coherent point source, moving closer and closer to the Source from which the entire creation has come forth. Such a person is permanently heart-centred and is capable of doing incredible feats well beyond the perceived limits of the natural world.

In scientific terms, as one meditates and removes the distortions in the consciousness, one moves centripetally towards the Source, like an implosion. A Yogi is a point source, with his awareness permanently located at the centre of his existence. This is the difference between thinking and being. Being is beyond the mind. Science seeks proof of the unified field in the physical universe when unity exists at the Being level, beyond physicality and thinking. Science can help us understand this intellectually but cannot help us be that unity we seek. To reach this unified state of Being, purity of intention, refinement of consciousness, simplicity of the heart, and effortless one-pointed focus of the mind are prerequisites. True knowledge does not come from thinking or rationality. It comes from an inner experience of being devoted to the Divine, thus becoming love in the process.

*The grand synthesis of Science and Yoga is the path of experimentation, observation, inquiry, learning, knowing, and becoming.*

# Wave Propagation and its Medium

## Propagation of Mechanical Waves

It is easy to visualise the mechanical disturbance on the water surface when we splash in a pool or drop a stone in a still lake. The mechanical energy displaces the water molecules, creating waves. The waves die out when the energy is exhausted or when pressure mediation is reached. Coherent waves can propagate faster, while incoherent waves cancel each other out. Waves in ropes and seismic waves similarly propagate through matter.

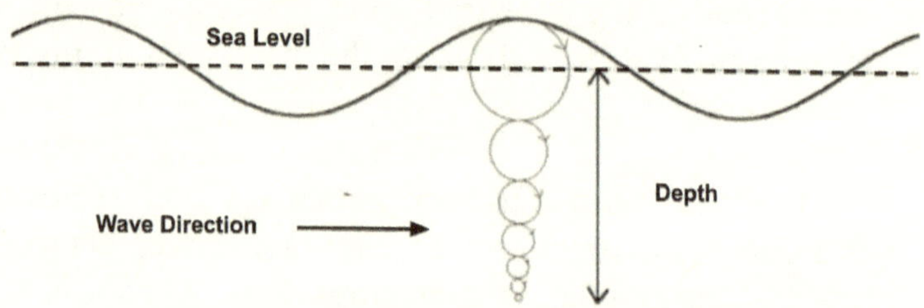



## Propagation of Sound Waves

What about sound? Sound disturbs air for propagation. The vocal cords or the speaker's diaphragm move the air, creating sound waves. Sound can be considered as a travelling wave of pressure in the air.

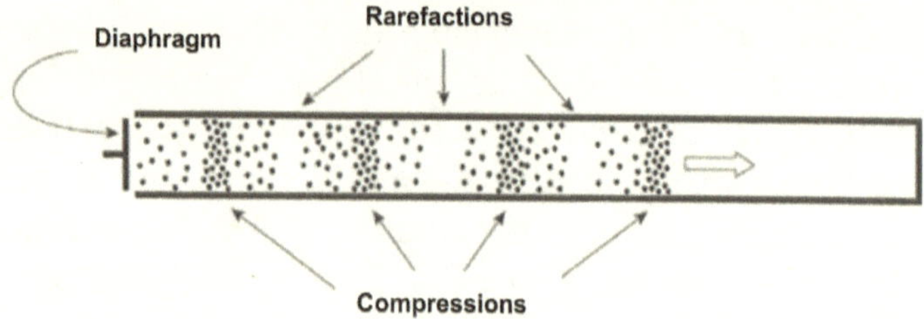



Sound travels a certain distance before pressure mediation is reached, and it can no longer propagate further. For greater audibility, we need to use amplifiers. The maximum speed of sound in air is the sound barrier, which can be surpassed. We witness it when jets, rockets and lightning fly, and their sound comes after them. The sound barrier is the saturation of the medium of air for propagation. Air cannot propagate sound any faster than that. We have seen other properties of sound through cymatics earlier; sound can create form and change or move matter and disintegrate objects.

## Propagation of Light Waves

What about light? Light is represented as an electromagnetic wave. The electric and magnetic fields are its two transverse components, and the direction of propagation shows the dielectric potential. These components are transverse, which means they are perpendicular to each other. Light, in essence, is a compound of dielectricity and magnetism.

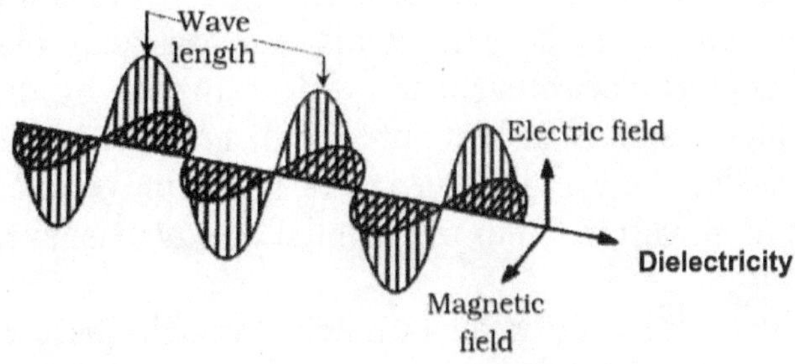


Shorter wavelengths of light have higher energy, and longer ones have less energy. Each cycle of the waveform can be visualised as a toric pulsation. The higher the number of pulsations, the greater the energy. Although the diagram above looks like the cartesian movement of the wave, light perturbation is toric.

Light disturbs ether for propagation, just like sound disturbs air for propagation. Lori Gardi, the Senior Software Developer at Robarts Research Institute, US, has developed interesting software to visualise wave propagation in different media. It demonstrates how surface waves on water propagate by the circular motion of the water molecules; similarly, light waves could propagate by the circular motion of ether. The water molecules do not travel longitudinally; they only create circular rotations at differing radii at varying depths of the water body. She similarly postulates that ether is set into circular motions for light propagation.

Scientists do not yet recognise ether as substantive because instruments cannot prove or detect it. However, scientists like Nikola Tesla and others stated the importance of ether in explaining the science of light and magnetism. Ether is one of the five basic elements, creating the other four perceivable elements: earth, water, fire, and air. It is the energetic and vibratory field in which all creation exists and is in constant motion. Light and matter manifest due to the motion in the ether. Ours is a constantly moving and changing electromagnetic world powered by the Source, which itself is at rest, unmoved, unalloyed, unchanging, just like the eye of a hurricane! In this universe of constant motion, vast amounts of potential energy exist everywhere.

Light seems to travel infinitely through space at a fixed speed, which gives astronomers a way to measure the universe. The distance a star or galaxy is can be determined by how long its light travels to us. What kind of light does a star emit? Is it shifting towards red or blue? These measurements give astronomers an idea about the star's composition and whether it moves away from or toward us.

We don't yet know what happens to light as it approaches a black hole, or for that matter, what a black hole is. It appears to be an entity that is the polar opposite of a star. A black hole and a star are like two poles of a pulsating torus. A black hole is also a point-source object, sucking everything into itself. A quasar is also a point source, although highly luminous, and it ejects vast amounts of electromagnetic and radio waves. These are some of the mysteries yet to be explained by science. However, from the point of view of torus geometry, these cosmic phenomena are explainable as giant polarised entities powered by the non-cartesian void at their centre.

**Propagation of Thought Waves**

How do thoughts propagate? Thought is energy, a wave, but subtler than light. Thoughts can travel far, fast and through everything. Have you ever experienced this fascinating synchronicity: you remember someone, and as soon as you pick up the phone to make a call, the exact moment the other person calls you instead? Thoughts seem instantaneous.

> *"We are what our thoughts have made us. So, take care of what you think. Words are secondary. Thoughts live; they travel far."*
>
> *- Swami Vivekananda*

Human life is all about navigating through the experience of various events and relationships. Similar events keep repeating unless we learn to live with equanimity and poise. Our thoughts create the circumstances we must navigate through. Taking care of our thoughts creates new life experiences rather than being on an old loop. Some of our relationships do not change, and although we might not confront the people involved with spoken words, our thoughts reach them faster and leave a lasting impact. Thoughts about someone are like holding one end of the rope, and the other end, attached to the other person, disturbs their consciousness. Even though words are not spoken, our thoughts reach them instantaneously.

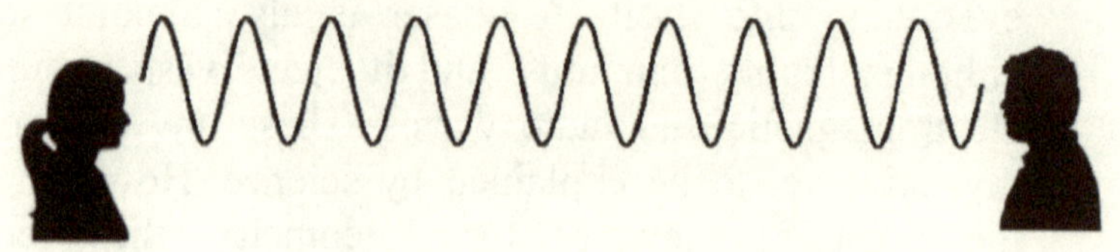

So, if you want your relationships to improve, you have two options. The first is to examine your thoughts about another person and convert negativity or expectations into affirmations and blessings. The second is to drop your end of the rope altogether. Then, you will help them and yourself as you will not be affected by the thoughts the other person has.

This is a direct result of yoga and meditation that we can experience. With yoga, we learn to withdraw the senses and mind within and curtail the outward tendencies of the mind. We learn to redirect our attention to the divine presence within and create positive thoughts and suggestions for the world instead. If we could understand the mechanics of thought propagation early in life, how well-equipped would we be to live to our full potential? When the mind is calm and there are no disturbing thoughts, then what do we radiate? We radiate the natural peace and love from our hearts; that is our true nature.

**Propagation of Scalar Waves**
Scalar waves are not a recent discovery, but their research is a recent phenomenon. A century ago, in 1905, Nikola Tesla wrote about scalar waves and experimented with scalar energy. He created the first scalar energy transmitter. James C Maxwell wrote 20 equations proving scalar waves, but later, his equations were reduced to just 4. This kept the scalar waves out of general education and research. In recent times, interest in scalar waves has been increasing. What are scalar waves in simple terms?

## Natural Scalar Waves

Natural scalar waves are described in various cultures as the life force or healing energy: Ki, Chi or Prana. The scientific or technical term to describe this energy is 'scalar'. The word scalar means 'a quantity' that does not have direction; it is there but not going anywhere. We feel the wind blow, water flow or fuel burn; we can view and feel the effects of this moving visible energy, but we miss noticing the scalar energy that exists all around us as an ocean of stationary energy. It can be described as tension in the ether that we live within. It extends throughout the universe, just like the ether, and it can not be seen or measured by conventional instruments as we are immersed in it. However, prana is the predominant energy in the universe. It is the energy of nature, the energy of our bodies, and the energy of healing. It is energy at all levels, from atomic to galactic.

Scalar energy is made up of standing or stationary waves. Through the science of resonance and cymatics, we have seen that a particle can be defined as a stationary wave energy structure that results when we get forward and reverse waves (incident and reflected) that become locked in resonance. There is no particle; everything is a wave or vibrating wave frequency. Some waves are in resonance and phase-locked with each other.

All matter and our bodies are zillions of such waves in phase-locked resonance. Our perfect health and awareness depend upon how well we maintain this phase-locked resonance. Our body and mind can then create phase-locking with others in our universe. The entire universe is a resonating mist of phase-locked particles/waves. When we see how hard some materials can be, like a diamond, we can understand how much energy there is between the phase-locked carbon atoms in the diamond's structure.

We have already seen some natural patterns in which scalar waves appear. Cymatics shows the patterns in which scalar energy shows up when different materials vibrate. Water drops always crystallise as hexagonal shapes. AFM images show atoms of various materials phase-lock together in scalar wave patterns. Shells, sand structures at sea-bed and dunes show scalar wave patterns. Mountain ranges, river tributaries, and even our fingerprints show scalar wave patterns. Crystals shapes are a 3D version of the ripples on water or sand, where atoms are phase-locked with each other. There are too many examples; the more keen eyes seek, the more they discover. The entire natural world is scalar generated. We are surrounded by such a massive amount of undetectable scalar energy, which we cannot perceive, but it announces its existence through observable patterns and phenomena.

**Artificial Scalar Waves**
Artificial scalar waves are two electromagnetic waves 180° out of phase, cancelling the magnetic wave components. Hence, artificial scalar waves are longitudinal compression waves in the ether, similar to sound waves, which are also longitudinal compression waves in the medium of air. Scalar waves do not have magnitude and can pass through everything. Due to this lack of magnitude, they are also not limited by space; they can travel without any transmission loss.

Some profound questions are: Why would artificial scalar waves be created in a science lab? Would they be used for healing or regeneration? As Tesla envisioned, would they be used for wireless free energy transmission without loss over great distances? Or would they be used for some other purpose? Only ethics could truly guide this research in a positive direction.

**Propagation of Prana**

Prana, the energy of the highest potency, comes from the Source. It is the Soul-essence. What medium would Prana use for propagation? Prana, the ultimate medium and power itself, is present everywhere, in every nook and cranny of the entire creation, so it can emerge anywhere, irrespective of time and space. Prana is everywhere as stationary potential energy and can be directed by thought. A yogi dives deep into his heart to access Prana and direct it. Pure thought and good intention backed by will can direct Prana.

Prana is subtler than Akash (Ether) and is also its cause. Because of this, Prana does not need Ether as the propagation medium. It is always present everywhere, so it seems infinite and instantaneous.

**What fills up the Creation?**

- *Prana* **(Lifeforce)** is the cause, the Soul Essence. It fills the entire creation. Prana is the infinite, omnipresent **manifesting power** of the universe. In a human being, Prana or lifeforce emanates from the heart as pure love.

- *Chitta* **(Consciousness)** is the mind-essence, a **subtle matter** or fine vibrations, that fills the entire creation. Motions of Prana power Chitta. In a human being, chitta or consciousness is the agency of awareness or knowing.

- *Akasha* **(Ether)** is the gross matter-essence. Akasha fills up the entire manifested creation. Akasha is the infinite, omnipresent **material** of the universe that gives rise to light and matter. Motions of Prana power Akasha. In a human being, The physical body is made up of gross matter.

What existed before creation? Swami Vivekananda said that before manifestation, Akasha existed without motion. Prana started the motion, causing the creation to manifest out of the Akasha. At the time of dissolution, all matter (both gross and subtle) resolves back to Akasha, which in turn resolves back to Prana, the Source. Prana is the highest, and all energies are a lower manifestation or stratification of Prana.

*"Out of this, Prana has evolved everything that we call energy, everything that we call force. It is the Prana that is manifesting as motion; it is the Prana that is manifesting as gravitation, as magnetism. It is the Prana that is manifesting as the actions of the body, as the nerve currents, as thought force. From the thought down to the lowest force, everything is but a manifestation of Prana. The sum total of all forces in the universe, mental or physical, when resolved back to their original state, is called Prana."*

- Swami Vivekananda

Prana is of the highest essence. Meditating with *Pranahuti* takes the practitioner to a sublime level in meditation, creating states of absorbency and helping clear the impressions from the energy field. *Pranahuti* is made available by a Yogi of high calibre, who, being connected to the Source, can tap into this energy and channel it to the seekers. In Heartfulness, a team of trainers also act as conduits to channel Prana to all practitioners worldwide like an interconnected network of light and love.

Yoga is truly scientific, a science of synthesis, while physical science is reductionist in comparison. However, both are needed for the full realisation of human potential. Personal experience and scientific research go hand in hand. Mainstream science restricts itself to observable physical phenomena; it fails to prove the electromagnetic 'fabric' of our reality of Ether through its instruments. The gross cannot perceive the subtle. To experience the subtle, we must wait for the future development of much more innovative technology. Alternatively, we can create subtlety in our perception through the science of Yoga, here and now.

Yoga says that when a Jiva embodies, it possesses a mind. Then, using the mind, it can transcend embodied existence. Jivas who evolved to higher levels must have been embodied once, except for *avatars* who descended into embodiment for particular purposes. All Jivas start their journey at the gross level and work their way upwards by increasing their vibrational frequencies, becoming potentiated, and moving ever closer to the Source or the singularity.

**Vortex**
Spirals or vortices tap into the energy field. Insects, fishes and birds can create vortices within their movements. Migratory birds make vortices to ease long-distance flying and resonate with other birds to create group movement in a V-formation. Plant tendrils create spirals to stimulate growth. Going with the natural energy flow in the environment helps conserve energy and makes impossible feats happen. Vortices can also have massive destructive power, like hurricanes or tornadoes. Vortices are

everywhere: in flowing water, rising smoke, air, galaxies, and black holes. Vortices can transfer energy by creating disturbances in the field.

There are vortices in our body structure, too. One is at the top of our heads, like a spiral hair parting. Every *chakra* or point in the energy body is a vortex, a fingerprint is a vortex, and the DNA double helix is a spiral structure. Natural energy is subtle and provides healing when invoked with positive affirmation and higher intent.

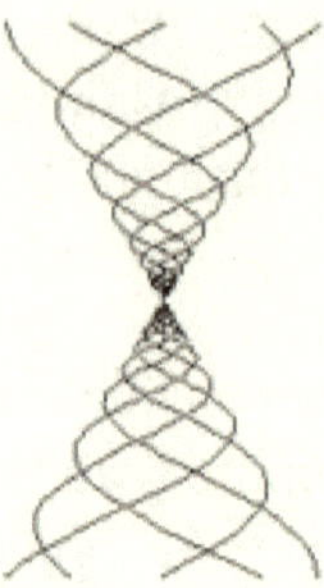

In Yoga, when we restrain our senses, control the outward tendencies of the mind, and turn our attention inwards, do we create such a spiralling vortex within us? Vortex seems to be the geometry for centring ourselves progressively and gaining proximity to the Source within.

# Part 3

# Synthesis

# Chapter 7
# Scientific Yoga

## Spiritual Journey (*Yatra*)

In the bestselling and widely popular books titled *The Heartfulness Way* and *Designing Destiny,* Daaji describes the milestones of the Heartfulness journey. In this spiritual journey, we learn how to meditate, clean the field of our consciousness and connect to the source within. We develop a keen perception of the inner processes. Time and effort in this journey vary from person to person, as each individual is unique regarding their karmic debt, tendencies, and motivations. However, with sufficient advancement, one can perceive the subtle steps of this journey.

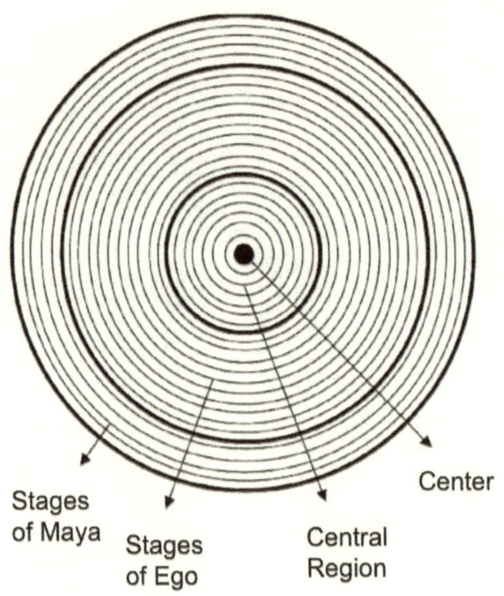


Source: www.heartfulnessmagazine.com

The journey has the following steps:

- Heart region: Points 1-5
- Mind region: Points 6-12
- Central Region: Point 13

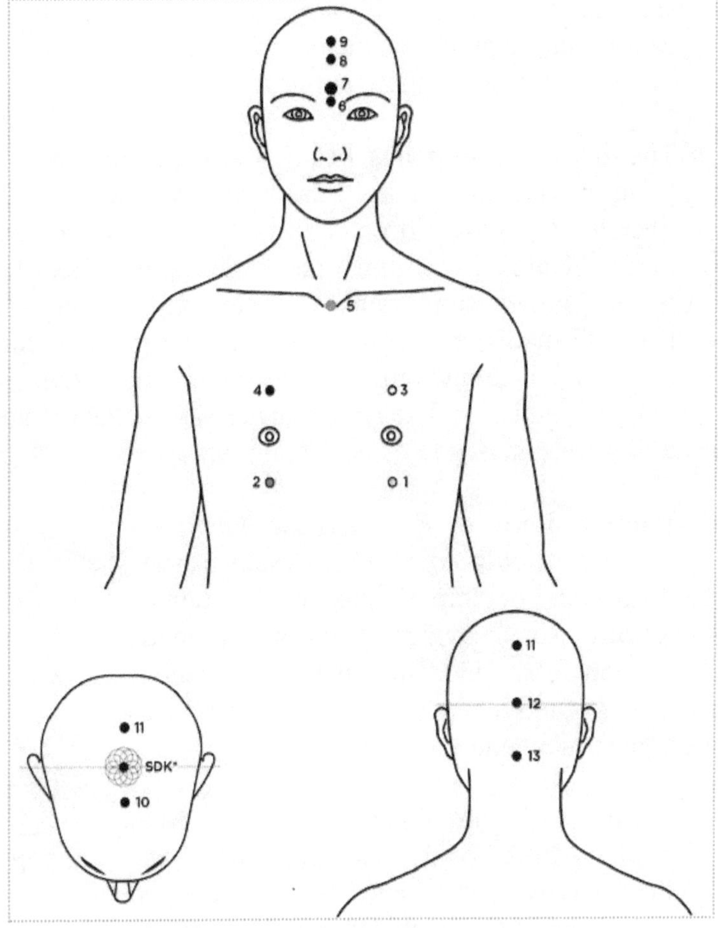


Source: www.heartfulnessmagazine.com

A depiction of the points in the human system
(Spiritual Anatomy as revealed by Daaji)

## The Heart Region

The heart region is the arena of duality. The first five points represent the physical world, which correlates to the five elements of Nature: Earth, Ether, Fire, Water, and Air. All elements are present at each point; however, one is dominant, giving it a unique quality. Each point has a specific location, colour, movement, or spin. Heartfulness details simple practices, including meditation, cleaning, and prayer, to transcend these points.

The journey from points 1 to 5 is in sequential order. After point 5, having crossed the heart region, the Jiva is liberated from the birth and death cycle, no longer needing to incarnate in the physical plane of dualities. Heartfulness is the journey from thinking to feeling to being. As we begin to meditate, the journey of these 5 points is mapped by the feelings and attitudes that emerge in us that change our perspective and behaviour. These appear as pointers for our onward march in the spiritual journey.

**Point 1**: Earth or *Prithvi is the dominant element at this point*. Our desires cause distortions or impressions at this point, leading to heaviness, discontent, and unhappiness. Once this point is cleaned and transcended, we experience contentment and acceptance.

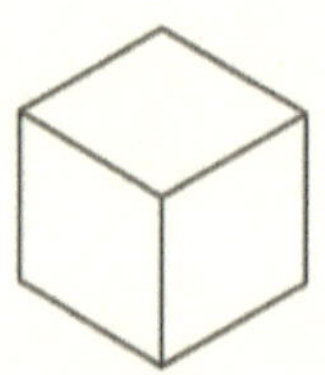

**Point 2**: The dominant element of this point is Ether or *Akasha*. Distortions or impressions at this point create restlessness. Once this point is cleaned and transcended, we experience deep peace.

**Point 3**: The dominant element of this point is Fire or *Agni*. Distortions or impressions at this point create anger. Once this point is cleaned and transcended, anger transmutes to love.

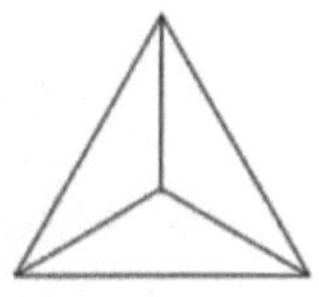

**Point 4**: Water or *Jal* is the dominant element at this point. Distortions or impressions at this point create fear. Fear is removed once this point is cleaned and transcended, and we feel courageous.

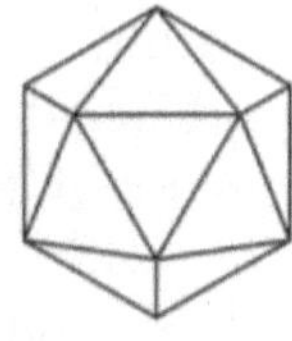

**Point 5**: The dominant element of this point is Air or *Vayu*. Distortions or impressions at this point create confusion and illusion. Once this point is cleaned and transcended, we experience clarity.

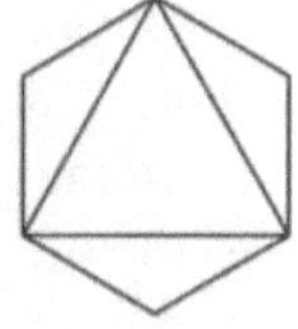

Desire is 'choice-making', which emerges from our impressions. Desire is a double-edged sword; its fulfilment leads to wanting more, and lack of it leads to discontentment and misery. Desires can be material or sensual. The impressions caused by these desires continuously deposit in the region of the first point. Hence, practice and vigilance are needed to clean them off and eventually cease their formation. Therefore, the journey of the heart region is about clearing the impressions and impurities lodged in it, which lead to the distortion of our consciousness, thus affecting our perception. This inner journey is made possible by the transformative power of meditation with transmission.

Action is better than inaction, but good action is better than any thoughtless action. Even better than good action is to forfeit the results of all good actions. A person transcending the heart region has gone beyond the need to act based on selfish choice-making. Instead, he engages in aware and desireless action aligned with his Soul's purpose.

**The Mind Region**
While the heart region is the journey to transcend duality, the mind region is the journey to refine ego or sense of identity. Here, the impurities distorting our consciousness are subtle ideas, beliefs, judgements, prejudices, and the sense of doership.

The mind region has seven points, from points 6 to 12. At the beginning of the journey, identity is self-centred (lower self), and as we progress in the mind region, we become more soul-centred. At the pinnacle, individual consciousness merges with universal consciousness. There is the oft-quoted analogy of the drop realising that it is the ocean and that it had always been the ocean but was covered in the illusory sheaths of ego and impurities, thus having forgotten its true nature.

The journey of the mind region is progressive non-attachment to one's ideas, thoughts, opinions and an illusory sense of identity. The following table shows the qualities and the feelings associated with the seven points of the mind region. This information is sourced from work titled *Spiritual Anatomy* by Daaji and *Heartfulness Yatra Garden* in Kanha Shantivanam, Hyderabad. I have taken the liberty to interpret the geometric representations as they correlate to the apparent scientific concepts. They somehow effortlessly point towards a synthesis of science and spirituality.

**Point 6**: It represents the subtle Earth or *Prithvi* element. The cosmic region, or the *Brahmanada Mandal,* distributes power to the lower planes. Having crossed the first 5 points, Jiva has moved beyond the limits of physicality and is now free from the birth and death cycle. The feelings associated with point 6 are expansion, limitlessness and holiness. It is the point of power. It is cleaned and bypassed so that the seeker moves on undisturbed.

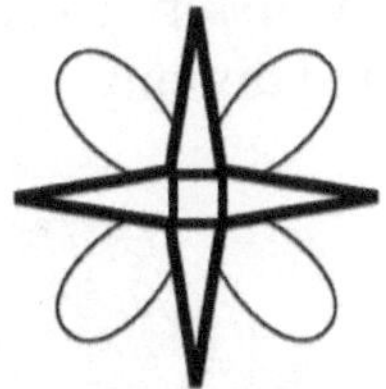

Power distribution- Atomic

**Point 7** represents the subtle Ether or *Akasha* element. It is the paracosmic region or the *Para Brahmanada Mandal*, the storehouse of power. The feelings associated with point 7 are further expansion, selflessness, and contained responsiveness.

The Electrical storehouse of Power with counter-rotating polarised motion

**Point 8**: It represents the subtle Fire element. It is the supra cosmic region. It is called the *Prapanna state,* and the feelings associated with point 8 are deep peace, humility, surrender and inner renunciation.

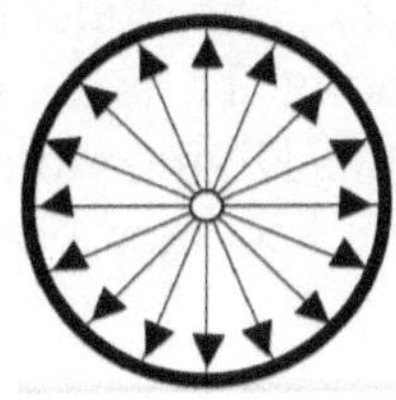

Power Generation

**Point 9** represents the subtle Water element. It is the *Prapanna Prabhu* state. The feelings associated with point 9 are further humility and surrender. The 'I-ness' recedes with greater inner renunciation, and the Absolute appears. Feelings of inner worship accompany this point, and the heart feels purity and divinity.

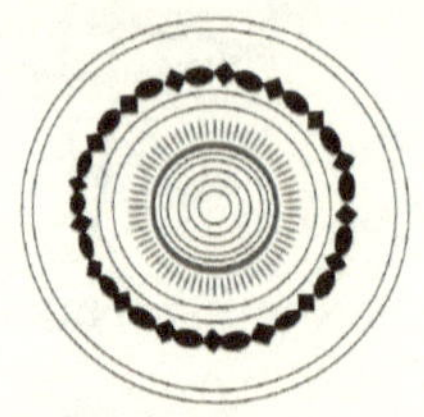

Sublime Magnetism

**Point 10**: It represents the subtle Air element. It is the *Prabhu* state. The feelings associated with point 10 are complete humility and surrender. With even greater inner renunciation, the 'I-ness' is completely gone, and only the Absolute remains. Feeling the presence of the Divine at all times, the seeker gets closer and closer to It.

Potential

**Point 11**: It represents the subtlest Earth element. It is the higher *Prabhu* state, the supermind of God. The feeling associated with point 11 is close inner proximity to the Divine. One radiates Divine vibrations, becoming a conduit for the Divine. Jiva becomes a witness; doer-ship is only of the Divine.

Between points 10 and 11 lies the crown chakra or *Sahasra Dal Kamal*, translated as 1000-petalled lotus. Traditionally, this point was considered the ultimate attainment on the yogic path, leading the seeker to a steady state of *sat-chit-ananda* or ultimate bliss. Heartfulness is the only yogic path that describes the journey beyond *Sahasra Dal Kamal*. In fact, *Sahasra Dal Kamal* is considered a trap where the seeker loses the motivation to move ahead due to infinite joy and bliss at that point. But with the help of the Guide, the seeker can transcend even this point and move further ahead. This point is also cleaned and bypassed so the seeker moves undisturbed.

**Point 12**: It represents the subtlest Ether or *Akasha* element. It is the highest *Prabhu* state of sublime purity. The feelings associated with point 12 are devotion, identicality with the Divine and total subjugation of the 'I-ness'. There is a renewed restlessness for mergence with the Source. This restlessness creates a forward momentum to propel the Jiva to the final summit of the spiritual journey, the Central Region.

Pure Potential

Flower of Life, Consciousness

The 12th point is superimposed by *Brahmarandra*, a point from which an evolved soul can enter or exit the body. It is represented by the Flower of Life pattern, the universal blueprint. This symbol, seen in all ancient cultures, represents consciousness and life as one interconnected whole.

**The Central Region**

The central region is the 13th point in the Heartfulness spiritual journey. Words cannot adequately describe it, but great souls who found a place in this region have called it Nothingness, Source, Center, or Absolute. This is the discovery of the Teachers of Heartfulness. Having reached the highest summit of spiritual elevation, the teacher returns to guide the seekers.

This region is the culmination of the spiritual journey, although the journey is still infinite; the seeker keeps moving towards the Source infinitely, continuously refining his approach at each stage. It is as if the seeker gives an opportunity to the Divine to view itself from an ever higher vantage point with each advancing step towards it. This is God's purpose of creation reaching its zenith.

The 13th point is represented by the dot in the middle: nothingness, source, void or *shunyata*. *Adi-Shakti* or Prana emanating from the Source illuminates everything, giving it life. The First Mind (circle containing the dot) creates tanmatras and panchabhutas, which are represented by the pentagrams in this beautiful heart-shaped symbol.

Indian traditional knowledge, folklore across various cultures, and sacred geometry describe the beginning of creation as the 'Source desiring to know itself, thus casting a reflection of itself'. Individuated Soul is analogous to how each point of the hologram contains the entire hologram. Each Soul has the capacity to reach this zenith to reflect the Divine as its existential Reality.

Heartfulness is the journey of the heart; hence, all the stages are descriptions based on feelings and experiences. How would you feel at each stage? Each stage is more refined, pure, and pious than the previous one. Once we embark on the journey, we can feel these points within, and the associated conditions of the heart guide our onward journey.

# Stratification of One



Walter Russell, born in Boston, US in 1871, wrote about the nature of light and matter in his remarkable books *The Secret of Light* and *The Universal One*, published in the first half of the 20th century. He laid out the phenomenon and the geometry of the electromagnetic nature of the universe, refuting the fundamentals of Newtonian science. He said that mainstream science only looks at one half of the cycle of creation, ignoring the two poles that perfectly void each other at all times, due to which perfect balance exists.

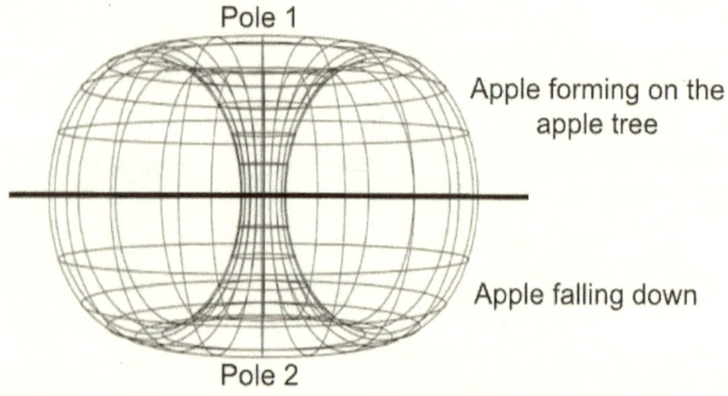


Walter Russell pointed out that Newton's apple is not falling towards the earth, but two bodies with mass are falling towards a null pressure point between them. In the case of Earth and the apple, the size difference fools the senses into making one think gravity attracts. He further says that the apple goes through creation and dissipation, perfectly balanced at all times, and we need to see this cycle in its entirety to understand the underlying phenomena. These scientific teachings of Walter Russell were considered esoteric just over a century ago, but now, with a better understanding of conjugate force fields and the technology to view them, there is greater acceptance of this phenomenon. It is also helping us understand the already unified forces of nature and their accurate inter-relationships. We are looking at the science of divine magnetism.

The smallest particle of matter, the hydrogen atom, is condensed light. It is a separate identity of matter apart from light, but it still is a pulse of light. The hydrogen then creates heavier and heavier elements of matter, as tabulated in the periodic table. Each element on the periodic table has a certain vibration. Hydrogen and oxygen bond to form water, thus creating the basis for organic lifeforms to emerge.

Eventually, compounds heavier than water form, leading further to complex molecules and finally to a living cell. Biological life eventually becomes more and more complex to develop delicate senses and a nervous system that can decode the electrical signals and guide the being with greater awareness, agency and self-interest for its survival and growth. We arrive at a diverse and increasing complexity of biological lifeforms, from microorganisms to fungi, plants, insects, animals and humans, with ever greater expression of the expanding consciousness.

Since all creation is from one source, it moves towards greater unity and balance back to that same source. It is integration, the opposite of entropy. Entropy is disorganisation or chaos from an ordered state. All systems left to themselves increase in entropy, but the self-organising principle in the universe is not entropic; it is, in fact, integrative. This is the genesis of the desire for evolution and returning to the Source at all levels of creation. This is the universal intelligence at play. The following diagram shows different levels of manifestation, from the subtle to the gross or from unity to multiplicity, in simple scientific terms.

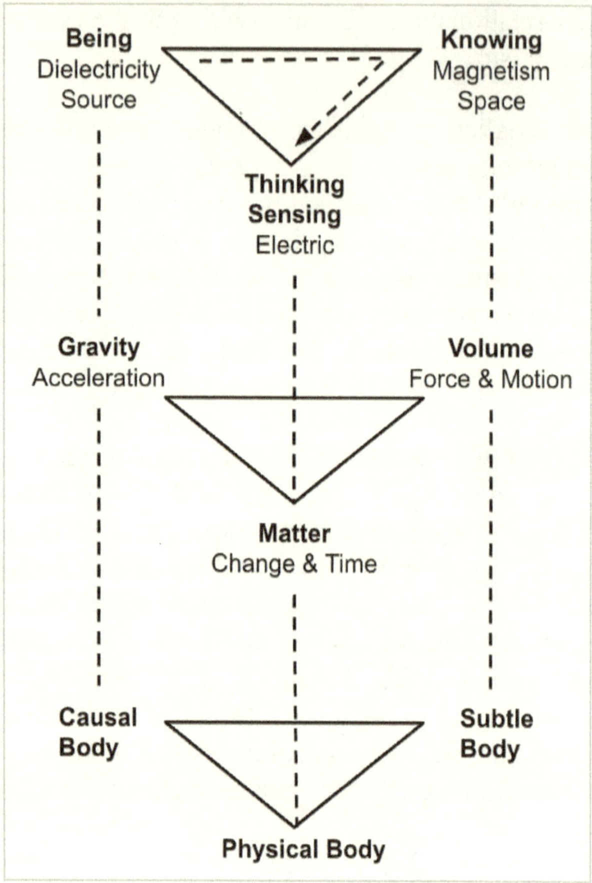


Dielectricity, pure potential or the non-cartesian centre, whatever we might call it, is the source of magnetism and gravitation. Later comes light or electricity, the polarised entity. Gravity is convergence to a point, while magnetism is divergence or spatial expansion. The geometry of the torus shows these conjugate forces.

*"When thought comes in contact with the soul, the third thing produces, and that is light."*

- Babuji

The evolutionary impulse of all creation is integrative and led by self-organising intelligence directed towards the source. Not only is all insentient matter moving up in an orderly way back to the source, but evolutionary instincts for survival and growth also lead all living beings to the source. However, human beings have a chance to **evolve consciously** due to the possibility of the willing expansion of consciousness through Yoga. Hence, there is a need to regulate the senses and the mind, as this journey back to the Source is beyond sensing and knowing; it is 'Being' itself. But of course, embodied beings in the creation are free to make their own choices based on their understanding and approach, thus leading to the phenomenon of free will and cause and effect.

**Peeling the Onion**

We can imagine these toruses as nested inside each other, with subtler levels closer to the centre and the grosser levels farther away. This is similar to the model of a Jiva, where the causal body is at the centre, while the subtle and gross bodies are farther away.

Side view

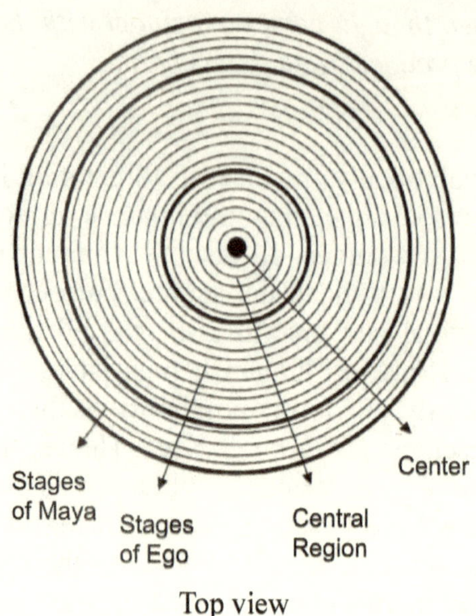


Top view

The top view of the nested toruses stratified by density is similar to the concentric circles model of the spiritual journey. We start from the outer circle of grosser levels of physical existence, then move into the subtle realms of light and finally enter the central region of pure potentiality. These concentric circles make a spiral, and the unwinding of the spiral is manifestation into the grosser levels, and rewinding it is evolution. The entire creation is One, only stratified due to differing levels of density or vibration. Let's take an analogy of the physical world; from the highest vantage point of a mountain climber, loss of altitude gives him another lower level. The higher and lower levels are still part of the same topology.

Another example could be light. The electromagnetic wave spectrum has numerous light frequencies, ranging from ultraviolet to infrared, yet it is all one light. Human eyes can see only the visible band, which is .0035% of the entire light spectrum. Interestingly, if our eyes were to capture more of the spectrum range, they would be dazzled by an onslaught of light, making the entire field of view incoherent. Further, the Earth's atmosphere permits only specific light wavelengths conducive to biological life.

Differing frequencies and densities stratify the entire universe. The higher the density, the lower the vibration and vice versa. Human beings at the physical level can only experience specific bands of frequencies. We can experience higher frequencies at the thought level, but the soul, the essence of the Source, is at *the* highest frequency. Yoga, which takes our awareness closer to the Soul, gives us the most elevated experience of living possible for a human being.

## Torus and the Transverse Wave Diagram

How can the current flow in a torus translate to a wave diagram? The image on the right with two circles is the cross-section of a torus. When rotated, these circles can create the torus or the doughnut form, as a tube with its ends joined together.

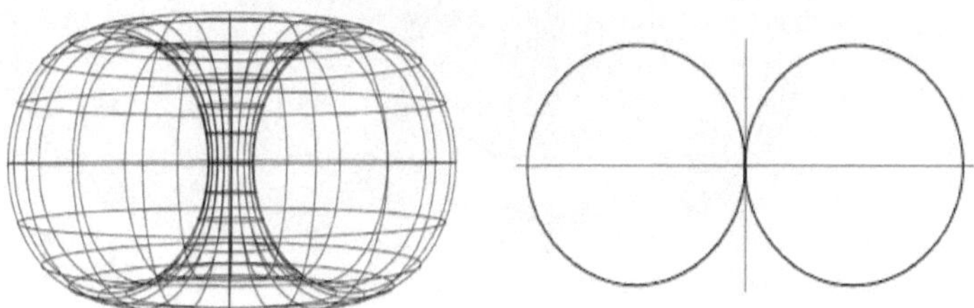

Current flow in the torus is simultaneous current flow in infinite circles of the torus. Let's take the example of current flow in just one circle. Tracing the circular motion of a point along the circumference of the circle would give us a transverse wave.

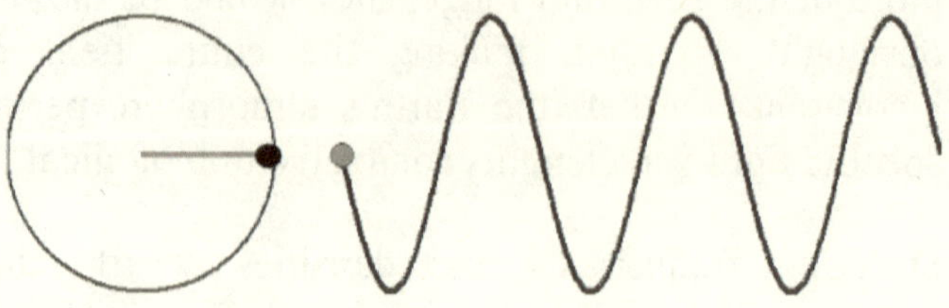

If there are nested toruses, infinite waves of all possible wavelengths and frequencies would be generated simultaneously, interfering with each other and creating standing waves at specific harmonic frequencies. This makes the electromagnetic world of waves we are a part of. Further away from the centre, the vibrations and frequencies are lower, hence denser the manifested reality. The closer to the centre, the higher the vibrations and frequencies, thus finer the reality. There is no motion at the centre, which is the potential or the prime cause. It is still abiding in *nothingness*.

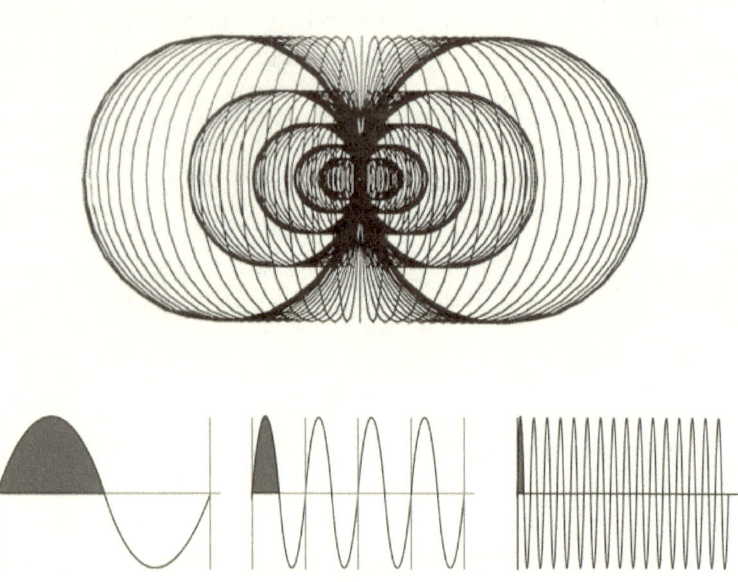

Layers of the torus and differing frequencies

Everything in nature follows the same principle: As above, so below. The entire manifested and unmanifest reality is vibrational. Our physical body, senses, and even the world of thought waves are vibrational hierarchies. Higher vibrations feel good, and God, the highest vibration, feels like pure unconditional love that radiates out on all like warm, nourishing Sunlight.

**Manifestation by Trinity**
Referring to the following diagram, point 1 is the beginning, and point 3 is the conjugate (opposite pair or polarity) of point 1. Point 2 is what manifests due to the interactions between 1 & 3. It is interesting to note how two things, at different levels of manifestation, become the cause of the third, as given in the table below:

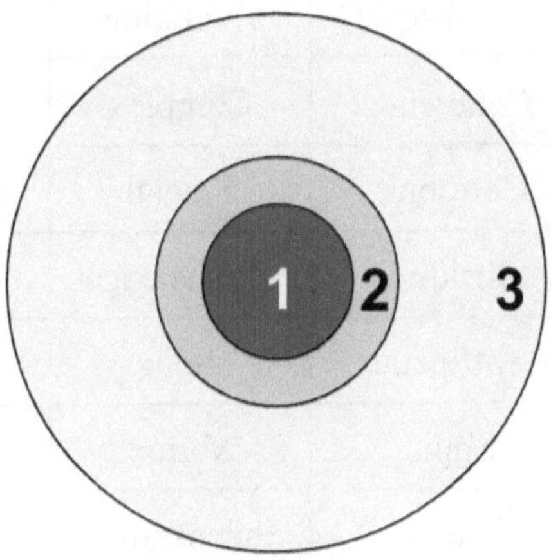


Read the table as 1 and 3 give rise to 2. For example, 'the cycle of birth and death creates life.'

| Beginning | Middle | End |
| --- | --- | --- |
| Birth | Life | Death |

| Beginning | Middle | End |
| --- | --- | --- |
| Electric Charge | Current Flow | Electric Discharge |
| Absorption | Energy | Emission |
| Stillness | Polarisation | Motion |
| Attraction | Mass/Gravity | Repulsion |
| Contraction | Resonance | Expansion |
| Stasis | Time | Change |
| Convergence | Integration | Divergence |
| Creation | Evolution | Destruction |
| Coherent | Complex | Incoherent |
| Isotropic | Fractal | Homogenous |
| Inside | On the edge | Outside |
| Centripetal | Spin | Centrifugal |
| Spin | Vortex | Counterspin |
| Absolute | Independent | Relative |
| Deceleration | Force | Acceleration |
| Fusion | Stable particles | Fission |
| Inhale | Breathing | Exhale |

| Beginning | Middle | End |
| --- | --- | --- |
| Silence | Music | Sound |
| Seed | Flower | Plant |
| Death | Afterlife | Rebirth |
| Female | Child | Male |
| Night | Twilight | Day |
| End | Transition | New Beginning |
| Sleep | Dream | Awake |
| Soul | Mind | Body |
| Silence | Thinking | Talking |
| Rest | Dance | Movement |
| Sat | Raj | Tam |

Manifestation of the entire creation seems to be born out of the Trinity, yet all is still One. The polarity creates the imbalanced electric potential to affect motion between the two poles.

# A Natural Synthesis

## All is One

All perspectives, be it Samkhya, Yoga, Greek philosophy, Geometry or Science, all point towards the idea that everything is from the One and tries to return to that One. Creation occurs on the principle of self-similarity. Creation is the *stratification* of the One, and the way back is *integration*. For a human being, the process is to integrate all aspects of oneself and become **coherent** in body, mind and soul. Then, **resonate** with higher vibrations and raise one's frequency to the next level. This is incremental growth towards the Source, the highest vibration experienced as universal love. Yoga is the path of unification to realise this Oneness.

## The Fallacy of Identification

The eternal question of *who we are* has been the basis of all human endeavours. Yogis took it upon themselves to answer this question as a direct experience. Instead of identification with the worldly personality (comprising body and mind), they attempted to expand the sense of identity to include the real essence, the Soul. Instead of fighting over appearance, possessions, achievements, ideas, beliefs and opinions, they learnt to identify as the witnessing presence.

*Neti Neti* (not this, not this) said the ancients who showed the path of negation to inquire into the nature of Brahma by eliminating everything that is not Brahma. By such discernment, they eliminated all terms that could not describe the perfect One, finally reaching *nothingness*. When all forms, words, ideas, descriptions and explanations fall short, then beyond that lies the direct experience of that Oneness.

Daaji reveals the true meaning of non-identification: facing up to our lower self, accepting it, and then surrendering it to the Higher Self. The ego or sense of identity gives us a foundation on which to stand. But then we shine a light on all its lower tendencies and transcend them with yogic practices. Imagine a ladder; we stand on one step and move upwards. Both the foundation and the final goal are equally important. At each step, the Higher Self is a motivator and a support system to lean on as we climb.

**Pressure Mediation**
Water flows from a higher to a lower level, air flows into a low-pressure area, and clouds precipitate and create rainfall in low-atmospheric-pressure regions. Earth moves effortlessly in its orbit around the Sun, on the plane of least pressure between them, considering their gravitational impact on each other.

Similarly, love and grace flow into a vacuumized heart. A clear, uncluttered, open mind becomes a receptacle for higher inspiration. The entire creation, at all levels, whether subtle or gross, works on the principle of pressure mediation. From this comes the adage: *empty your cup to receive what is worthwhile*. The spiritual journey is the journey of increasing inner lightness so that the divinity within each one can radiate forth.

**An Ode to Devotion**

How necessary is knowledge in the spiritual quest? Just enough to choose the right path, follow the path, and persevere on the path. True knowledge is a byproduct of a spiritual quest. The most crucial element in such a pursuit is devotion, the subtle thread that binds the seeker to the sought. Another essential element is the engagement of the heart in the practice, as the entire spectrum of spiritual states is felt as conditions of the heart. And the final element is to allow the finer and finer conditions of the heart to percolate into our communication, work, relationships and lifestyle. The way to the divine goes through a devoted human heart.

> *"The glory of God is reflected only in the heart which is pure like mirror."*
>
> — *Babuji*

# Appendix 1

## The Vast Library of Ancient Indian Literature

This is a glimpse into ancient Indian literature for reference, but this list is incomplete. This simple compilation of some of the most well-known and widely available works can help a seeker navigate this library. As an evolving civilisation, we can gain much by taking a greater interest in what our ancients were saying. An important point to remember is that ancient literature is anthropomorphic, allegorical, visual, depictive, story-based and poetic. Hidden within them are some great spiritual and scientific truths waiting to be revealed to a sincere seeker. Where to start? Choose what interests you and practice to realise.

### *Vedas*

1. ***Rigveda****:* A collection of 10 books, *Rigveda* is considered the oldest text containing chants praising Vedic *devatas*. It also contains the famous *Gayatri mantra*. The stories in *Rigveda,* called the *suktas,* reflect the philosophy and belief systems of ancient Indian society. Modern mathematics, computing, and other branches of science trace their roots to Rigveda.

2. ***Yajurveda****:* A handbook for performing *Yajnas.* Generally, *Yajna* is associated with *havan* or fire ritual, but *Yajna* means 'sacrifice'. It is not a sacrifice of objects in the fire but rather a way of life that sacrifices or gives up lower tendencies for higher attainment. In the Vedic context, *Yajna* is regarded as a homage or an offering to the *devatas*. The concept is that humans perform *Yajna* to honour *devatas*, and they, in turn, ensure the proper functioning of

nature, providing for humans through rain, plants, light, fire, fertile land, food and life-sustaining cycles. This points towards a symbiotic relationship between different realms. Although the ceremonial import of *Yagna* is lost in the current times, the spiritual relevance of *Yagna* is very much alive; that is, to consider one's life as a *Yajna* and offer it to the divine.

3. ***Samaveda****:* A Veda of *mantras* or chants consisting of melodies to be sung during worship and the performance of *Yajna*. Mantras produce effects both in the person chanting and also those listening. Cymatics has shown how sound affects the environment.

4. ***Atharvaveda****:* This collection of 20 books contains hymns, mantras, and incantations. It also outlines the rites and rituals to be performed in daily life.

## *Upa-Vedas*

1. ***Ayurveda****:* It deals with the science of health and medicine. There are two primary texts: *Charaka Samhita* and *Sushruta Samhita.* 'Samhita' means a collection or a treatise. *Ayurveda* describes the human body as consisting of *prana* (energy), *nadis* (pathways or channels) and *chakras* (energy vortices). It identifies the body based on *Tridoshas* (3 forces of the body). The books give details of natural herbal medicine formulations, disease management, and surgical methods.

2. ***Dhanur-Veda****:* The science of warfare and archery practised in ancient India. A master could add potency to the arrow through his thought power or with specific mantras.

3. ***Gandharva-Veda****:* The science of sound and music. It shows how music balances the mind and body through the sense of hearing. Indian classical music is entertaining, soothing and spiritual at the same time. The *raga* is a musical piece, literally meaning 'that which can colour the mind', which can produce different effects on the listener. A musical composition comprises notes (*swara*), time (*laya*), rhythm (*tala*), structure (*raga*) and lyrics (*sahitya*).

4. ***Arthashastra****:* It examines history, economics, politics, and management. The fundamental guiding principles are social welfare and individual enterprise.

5. ***Shilpa-Veda****:* The science of mechanics, manufacturing, artistry and architecture. It deals with all matters of construction. The measurements are geodesic, and one finds the use of universal constants in construction, alignment, and symmetry.

## *Vedangas*

1. ***Shiksha****:* Sanskrit Language and its pronunciation.
2. ***Vyakarana****:* Sanskrit grammar detailed by Sage Panini.
3. ***Chhanda****:* Sanskrit poetic metre and verse.
4. ***Nirukta****:* Sanskrit etymology detailed by Sage Yaksa.
5. ***Jyotisha****:* Astronomy, astrology, and mathematics (*Vedic Ganit*). Indian Astronomy has been heliocentric since ancient times, as the *Surya Siddhanta* (Sun Treatise), one of the oldest texts available, explains.
6. ***Kalpa****:* Rites and rituals for different stages of life.

# *Upanishads*
(12 Upanishads published by Chinmaya Prakashan)

**1. *Kenopanishad***: Self- Different from Known and Beyond Unknown
This text is a dialogue between a student and a teacher. The student wants to know, 'What is the cause behind the senses and the mind?' The Kenopanishad highlights the importance of seeking the truth. It also explains the role of a Guru who not only knows the scriptures but is also established in Truth.

**2. *Aitareya Upanishad***: Truth- Before & After Creation
This text describes the creation of the worlds, the cosmic man and the human, in poetic terms. Analogies explain the sequence of events in creation. It gives a detailed description of the human system at gross, subtle and causal levels.

**3. *Kathopanishad***: A Dialogue with Death
Lord of Death Yama reveals spiritual secrets to Nachiketa. This text explains the divine laws, the nature of the Soul, and how to extricate oneself from the sufferings of life and uphold righteous conduct.

**4. *Mundakopanishad***: Tale of Two Birds- Jiva and Isvara
Saunaka asks Rishi Angira, 'What is That, having known which all there is becomes known'? In reply, the rishi explains two types of knowledge: terrestrial (*apara vidya*) and transcendental (*para vidya*), and thus sets the stage for an elaborate response to this question.

This text contains the famous analogy of the two birds on a tree. One bird indulges in action (identifying with the ego), and the other just witnesses (the Self). *Mundakopnishad* clearly states the importance of a Guru for gaining *Brahma vidya*, as it is a practical approach, not just an intellectual exercise. It suggests meditating on the Divine seated within the 'cave of the heart' to realise Him.

### 5. *Taittiriya Upanishad*: Self beyond Sheaths

This text provides a detailed study of the bodies or sheaths of a Jiva. It also demonstrates the importance of nurturing both the inner and outer worlds and outlines the essential practices of Vedic life.

### 6. *Svetasvatara Upanishad*

Reveals the true nature of God/Truth and establishes our essential oneness with Him/It.

### 7. *Isavasya Upanishad*: God in and as Everything

*"The Atman moves, and It moves not; It is far, and It is near; It is within all this, and It is also outside all this."*
It explains in words what is essentially inexplicable and can only be realised as an inner experience.

### 8. *Prashnopanishad*: Six Disciples, Six Questions, One Truth

*Prashna* means a question. In this *Upanishad,* six seekers ask questions about creation, life, and purpose. A great sage named Pippalada answers them.

### 9. *Mandukya Upanishad*

This text describes AUM as eternal existence, consciousness and bliss. It also explains the states of consciousness: waking, dreaming, deep sleep and *turiya*. Truth witnesses everything.

### 10. *Kaivalya Upanishad*: I am in all; all are in me.

In this text, the Creator Himself is the Teacher. He describes creation, its constituents, who He is, and how to reach Him. He says,

*"...I am the one who is in the cavity of the heart, who is without parts, without a second, the witness of all, beyond existence and non-existence...devoid of all forms, of incomprehensible power, I am knowing, and there is none that knows Me. I am ever pure knowledge."*

### 11. *Ganapati Atharvashirsha Upanishad*
Reveals the true nature of Lord Ganapati, who is considered the very embodiment of ॐ (AUM or OM).

### 12. *Amritabindu Upanishad*: A Drop of Immortality
What is the role of the mind? How can we separate the mind from the objects? What is the importance of meditation? Truth, Self, Brahma, and knowledge are dealt with in this text.

## *Itihasas*

1. ***Ramayana*** (by Sage Valmiki): An epic Treta Yuga story of exiled Prince Shri Ram, who travels across India to defeat a demon king Ravana and liberate the people from Ravana's tyranny. Later-day sages also wrote *Ramayana* in different languages, for example, *Ramavataram* by Tamil poet Kambar in the 12th century and *Ramcharitmanas* by Tulsidas in the Awadhi language in the 16th century. *Ramayana* has travelled worldwide and is still considered a cultural heritage in many East Asian countries. *Ramayana* has many versions in multiple languages across entire Asia.

2. ***Mahabharata*** (by Sage Ved Vyas): This saga of gargantuan proportions, set in Dwapara Yuga, details the life and times of Lord Krishna and the royal families around 3100 BCE. It is about upholding divine order and righteousness (*Dharma*).

3. ***Srimad Bhagwat Gita****:* This is a subtext of the
*Mahabharata* in which Shri Krishna explains the Vedic
principles to warrior prince Arjuna on the battlefield of
*Kurukshetra*. Many commentaries on The Gita have added
to our understanding of this profound text. The Gita
explains creation, human life, and the path to growth
(Yoga) in detail. It summarises Vedic knowledge; hence, it
is also called Vedanta.

## *18 Maha-Puranas*

1. ***Brahma Purana****:* The first and most prominent Purana.
It deals with the formation, periodic dissolution and
re-creation of the universe, cosmic cycles and cosmological
timescales.

2. ***Naradiya Purana****:* Narada is the sage who initiated Sage
Valmiki to write Ramayana and Sage Ved Vyasa to write
Mahabharata. It tells us about Sage Narada and lays out
details of worship to Vishnu.

3. ***Padma Purana:*** This text describes the birth of Brahma,
the creation of the universe according to Sankhya tradition,
different ceremonies, and the importance of various months
in a year.

4. ***Garuda Purana****:* This is a conversation between Vishnu
and his *vaahana* (vehicle), *Garuda* (an eagle). It discusses
death, the afterlife, liberation, and the role of *Yama* (the
deity of death) and his assistant, *Chitragupta*. It describes
how *moksha* (liberation) can be achieved with yoga and
*bhakti* (devotion).

5. ***Varaha Purana****:* The incarnation of Vishnu as *Varaha* (a boar). It describes sorrow and happiness for a human being. It also mentions *Yama* and his work.

6. ***Bhagavata Purana****:* Bhagavata Purana is a conversation between King *Parikshit* and *Sukdevji*. It details Vedic knowledge and discusses Vishnu and his various incarnations.

7. ***Matsya Purana****:* This is an index of all the Puranas and a table of contents for all 18 Maha-Puranas. Ved Vyasa made this systematic arrangement so the Puranas could have a fixed structure.

8. ***Kurma Purana****:* Narrated by Vishnu as *Kurma* avatar (a tortoise), it details the 'churning of the milky ocean' by *devatas* and *asuras* for *amrita* (the nectar of eternal life).

9. ***Shiva Purana****:* This text describes Shiva's greatness and mentions the emergence of *Nandi* (the bull) and *Dhruva* (a devotee of Shiva).

10. ***Skanda Purana****:* It describes the entire history and geography of *Bharatvarsha* (ancient India).

11. ***Agni Purana****:* It praises Agni (Fire), a form of Vishnu. It also talks about *Alankara Shastra,* the science of figure of speech. The Sanskrit language has literature that shows graceful speech and fine poetry. Agni Purana also describes the *Navarasas*- the nine expressions humans often show. These are love (*shringaar*), laughter (*haasya*), compassion (*karuna*), anger (*rudra*), courage (*veera*), fear (*bhayaanaka*), disgust (*bheebhatsya*), wonder or surprise (*adbhutha*) and peace or tranquillity (*shaantha*).

12. ***Brahmanda Purana***: It details *Lalita Sahasranama* (1000 names of *Shakti*, the feminine divine principle).

13. ***Vayu Purana*** describes the creation and re-creation of the universe, the measurement of time, the origins of various rishis and deities, and elements of Nature, such as animals, birds, and plants. It also predicts the Gupta Dynasty of *Magadha* in *Kaliyuga*.

14. ***Markandeya Purana***: Narrated by Rishi *Markandeya*, as questions and answers, it describes the worship of the feminine divine principle *Shakti*. It starts with the story of 4 birds who are aware of moral conduct and can explain the reasons for people's actions in the past.

15. ***Bhavishya Purana***: *Bhavishya* means 'future'; hence, this Purana tells stories of the future. It also extols the spiritual importance of the Sun (*Aditya*).

16. ***Brahma Vaivarta Purana***: It details the stories of *Ma Radha* and *Shri Krishna*.

17. ***Vamana Purana***: It tells the popular story of King *Bali* and *Vamana* (a dwarf boy), the avatar of Vishnu.

18. ***Vishnu Purana***: Sage *Parashara* (father of Ved Vyasa) narrates this *Purana* to *Maitreya*. It describes creation, *Purusha* (Pure consciousness) and *Prakriti* (Nature), various avatars of Vishnu, and also talks about Kaliyuga.

# *Darshana Shastra*
## 6 Prominent Schools of Philosophy

There are six prominent schools of thought in Indian philosophy, of which *Samkhya, Vedanta,* and *Yoga Shastra* are explained in greater detail in this book. Below is a brief introduction to the other three schools: *Nyaya, Vaisheshika, and Mimansa.*

1. **Sankhya Darshana** (by Kapila Muni): *Samkhya Darshana* is the foundation of Vedic or Hindu philosophy. It describes creation at all levels of manifestation and the ways and means to achieve Union with the Ultimate Being.

2. *Vedanta* (by Ved Vyasa): Vedanta is made up of the words *veda+anta,* meaning 'end of Vedas'; hence, Vedanta is the essence of Vedas. Since the Upanishads contain the philosophical basis and concepts of the Vedas, they are also referred to as Vedanta. Vedanta could also mean the highest thought, the very end of thought, or even beyond thought. *Brahmagyan* (the divine knowledge) is beyond thought; it is the essence of Being.

3. *Yoga Shastra* (by Sage Patanjali): While *Sankhya* is philosophy, and *Vedanta* is the essence of Vedas, Patanjali's *Yoga Sutras* are a path to the highest. The *Yoga Sutras* are in Sanskrit, in a coded form; hence, many authors have given their perspectives and commentaries. *Authentic Yoga* by Shri PY Deshpande's masterpiece Authentic Yoga is one such commentary presented in a very lucid and scientific manner. Swami Vivekananda's commentary is also an excellent guide to understanding the *sutras.*

4. *Nyaya* (by Sage Akshapada Gautama): *Nyaya* philosophy is closely linked to *Vaisheshika.* It deals with logic-based epistemology (theory of knowledge). Its main objective is to eliminate suffering by removing ignorance

and gaining knowledge. It relies on four sources of knowledge or valid proofs (*Pramana*): *Pratyaksha* (Perception), *Anumana* (Inference), *Upamana* (Reasoning by analogy) and *Shabda* (Testimony). It also explains four invalid means of gaining knowledge: *Smriti* (Memory), *Samsaya* (Doubt), *Viparyaya* (Error), and *Tarka* (Hypothetical Reasoning).

5. **Vaisheshika** (by Sage Kanada): *Vaisheshika* means 'particular or distinction'. Called the atomistic school of Indian Philosophy, *Vaisheshika* philosophy explains seven elements of matter (*Sapta-padartha*) - *Dravya* (substance), *Guna* (qualities), *Karma* (activities), *Samanya* (general traits), *Vishesha* (speciality), *Samavaya* (inter-relatedness) and *Abhaava* (absence). It is similar to Greek philosophy, where the search is for the basic substance of the universe.

6. **Mimansa** (by Sage Jaimini): *Mimansa* means 'reflection'. *Mimansa darshana* is based on the *Karma Kanda* part of the Vedas. It encourages people to follow the directives of Vedic rituals by performing various *Yajna* (sacrifices, efforts and good deeds). The sacrifice is not only about performing fire homage (*havan*) but about a life lived consciously with good thoughts and deeds. Some *Yajnas* are suggested for a householder to attain *moksha* (liberation), and others are for a King or a royal, which is not so relevant in the current times.

ॐ सर्वे भवन्तु सुखिनः। सर्वे सन्तु निरामयाः।
सर्वे भद्राणि पश्यन्तु मा कश्चिद्दुःखभाग्भवेत।
ॐ शान्तिः शान्तिः शान्तिः॥

May all be happy and in good health.
May all see what is spiritually uplifting.
May no one suffer.
May there be peace, peace, peace.

# Bibliography


Bala, Saroja. Mahabharat: Retold With Scientific Evidence. Gurugram, Haryana. Garuda Prakashan, 2021.

Bala, Saroja. Ramayan Retold With Scientific Evidence. New Delhi. Prabhat Prakashan, 2019.

Georg Feuerstein & Frawley David & Kak Subhash. In Search of the Cradle of Civilization. Delhi. Motilal Banarsidass Publishers Pvt Ltd, 2008.

Oak, Nilesh. When Did The Mahabharata War Happen? The Mystery of Arundhati. The US. Danphe Inc, 2011.

Oak, Nilesh. Dating of the Ramayana and Mahabharata. #SangamTalks. Jan 1, 2017.

Sanyal, Sanjiv. The Incredible History of the Indian Ocean. Gurugram, Haryana, Penguin Random House India Pvt Ltd. 2020.

Sanyal, Sanjiv. The Ocean of Churn. Gurugram, Haryana. Penguin Random House India Pvt Ltd. 2017.

Sanyal, Sanjiv. Land of the Seven Rivers. Gurugram, Haryana. Penguin Random House India Pvt Ltd. 2012.

Malhotra, Rajiv. Being Different. Noida. Harper Collins, 2018.

Sai, J Deepak. India That is Bharat. New Delhi. Bloomsbury Publishing India Pvt Ltd, 2021.

Verma, RR, The Bhagwat Gita. New Delhi. Prakash Books India Pvt Ltd, 2020.

Bhave, Vinobha. Talks on the Gita. The Heartfulness Way Series. Kolkata. Spiritual Hierarchy Publication Trust, 2019.

Saraswati, Prakashanand Swami. The True History and the Religion of India. Delhi. Motilal Banarsidass Publishers Pvt Ltd, 2004.

Frawley, David. Ayurveda and the Mind: Healing of Consciousness. Delhi. Motilal Banarsidass Publishers Pvt Ltd, 2018.

Chinmayananda, Swami. Ashtavakra Gita: A Commentary. Mumbai. Chinmaya Prakashan, 2021.

Malhotra, Rajiv & Dasa, Satyanarayana Babaji. Sanskrit Non-translatables: Importance of Sanskritizing English. New Delhi. Manjul Publishing House Pvt Ltd, 2020.

Deshpande, PY. The Authentic Yoga: Yoga Sutras of Patanjali. Telangana. Heartfulness Education Trust, 2021

Patel, Kamlesh. Tales from the Vedas and Upanishads. Heartfulness Education Trust. Chennai, Tamil Nadu. Westland Publications Pvt Ltd, 2021.

Selbie, Joseph & Steinmetz David. The Yugas: Keys to Understanding Our Hidden Past, Emerging Present and Future Enlightenment. Commerce, CA, USA. Crystal Clarity Publishers, 2011.

Giri, Swami Yukteshwar. The Holy Science. Kolkata. Yogoda Satsangh Society of India, 2021

Patel, Kamlesh. The Planet was there Before us, and will be there After us. Article published in the Heartfulness magazine of April 2022.

Tully, R., Courtois, H., Hoffman, Y. et al. The Laniakea supercluster of galaxies. Nature 513, 71–73 (2014).

Patel, Kamlesh. The Heartfulness Way: Heart-Based Meditations for Spiritual Transformation. Oakland, CA, United States. Reveal Press, 2018.

Patel, Kamlesh. Designing Destiny: Heartfulness Practices to Find Your Purpose and Fulfill Your Potential. Carlsbad, California, US. Hay House Inc, 2019.

Chandra, Ram of Fatehgarh. Truth Eternal. Chennai, Tamil Nadu. Westland Publications Pvt Ltd, 2018.

Patel, Kamlesh. Truth Eternal: Lecture Series. 2021. https://www.sahajmarg.org/literature/online/speeches/truth-eternal

Chinmayananda, Swami. Upanishad Series. A commentary. Set of 12 books. Mumbai. Chinmaya Prakashan, 2021.

Debroy Bibek & Dipavali. The Holy Puranas (Set of 3 Volumes). Delhi. BR Publishing Corporation, 2021.

Debroy, Bibek & Dipavali. The Holy Vedas: Rig Veda, Yajur Veda, Sama Veda, Atharva Veda. Delhi. BR Publishing Corporation, 2020.

Saraswati, Niranjanananda Swami. Samkhya Darshan: Yogic Perspectives on Theories of Realism. Bihar, India. Yoga Publications Trust, 2009.

Vivekananda, Swami. The Complete Works of Swami Vivekananda. Kolkata. Advaita Ashrama Publication Department, 2016.

Monika Khanna, Aristotle: Life and Works. Delhi, India. Farsight Publishers and Distributors, 2017.

Patel, Kamlesh. Yogic Psychology. Heartfulness Magazine Collector's edition, Dec 2019.

Sparks, Ben. #Numberphile. The Golden Ratio (why it is so irrational) Understanding the real significance of the golden ratio. May 9, 2018. https://youtu.be/sj8Sg8qnjOg

Wheeler, Ken. Uncovering the Missing Secrets of Magnetism. Kindle Edition, 2014. Available on archive.org. 2014.

Leedskalnin, Edward. Magnetic Currents. Available on archive.org.

Emoto, Masaru. The Healing Power of Water. Singapore. Hay House Inc, 2007.

ISRO's Geoportal | Gateway to Indian Earth Observation | Applications https://bhuvan-app1.nrsc.gov.in/saraswati/saraswati.php#.

The Stages of Embryo Growth. Youtube. #UPMC. May 20, 2016. https://www.youtube.com/watch?v=1TRLaeH2GBQ&t=48s

Blastocyst Development - Day 3 to Day 5. Youtube. #London Women's Clinic (Cardiff). Aug 4, 2016 https://www.youtube.com/watch?v=uCn1PQP2yAo

HeartMath Institute. Science of the Heart. Boulder Creek, CA, USA. HeartMath Research Center, 2015.

Chandra, Ram (of Shahjahanpur, UP). Complete Works of Ram Chandra (5-book series). Published by Heartfulness, 2019.

Dinu, Ionel & Gardi, Lori. (2020). Fundamentals of a Theory of Aether - Part 1. 2021.

Gardi, Lori. Steinmetz Analogy Between Magnetic and Dielectric. Gardi, Lori. An Aether Model of Electricity: The Missing Secret of Magnetism.

Patel, Kamlesh. Evolution of Consciousness. Heartfulness Magazine Vol 2 Issue 12, 2016.

Lipton, Bruce.  Biology of Belief. New Delhi. Hay House India, 2016.

Allen, James. James Allen: Complete Premium Collection. Audiobook Audible. Narrated by Andrew Farell. 2019.

Russell, Walter. The Secret of Light. The book is available as an open-source document on archive.org. Also available as an audiobook.

Russell, Walter. The Universal One. The book is available as an open-source document on archive.org. Also available as an audiobook.

The World's First MRI of a single atom. Youtube. #Seeker. Aug 21, 2019.  https://www.youtube.com/watch?v=pjiD0FrUNN8

MRI of a single titanium atom. Youtube. #O. Rood. Sep 16, 2020. https://www.youtube.com/watch?v=C2t37TUH_qw

Kumar, Alok. Ancient Hindu Science: Its impact on the ancient and the modern worlds. Mumbai, Jaico Publishing. 2019.

Heartfulness Research Institute. https://www.heartfulnessinstitute.org/research.

Devam, Y. (2024) 'A cryptanalytic decipherment of the Indus Script,' www.academia.edu [Preprint]. https://www.academia.edu/78867798/A_cryptanalytic_decipherment_o f_the_Indus_Script.

# Glossary of Sanskrit Words

Abhinivesha: Fear of death.
Adharma: Unrighteousness.
Adhyatma: Spirituality.
Adi-Shakti: Supreme or Primal Power.
Aditya: Name of the Sun deity.
Advaita: Non-dual, represents Oneness.
Agni: The fire element.
Ahamkara: The ego, or the sense of I.
Ahimsa: Non-violence in thought and deed.
Akarma: Desireless devoted action, inspired by the Divine.
Akarmanyata: Laziness, lack of action.
Akarta: Non-doer; one who does not act and stays still, while being the power behind all creation and all actions.
Akasha: The space or ether element.
Alabdha-bhumikatva: Failing to attain higher stages in spiritual pursuit.
Alasya: Laziness, sloth.
Anand: Joy, bliss.
Anavasthi-tatvani: Inability to maintain a stage in a spiritual pursuit.
Angam ejayatva: Nervousness.
Annamaya kosha: The physical body made by consuming food.
Anoraniyan: Smaller than the smallest.
Apara-Prakriti: The manifest Nature.
Aparigraha: Being Non-Possessive.
Aranyakas: Treatises of knowledge, which are a part of Vedic Jnana. Kanda. They describe the philosophy of the Vedic mantras and rituals.
Asana: Postures.
Ashtanga Yoga: The eight-fold Path of Yoga by Sage Patanjali.
Ashwini Kumars: Twin sons of the Sun deity.
Asmita: Sense of identity or separateness.
Asteya: Non-stealing, being non-covetous.
Asuric: Demonic, lower entities.
Avatar: Incarnation of God, supreme entity.
Avidya: Ignorance, lack of knowledge of Self.
Aviratti: Lack of abstaining.
Avyakrit Or Antaryamin: 'The one who dwells within', the subtle body of Brahma.
Avyakta: Manifested, expressed.
Ayurveda: Vedic science of life, health and healing.
Bandhas: Energy lock, one of the Hatha yoga practices.
Bhakti: Devotion to God.
Brahma: The Divine Principle of Creation.

Bhranti-darshana: False perception or delusion.
Brahmacharya: Moderation of senses and faculties.
Brahman: The one who dwells on Brahma.
Brahmanda Mandal: Brahma's entire creation.
Brahmarandra: The point in the mind region from where a realised soul exits the body.
Buddhi: Intellect.
Chakras: Energy points that are visualised as wheels, vortices, or whirlpools.
Chandra Nadi: The energy channel corresponding to the parasympathetic nervous response, responsible for rest and relaxation in the body.
Chatuburj: With four arms.
Chaturyuga: Four yugas comprising one yuga cycle.
Chit: the field of consciousness.
Daivic: Related to devatas or gods of the heavenly realm (lokas).
Dama: Natural control of senses.
Darshana: Direct inner perception, a perspective or philosophy.
Daurmanasya: Despair and depression.
Devatas: Higher beings or energies of Nature that maintain balance in the Earthly realm.
Dharana: Yogic practice of developing focus and unwavering attention.
Dharma: 'That which supports', dharma is the foundation of divinely inspired and duty-bound actions for the welfare of all.
Dhyana: A vehicle that can take us beyond the mind. The practice of transcending the mind to realise the soul as one's true essence.
Duhkha: mental and physical pain.
Dvaita: Dual, 'of two'.
Dvesha: Aversion.
Ekagra: Single-pointed focus.
Guru: A self-realised Teacher of spirituality.
Guru-Shishya Parampara: The teacher-disciple relationship, a tradition based on mutual respect and reverence for the Guru.
Gurukula: 'Family of the Guru', the ancient education system, where the students live in a natural environment and learn from the Guru.
Hatha: A path of yoga that deals with the regulation of the physical and energetic body.
Hiranyagarbha: 'The golden egg', a description of Brahma's causal body.
Ishwar Pranidhana: Devotion and surrender to God.
Itihasa: 'As it happened', the historical accounts of Bharat, comprising the epics Ramayana and Mahabharata.
Jada: Inanimate.

Jal: The water element.
Jivas: Living beings.
Jnana Kanda: The Vedic treatise for knowledge.
Jnanendriyas: The organs of perception.
Kaivalya: Alone, the only One.
Karan Sharir: Atman, the causal body.
Karma: Action.
Karma Kanda: The Vedic treatise for rituals and chanting.
Karma, Bhakti and Jnana Marg: The traditional paths to God are action (Karma), devotion (Bhakti), and knowledge (Jnana). Raja yoga combines all three into one grand synthesis.
Karmendriyas: The organs of action.
Kleshas: Mental afflictions or colourings.
Koti: Supreme, type or category.
Kriyas: Processes. Yoga defines various cleansing processes to refine perception.
Layaavastha: In a state of mergence.
Lokas: Worlds or realms.
Maha-Kaal: Time.
Mahatomahiyan: Greater than the greatest.
Mahavakyas: Great sayings.
Mahayana Buddhism: A branch of Buddhism.
Mahesh: The Divine Principle of Destruction, also called Shiva.
Manas: Mind.
Manomaya Kosha: The subtle body: one of the five sheats of the human constitution. It comprises the mind, identity and consciousness.
Maya: Illusion.
Moksha: Salvation, a temporary relief from the life and death cycle.
Mudras: Subtle psychic gestures.
Mukti: Liberation, a release from the life and death cycle, as the soul continues on other planes of existence.
Mumukshutva: Intense longing for the goal of self-realisation.
Nadis (Ida, Pingala, And Sushumna): The three primary energy channels in the human energy body, the Pranamayakosha.
Neti Neti: 'Not this, not this', the path of negation to realise Brahma by eliminating all words, objects, sounds, and concepts that are not Brahma.
Nidra: Sleep.
Nir-Bija Samadhi: A meditative state with pure-seeing-based absorption in the divine, where the sense of I is absent.
Nirguna (Nirakar): Indeterminate Absolute, without form or qualities.

Nir-Vichara Samadhi: It is the stage in meditation when the realm of subtle thoughts is transcended, and the meditator develops effortless, single-pointed focus.

Nir-Vitarka Samadhi: It is a stage in meditation with pure perception.

Niyama: Routine or discipline.

Paapa: The result of negative actions.

Panchabhutas: The five fundamental elements are air, fire, water, space, and earth.

Panchakona: Pentagon.

Para-Brahmanda Mandal: The sphere of reality before Brahma, the cause of Brahma.

Para-Prakriti: The sphere of reality before manifested Prakriti (Nature)

Paradharma: Someone else's duties.

Paramatman: The supreme Soul, the Divine oneness, Brahma.

Pashupati: The God of all living beings, another name for Shiva.

Pinda-Pradesh: The physical world of matter and dualities.

Prabhu State: The region of nearness to the Divine in the spiritual journey. When a seeker reaches this region, he is in the Prabhu state.

Pradhana: Prime or chief; a word used to describe Prakriti (The Original Nature).

Prakriti: Nature, the original condition that led to the manifestation of the natural world.

Pramada: Carelessness, negligence or haste.

Pramana: Proof of right knowledge.

Prana: The vital force or energy that gives life.

Prana Vayus: the five subtle energy channels that control different functions in the human body. These are Apana, Samana, Prana, Udana, and Vyana.

Pranahuti (Pranasya Prana): Transmitting of Prana for spiritual elevation.

Pranamaya Kosha: The causal body or Atman, composed of bliss and joy.

Pranayama: Breath regulation through breathing exercises to balance the pranas in the body.

Prapanna Prabhu State: This is the region in the spiritual journey where one surrenders to the Divine. When a seeker reaches this region, he is in the state of Prapanna Prabhu.

Prapanna State: Prapanna means 'one who is ready'. Prapanna State is the spiritual region where the seeker seeks the Divine as their only refuge and goal. When a seeker reaches this region, he is in the Prapanna state.

Prarabdha: The portion of past karma experienced in the present life.

Pratyahara: Withdrawal of the senses and mind within to rest attention on the heart.
Pravasa: Irregular exhalation.
Prithvi: The earth element.
Punya: the result of good actions.
Puranas: The records of the very ancient history of Bharat.
Purusha: Pure consciousness.
Raga: Attachment.
Raja Yoga: The path of yoga that helps in mind regulation.
Rangoli: Intricate symmetrical patterns made on the floor, usually with finely ground rice powder and colours.
Rta: The cosmic intelligence that governs creation.
Rudras: These are the subtle and causal aspects of the human being. If unregulated, it can cause suffering.
Sa-Anand Samadhi: A steady, settled, meditative state of inner tranquillity, joy and bliss.
Sa-Asmita Samadhi: A meditative state is beyond bliss, with just pure awareness or Is-ness.
Sa-Bija Samadhi: A meditative state of absorption in the divine, where the sense of I is still present.
Sa-Vichara Samadhi: A meditative state in which thinking can happen, but the mind is quiet and regulated.
Sa-Vikalpa Samadhi: A meditative state in which thoughts are present but do not disturb. The meditator is aware of self and the world.
Sa-Vitarka Samadhi: A meditative state in which the mind is regulated, and the meditator can use logic and reasoning to arrive at conclusions.
Saadhana Chatushtaya: The fourfold means of successful spiritual practice.
Sadhana: spiritual practice, meditation.
Saguna or Saakar: Determinate Absolute, with form and qualities.
Sahaj Samadhi: The ultimate state of effortless union with the Divine.
Sahasra Dal Kamal: The 'thousand-petaled lotus' refers to the crown chakra, associated with sat-chit-ananda (truth, consciousness, and bliss).
Samadhaan: A state of being self-settled on the goal.
Samayama: Once dharana, dhyana and samadhi are established in a yogi, he can practice these three together as samayama to gain knowledge of the world.
Samhita: A collection.
Samsaya: Dilemma or indecision.
Samskaras: Impressions, or subconscious conditioning due to emotional imprints.
Sanatana: Eternal.

Sandhi: Conjunction.
Sankhya: A philosophy propounded by Sage Kapila that deals with the dualist nature of Creation, as being composed of Purusha (Pure Consciousness) and Prakriti (Inanimate Nature).
Santosh: Being content and in a state of acceptance.
Sat-chit-ananda: The state of experiencing Truth, Pure Consciousness and Bliss associated with the crown chakra, Sahasra Dal Kamal.
Satya: the existential Truth, Oneness or Reality.
Satyam Shivam Sundaram: The fundamental nature of Reality known as 'Truth, Goodness and Beauty'.
Saucha: External and internal hygiene and purity.
Shabda: The sound of AUM, the highest vibration of Creation.
Shakti: The Divine Power.
Shama: Regulation of mind (by Ashtanga Yoga).
Sharnagati: The act of surrendering to the Divine.
Shat-Sampatti: Six virtues or attainments that help a seeker on the spiritual path.
Shatkarma- Six purification techniques in Hatha Yoga.
Shatkona: Hexagon.
Shiva: The Divine Principle of Destruction, also called Mahesh.
Shlokas: Sanskrit verse or stanza typically consisting of two lines, each with 16 syllables.
Shraddha- Faith and devotion.
Shruti: 'That which is heard'. It refers to the Vedas.
Shunya: Zero.
Shunyata: Nothingness, state of being zero.
Smriti: 'From the memory'. It refers to the ancient texts of Upanisads, Puranas and Itihasas.
Sthitaprajna: The state of inner stability and balance.
Sthula Sharir: The gross body.
Styana: Mental laziness or dullness.
Sukhma Sharir: the subtle body.
Surya Nadi: The energy channel corresponding to the sympathetic nervous response responsible for flight or flight.
Sutras: A type of concise text in Sanskrit that encodes profound wisdom.
Svasa: Irregular inhalation.
Swadharma: One's duties.
Swadhyaya: Self-study.
Tantra: Technique.
Tapasya: Sadhana, practice of self-discipline, self-sacrifice and austerity.
Tarka: Inferential reasoning.

Titiksha: Fortitude and total satisfaction.
Tribhuj: Triangle, a form with three arms.
Trigunas (Sat, Raj and Tam): Three qualities of Prakriti (Nature).
Tulsi: The holy basil plant.
Turiya: A fourth state of consciousness beyond awake, sleep and dream states.
Turiyateet: A state of consciousness even beyond Turiya.
Upa-Vedas: The supplementary texts to the Vedas.
Upanishads: The essence of Vedic knowledge.
Upratti: Self-withdrawal, settled within.
Vairagya: Neutralising likes and dislikes.
Vasudeva Kutumbakam: The world is one large, extended family.
Vasus: The eight deities of our world that help govern it.
Vayu: The air element.
Vedangas: the limbs of Vedas, extension of Vedic knowledge into specialised branches.
Vedanta: End of Vedas, the essence of Vedic knowledge.
Vedas: The foundational texts of Hindu civilisation.
Vedic Ganita: Vedic mathematics.
Vichara: Thought.
Vid: The root word of Veda, vid means 'to know'.
Vighnas: Diseases.
Vijnanamaya Kosha: The sheath of the human system comprising the intellect.
Vikalpa: Fantasy or imagination.
Vikarma: Short form for vishishta (distinguished) karma. It is desireless action done for the welfare of all with love and devotion (bhakti).
Vikshepas: Debilitating habits and obstacles.
Viparyaya: False or wrong knowledge.
Virat: The gross body of Brahma.
Vishnu: The Divine Principle of Sustenance of the Creation.
Vishnu-Nabhi: 'The naval of Vishnu'. The singularity at the centre of creation that powers it but remains still.
Vitarka: Logical reasoning.
Viveka: Power of discrimination, discernment.
Vritti: A modification of the field of consciousness or a tendency.
Vyadhi: Disease or illness.
Yajnas: Homage to the gods.
Yama: God of Death.
Yoga: Made from the root word 'yuj', yoga implies uniting, joining, or integrating.
Yuddha: Righteous wars to uphold natural laws.
Yuga: The cycle of time and consciousness.

www.ingramcontent.com/pod-product-compliance
Lightning Source LLC
Chambersburg PA
CBHW032008150726

47990CB00005B/1885